BRITANNIA
THE FAILED STATE

T0322558

questions about the end of Roman Britain. So it may be worthwhile to explore a hypothesis in the light of the available evidence, while always granting priority to the archaeology rather than any modern concerns. This is not intended to be the last word in the debate over what happened at the end of the fourth century and beginning of the fifth, but if it's the next word that at least would be something.

For many people in Britain today, particularly among the over-35s (a demographic group that includes much of the academic and archaeological establishment), the quintessential war remains the Second World War. They are, of course, well aware of the many other different types of war that have existed and continue to exist, but many of their attitudes and ideas about armed conflict seem still to be dictated by the period 1939-1945.

This is, in many ways, entirely understandable and inevitable. The Second World War achievement is something many Britons remain hugely proud of and it dominated a number of aspects of the childhood of those who grew up in the 60s and 70s, a mere 15-35 years after the end of the war. One has only to think of the Second World War construction kits that occupied so many schoolboy hours and the Second World War films and series that filled so much cinema and television time – not to mention, of course, the frequent recurrence of Second World War themes in political rhetoric through the years of the Cold War (and continuing in today's 'War on Terror'). The 'bad guys' are always likened to Hitler, however unlike Hitler they may be, and the 'good guys' are often likened to Churchill, however unlike Churchill they may be.

In terms of understanding history, though, (or indeed making it) this dominant position of the Second World War can be very unhelpful because the Second World War was, by the broad standards of history, an immensely unusual armed conflict. The paradigm of highly united nation states facing each other in a lengthy, determined fight to the finish, with good clearly on one side (if one ignores Stalin and contentious issues like the bombing of Dresden) and evil clearly on the other, is one that occurs in history comparatively rarely. In most armed conflicts, support for war is far less united and the moral boundaries are far more blurred.

The good-versus-evil moral paradigm has had an undeniable effect on views about the end of Roman Britain and the beginning of England, with a number of historians appearing to take sides; some perhaps subconsciously, some more obviously. There is still some evidence of a pro-Celtic faction who essentially find it regrettable that England is not a Celtic nation today and have seen the Anglo-Saxon arrival as, therefore, something bad which the Britons of the time would and should have resisted but were unable, for some reason, to defeat. Less common today (though widespread in Victorian times) is the opposing view – that the Anglo-Saxon arrival was the invasion of a force with superior characteristics of hard work and morality, sweeping away the decaying remnants of a corrupted Romano-British culture. Even more damaging, though, in terms of modern historiography are underlying beliefs about the concept of a nation state uniting every member of society to face its enemies.

Today's historians are clearly too knowledgeable and sophisticated to apply this model in its fullest form to the transfer of power from Roman Britain to Anglo-Saxon England. However, many of its core assumptions still flavour the debate about the period. Just as the Romans referred to *Britannia* and *Brittones* as if they were one unified homogenous force, so we refer to Roman Britain and Britons, ignoring the many different peoples, nations in many senses, that made up Britain at the time and who were often separated from each other by huge cultural and political differences.

Referring to 'Britons' in the Roman period as a homogenous group makes little more sense than referring to Europeans, for instance, in the same way at the same time. On one level it is a harmless and, perhaps, inevitable shorthand for the different tribes living in Britain, but on another it skews the whole debate in a very unhelpful way.

Many people find it hard to understand how Roman Britain, with a population of perhaps 2-4 million in the early fourth century,[1] could in the fifth century allow its central eastern areas to become culturally, and on some level, politically, dominated by a far smaller number of Germanic immigrants. If Roman Britain had been a single political entity then it would, indeed, be hard to comprehend.

The Second World War's hold on modern British imagination is, however, now beginning to slip. As veterans grow older and die the period is slowly moving beyond living memory. Equally Britain and Britons have recently become involved in armed conflicts which are, in many ways, far more typical of war throughout history and which suggest new ways of examining the end of Roman Britain and the beginning of Anglo-Saxon England. The first of these conflicts was the war in Bosnia or, in more general terms, the break up of the Former Yugoslavia. Some of what happened there I saw at first-hand as an aid worker. Inevitably with such a recent and so bitter a conflict much of what occurred, and why, remains controversial. However, the broad outlines are clear and have some potential analogies with the period in Britain at the end of the fourth century and beginning of the fifth.

Yugoslavia was knitted together at the end of the First World War from disparate cultural groups with independent identities – the most politically prominent ones at that stage being the Serbs, Croats, and the Slovenes, and indeed this period of Yugoslavia's history is referred to as the Kingdom of the Serbs, Croats and Slovenes.

Under the Germans, and with nationalist pressure from the Croats, Yugoslavia briefly fragmented during the Second World War, only to be reconstituted in its post-war form under Tito. This was modern Yugoslavia, recognising within its boundaries now not just Serbs, Croats and Slovenes but also other groups with their own identities, including Montenegrins, Macedonians, Bosnian Muslims, Albanian Kosovars and the Hungarians in Voivodina. Even this line-up (probably like Ptolemy's list of British tribes discussed in Chapter 1) was an over-simplification of the ethnic and cultural jigsaw that was Tito's Yugoslavia but it gives some idea of the mixed identities that were brought, for a time, together. Similarly, Rome's territory Britannia was formed by forcing together a number of tribes who before the arrival of Rome were independent of each other and very probably, on occasion, at war with each other. Like the Roman Empire in Britain, Tito's rule in Yugoslavia ultimately relied on force to impose unity. Under Tito, a number of prominent nationalists who attempted to publicise their view were imprisoned. However, again as in Roman Britain, the unity of Tito's Yugoslavia was undermined by the retention of internal borders linked to cultural identity to define areas of local administration. Just as Roman Britain had the *civitates* based on pre-Roman tribal territories, so Tito's Yugoslavia was a Federal Republic composed of 'separate' Republics and a number of autonomous provinces based on the constituent ethnic and cultural groups.

The beginning of the end of Yugoslavia can, in some sense, be traced back to the death of Tito, perhaps the man who believed most in keeping Yugoslavia united. With him gone, ambitious politicians used the historical animosities and cultural differences between the various groups in Yugoslavia to lever them apart (*1*). In the process they briefly furthered their own careers, but ignited a series of wars fought over disputed areas where different ethnic and cultural groups had mingled and could not be easily torn apart. These wars sliced up the previously affluent Yugoslav economy and in a couple of years reduced the standard of living in the areas most affected from something comparable with that of parts of Western Europe to, in many places, little more than subsistence farming.

There are many similarities between Bosnia in the early 1990s and the picture archaeology has revealed of the end of Roman Britain. Rubbish piled up in the streets, bodies were buried in town centres, mass manufacturing ceased, people lived in the shells of formerly rich buildings lighting fires on fine floors, and roads were blocked (*2, 3*). If the effects were similar, maybe the causes of the decline were too.

It is sometimes suggested that national identities and the ethnic and cultural prejudice that often accompanies them, are modern constructs. While the modern nation state itself may be a product of the nineteenth century, there is plenty of evidence in the corpus of classical literature to suggest that ethnic/

1 In Bosnia the abrupt decline was caused by war over tribal boundaries. This could also have been the case in late and post-Roman Britain

2 Rubbish piled up in the towns of Bosnia in the early 1990s, as it did in the towns of early fifth-century Britain

3 People continued to live and work in partly derelict buildings in Bosnia, as they did in Britain at the end of the Roman period

cultural identity and ethnic/cultural prejudice were already powerful forces in the classical world. There is, for instance, the Athenian view that Athens was humane and urbane as opposed to Sparta, which was viewed as militaristic, boring and boorish. Or look at the Romans' contrast of 'simple Roman virtues' with the common view in Roman culture that people from the east were soft and obsessed with luxury, and that Celts were undisciplined and emotional. There is no reason why such tensions could not have been widespread between the tribes in pre-Roman and Roman-period Britain. Any conflict at the end of Roman control of Britain may have been about power but one should not discount ethnic and cultural prejudice as factors too.

The other war that has concentrated British attention on the potential conflicts between different ethnic and cultural groups is, of course, Iraq. The pattern is familiar. Iraq was knitted together, this time by the British Empire, from separate Ottoman provinces after the end of the First World War. Here, three main groups, all with separate identities, were united. In the south was the largely Shia province focused around Basra, in the centre was the largely Sunni province focused around Baghdad and in the north lay the largely Kurdish province focused around Mosul. Britain took the three provinces and created Iraq, partly to ensure control of the already important oil fields around Mosul. In the early days it was, therefore, Britain that held the three areas together by force. In later periods it was monarchs followed by assorted strongmen.

Saddam has, however, been replaced by a government struggling to bring unity to the three groups and, once again, areas where the groups have mingled most have lain at the heart of bitter battles for control. As in Bosnia, this process has been assisted by ambitious men who see advantage for themselves in setting the separate cultural groups against each other.

Late fourth- and fifth-century Britain is bound to have had its fair share of such men. Unlike Bosnia though and unlike fifth-century Britain, Iraq has a large powerful American army attempting to prevent cultural divides leading to full-scale civil war (though, of course, the American presence has also introduced a wholly different set of issues).

It is harder to quantify the economic damage done to Iraq by the civil conflict there, due to the question of damage already caused under Saddam and due to the destruction inflicted during the invasion. However, the difficulties that have been faced by oil-rich Iraq in recovering from such setbacks must be largely put down to the war against the US presence and the civil conflict, mainly between Sunnis and Shias but also including, at times, the Kurds.

Bosnia and Iraq are the two cases of a power vacuum leading to fragmentation and conflict that most quickly spring to mind for most modern Britons. However, there are, of course, a number of other countries around the world presently facing similar problems. Somalia and Afghanistan are obvious instances.

Moreover, history offers many examples of the same phenomenon across the centuries. Where a strong central power forcibly unites different groups with a history of hostility and then, after a period of limited integration among the different elements, that central power is suddenly removed, the resulting power vacuum often causes fragmentation and conflict.

The break-up of Alexander the Great's empire is an obvious ancient example, with the successor states left in a condition of chronic warfare, battling over borders. The fragmentation of Charlemagne's empire is another instance. The break-up of the Ottoman Empire in the Balkans provides a more recent historical example. For those who think that the end of the twentieth century was a bad time for the Balkans, it is worth remembering that the end of the nineteenth century and beginning of the twentieth century were bad as well. In this case, after hundreds of years of occupation, longer than the period spent by the Romans in Britain, Ottoman power disappeared in a fairly short space of time. In the aftermath, ethnic and cultural groups forced into the Ottoman Empire back in the fourteenth and fifteenth centuries re-asserted their independence, and it took a long period of intermittent conflict to establish final borders.

In fact on the basis alone of Rome pulling together separate British tribes, many with a history of conflict with each other, and then leaving behind a power vacuum, a strong case could be made that chronic conflict inflicting huge damage on the British economy and on any possibility of British unity is almost certain to have occurred. Such a conflict would, almost inevitably, have created a situation vulnerable to exploitation by external forces (either through collaboration with local Britons or by conquest) such as Anglo-Saxons looking for brighter prospects outside their continental homelands. It is a perfectly viable, and indeed probable, scenario to explain the 'Roman Britain ends and then a few decades later Anglo-Saxon England begins' conundrum. However, rather than relying on that as an (albeit valid) assumption, let us turn to the evidence.

I shall examine how the different cultural and ethnic groups in Britain responded to each other in the period before the arrival of Rome. I will consider too how they were involved in the three great, but little understood, convulsions that struck Roman Britain in 60/61, 155-211 and 367. I shall also explore their reaction to the ending of Roman power and how they related to the incoming Anglo-Saxons. These are questions that lie at the heart of both what it means to be British and what it means to be English and they are of significance to all people who consider themselves either or both, or who are at all interested in the origins of England and Britain.

CHAPTER 1

The Tribes

The first modern humans came to Europe perhaps some time around 50,000 years ago[1] and gradually moved north towards Britain. They were, of course, just the first of many immigrants to this island. There must have been a number of waves of immigration in prehistoric times about which we now know little or nothing. Genetic evidence is beginning to probe these questions, exploring, for example, links both to the Iberian Peninsula and the Black Sea region,[2] but it is still a comparatively new science and many of the conclusions offered by it remain controversial.

In previous generations there was an assumption that every time a culture from Europe was adopted in Britain this represented a mass immigration. Thus, for instance, it was originally assumed that the appearance of the Beaker Culture during the third millennium BC must have represented the arrival of a large group of immigrants to Britain, bringing with them a new culture which was imposed either by force, or on some more voluntary basis, upon the locals.

In recent decades, by contrast, there has been a reaction against this view and the alternative assumption tends to have held sway – that these waves of new culture do not represent significant movements of people into this country. The truth, as is so often the case, probably lies somewhere between the two extremes. A widespread adoption of a culture from the mainland of Europe need not imply a widespread arrival of new immigrants from Europe but, equally, it is unlikely to have taken place without the arrival of at least a significant number.

We have no tribal names, at this stage, for either the people in Britain or the new immigrants arriving. We do not know what they called themselves or what others called them and we know little about any group entities that may have existed. We do, however, know that such groups existed. Humans are social animals and, from the first, it must have been natural for them to join together to cope better with the challenges of life. At its simplest level this could mean one family living together in a single dwelling but, by around 3000 BC, large-scale construction projects like Avebury and Stonehenge clearly demonstrate the ability of the inhabitants of Britain to form much larger social groupings, whether short term or long term. In the first millennium BC the construction of significant numbers of hillforts across a wide swathe of central and southern Britain suggests that social groupings had acquired a military dimension.

It seems likely that British society in the pre-Roman period was, on some level at least, a society in which military activity was taken for granted and generally regarded as praiseworthy. There is ample evidence for such an approach to warfare in Britain, including the regular ritual deposits of weapons, the skill and care often used in the creation of military equipment like scabbards[3] and the depiction of warriors in art.[4] The Irish epic poems, such as the *Cattle Raid of Cooley* (though later and no doubt incorporating many later elements) give some idea, with their emphasis on valour and combat, of what kind of a society this might have been. Creighton has recently developed a concept of horse-and-chariot-borne bands of warriors transforming the cultural landscape of Britain at the beginning of the Late Iron Age.[5]

There has been a tendency in recent years to downplay the military aspects of hillforts, emphasising, for instance, their role as ostentatious displays of wealth and power. One should not, however, underestimate the sheer amount of effort needed to build, for example, the complex multivallate hillforts of the late pre-Roman period. These represent huge investments in terms of man (and no doubt woman) hours by the local community and it is hard to see them as anything but a reaction to a very real threat of attack. There is a limit in most societies to the amount of time, money and effort people are prepared to put into being 'one up' on the neighbours. Ostentation, in any event, has always been a part of warfare. The stronger defences look, the less likely they are to be attacked.

Equally, archaeology has provided indications of actual fighting in and around some of the few early hillforts to be thoroughly investigated. For instance, at Danebury the remains of at least 10 bodies were found showing signs of war injuries, and in eight of these cases, the person seems to have died from the injuries. Thousands of sling stones were also found in and around the gate.[6] Such evidence suggests, unsurprisingly, that the entrance was one of the weakest spots on a hillfort and the one most likely to be attacked. Caesar records that the Gallic way of warfare was to surround a hillfort, throw stones to drive the defenders off the ramparts and then attack the gate.[7] The gates of the early fort at Danebury seem to have been burnt in the fourth century BC and the main gate was burnt again around 100 BC.[8]

The architecture of hillforts in the centuries before the Roman invasion shows increasing complexity in the layout of defences around gateways. These look pretty in aerial photos, almost like Celtic artwork with their repeated sinuous twists and turns. However, on the ground, they are complex pieces of defensive planning which would have slowed the approach of attackers and exposed them to hostile fire from a number of angles as they advanced towards the interior of the hillfort. Again, ostentation no doubt has a part to play, but that need not invalidate a view of defensive capacity being paramount in these sophisticated constructions.

Hillforts were never as widespread in the south-east and east of England as further west. In any event, in the first century BC, many of the hillforts that did exist in this area seem to have been abandoned. This should not, however, be taken as a sign that times had become more peaceful. The south-eastern tribes that Caesar faced were evidently, from his descriptions, well equipped for and well used to warfare. It may simply be that the growth of larger political entities in the south-east, enabling the raising of larger armies, was making hillforts militarily less viable (something the Durotriges probably discovered to their cost when Vespasian swiftly fought his way across their territory after the invasion of AD 43). This time and this region see the appearance of so-called *oppida*. This is simply the Latin word for towns, but in terms of pre-Roman Britain it has come to be used for what is not exactly a town but a type of large lowland settlement protected by extensive linear defence systems which presumably better reflected the needs of the increasingly affluent tribes of the south-east.

Although it is currently a matter of fierce debate (with many archaeologists reluctant to recognise the existence of large-scale political entities in Britain before the first century BC) it is possible that in the same period as the rise of the hillforts we can also see the first, faint beginnings of what were to become the classic tribes of Britain, as later encountered in the classical, historical sources.

Cunliffe has identified regional pottery groups from as early as the sixth to fifth centuries BC, that he argues represent prototype groupings of the peoples who would later become the Dobunni, the Durotriges and the Atrebates.[9] Naturally different political entities can use the same artefacts, just as different regions of one political entity can use different artefacts, but it is interesting nonetheless. Perhaps more significantly, there is historical evidence from Gaul which suggests that a number of the tribes mentioned by Caesar were already in existence, and in at least roughly the same locations, by at least the fifth century BC.[10] One should certainly envisage a significant element of fluidity in British political geography in the pre-Roman period, but there seem no grounds to deny a significant element of continuity as well.

Our knowledge of the actual names of the classic British tribes and their basic location is derived largely from the works of the geographer Claudius Ptolemy,[11] backed up by scattered references in other Roman historical sources and a number of inscriptions. Ptolemy seems to have been writing some time in the first half of the second century AD, so the picture he gives of British tribal

4   Location of the tribes of Britain as indicated by Ptolemy

geography is as it was cemented into place by the Romans when, around the end of the first century AD, they created the *civitas* system of local administration based on the pre-existing tribal territories.

The few references to British tribal identities in Caesar writing over 150 years earlier include only one, or possibly two, of the names mentioned by Ptolemy. The Trinobantes or Trinovantes are mentioned and it is possible that the Cenimagni should be seen as a mangling of the phrase '*Iceni magni*', the 'great Iceni'. Caesar does, however, include a small number of other tribal names which seem to have dropped from view by the time Ptolemy was writing. It may be that these were minor tribes, later subsumed into a larger tribe, or alternatively were constituent parts of a bigger tribe, like the Scottish Septs.

Whatever the situation, by the late first century BC, distribution of coinage and some other artefacts can be interpreted to support the existence of tribal groupings potentially identifiable with Ptolemy's tribes at the beginning of the second century AD (*4*). Obviously, we do not know whether the names Ptolemy gives the political entities in question were how they were known in pre-Roman or early Roman times, but in the absence of other evidence and for the sake of convenience, I will use Ptolemy's names. Their use as labels is not perfect but it enables easy discussion of the peoples of Britain in a way that becomes much more difficult if we have constantly to identify nameless groups by their attributes. The use of terms such as 'southern kingdom' or 'eastern region' or even the use of modern county names (as sometimes now happens) to denote groups of Britons in the pre-Roman period may be neutral but seems rather to duck the issue. We know for certain that the Britons in question did not refer to themselves in any of those ways, but there is at least a possibility they used some, or all, of the names of the Roman period as listed by Ptolemy.

To reach some definition of the actual extent of the territories of British tribes involves an inevitably rather messy mix of literary references (especially Ptolemy, who attributes different towns to different tribes, and the *Antonine Itinerary* and *Ravenna Cosmography* which give some names of tribal capitals incorporating the tribes' names), cultural artefacts (especially coins) and an understanding of the sheer physical geography of Britain. It is far from being an exact science and in terms of artefacts is to a certain extent open to an accusation of circularity[12] but overall the picture produced, while hardly uncontroversial, has a certain coherence.

Obviously, the presence of a coin attributed to one tribe in a specific area does not necessarily indicate that that tribe controlled that area. For a start, as with so much pre-Roman archaeology, there is controversy over exactly how coins were used. However, by the late first century BC, at least in some areas, there is a coinage which echoes features of Roman coinage, carries the names of rulers and, like Roman coinage, comes in copper alloy, silver and gold units.

It seems reasonable, therefore, to see that coinage as fulfilling many of the same functions as Roman coinage, and it seems reasonable to infer that the same is true of a fair proportion of predecessor coins. The presence of a tribe's coins in an area, therefore, does indicate direct or indirect contact, be it commercial, political or military, or a combination of all three. It also seems reasonable, in an area where the coins of one tribe are dominant, in the absence of other evidence to the contrary, to make a working assumption of political control by that tribe (5).

Equally, while dating pre-Roman coins closely is a difficult and often controversial task, such dating evidence as can be attributed to different coins can help provide something of a picture of changing contacts and influence in pre-Roman Britain. Again, while obviously the replacement in an area of coins of one tribe by coins of another need not necessarily imply violent conquest, it must imply something about a changing zone of influence, and one should certainly not ignore the possibility of military activity as a major, perhaps *the* major, factor in political change in this period. Warlike themes are a recurrent motif on pre-Roman coinage and in the earliest historical account of the British tribes, Caesar says that prior to his arrival, the British chief Cassivellaunus had been engaged in constant warfare with other British tribes.[13] Our generation, brought up with the knowledge that they are unlikely to experience any personal involvement in war (apart from possible rapid nuclear annihilation or being affected by terrorism), is commendably hostile to war and reluctant to see it as a 'normal' part of human activity. Nevertheless we should understand that we are, in that respect, in an extremely unusual position in terms of human history. Many periods of history and many cultures have seen states of almost continual armed conflict, whether of high or low intensity. Even in terms of sheer mathematical probability, it is far more likely that the situation in pre-Roman Britain was like that than like the settled calm of modern Western Europe and North America.

If we are to understand the development of Britain during the Roman period and at its end we need to understand the Britons of the period. Only by doing this can we establish whether the Bosnia/Iraq scenario can provide a likely explanation for the end of Roman Britain (see Introduction).

It is time to meet the British tribes. We shall concentrate on the tribes of modern-day England (in particular, those of the centre, south and east of England) because these tribes are likely to have had most influence on the transition from Roman Britain to Anglo-Saxon England. However, it is also worth taking a brief look at the tribes elsewhere in Britain. The pre-Roman period is not the focus of this book, so this overview is not intended to be a comprehensive review of all the current controversies surrounding that era. It is merely intended to give an outline of the main British players in the subsequent period.

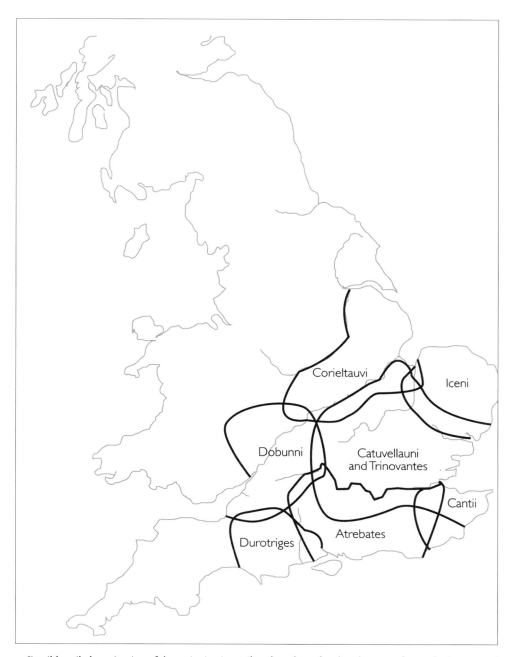

5 Possible tribal territories of the coin-issuing tribes, based on the distribution of coin finds. Areas of overlap show areas that may have been subject to competing influences or change of control.
After Cunliffe and Jones & Mattingly

TRIBES OF CENTRAL AND SOUTHERN BRITAIN

Cantii / Cantiaci

The Cantii, as their name suggests, occupied the area roughly covered by the modern county of Kent. It seems possible however, that some of present-day East Sussex to the east of Pevensey may also have been part of the territory of the Cantii (rather than being connected to Atrebatic territory next door in present-day West Sussex). Cunliffe suggests that pre-Roman pottery in parts of East Sussex has more in common with that found in Kent than with that found in Atrebatic areas, suggesting at least significant commercial links with Kent.[14] Caesar mentions four kings in Kent.[15] It is probable that these were the kings of different areas within the territory of the Cantii and one of the four separate regions could have been the eastern part of East Sussex.

The Cantii, because of their geographic location, are likely to have had a close relationship with the inhabitants of the continent across the Dover straits. They may, for instance, have been the first tribe to commence the continental practice of issuing coins. They also adopted a number of other continental customs in the second half of the first century BC, including wheel-turned ceramics and the use of cremation for some of their dead. A linked feature is the increasing appearance of goods from the Mediterranean region, including large wine amphorae and table wares. Similar artefacts and practices are also present in northern France across the so-called Southern Belgic area.

This suggests strong commercial links, at least, between the two areas, and there is even the possibility of some form of political control stretching across the Channel in this region. At one point Caesar refers to the chief of the Suessiones in Gaul exercising control over part of Britain.[16] If so, bearing in mind the location of the Suessiones in north-eastern France and the proximity of Kent, then the Cantii are one of the more likely candidates for Gallic political influence. It is possible that Caesar's invasions caused extensive damage to the area's economy, perhaps through political turmoil created in the aftermath, or possibly because trade between the Cantii and the continent was hindered due to the Cantii's resistance to Caesar. Certainly, there is no sign in Kent of the elaborate, rich burials found in Catuvellauni and Trinovantes territory just to the north in the late pre-Roman period and the Cantii stopped issuing their own coins around the end of the first century BC. This also seems to be about the time when Kent became a zone of dispute between the expanding power of the Atrebates in the west and the widening influence of the Catuvellauni to the north.

The impact of this rivalry, which we will examine in greater depth in the next chapter, was probably felt most acutely in West Kent, the region closest to the Catuvellauni and also bordering on Atrebatic territory. It may be that the competition of the two neighbouring powers expressed in this region helped mould a distinct identity for West Kent, or it may be that it exaggerated a difference that was already evident. The territory of the Cantii includes a small number of *oppida*. Two of these were located at Rochester and Canterbury, and these sites subsequently became the two major Roman centres in the *civitas* of the Cantii, one in West Kent, the other in East Kent. It may be that this arrangement represents some kind of administrative division in the Roman period. Certainly, separate identities for East and West Kent existed in the post-Roman period, with differences in the initial Anglo-Saxon cultures of the two areas, and subsequently separate dioceses, being based around Rochester and Canterbury (see Chapter 8).

Ptolemy also lists London as a town of the Cantii. London does not seem to have existed as a significant settlement in pre-Roman times and its position in the Roman administration of Britain is at times unclear. It is hard to know how it fitted into the layout of the *civitates* in the period when Ptolemy was writing in the early second century. South of the Thames, coinage distribution suggests the territory of the Cantii may indeed have stretched as far west as the area of present-day Greater London, but whether it ever stretched north of the river is unclear.[17] The land of the Cantii remained a major gateway to the continent throughout the Roman period (as, of course, it does today).

A thriving pottery industry emerged in West Kent in the Roman period and the area also provides some evidence for commercial salt extraction. In addition, it seems to have been one of the more heavily farmed parts of the territory of the Cantii with, for example, large numbers of villas situated in the area.[18]

Catuvellauni, Trinovantes

The other two main tribes adopting cremation for some of their dead in the latter half of the first century BC were the Catuvellauni and Trinovantes in their tribal territories to the north of the Thames. With the Catuvellaunian/Trinovantian confederation we are in the major league of British tribes and we will examine their rise to tribal superpower status in more detail in the next chapter.

By the time of Ptolemy, the Catuvellauni occupied one of the largest areas of any tribe, including most of present-day Hertfordshire, Bedfordshire, Buckinghamshire, Oxfordshire, Cambridgeshire and Northamptonshire. In the south was a lowland area around the Catuvellaunian capital at Verulamium, with, to the north, the Chilterns and beyond that, territory in the Nene Valley and the fenlands.

The origins of the Catuvellauni are obscure. Caesar, for instance, does not mention them. Nevertheless it is possible that Cassivellaunus, the British leader who resisted Caesar, is effectively the first recorded Catuvellaunian leader. Caesar locates his territory north of the Thames and indicates that he was, at that time, in conflict with the Trinovantes (who occupied territory in what is present-day Essex). It seems an inevitable conclusion therefore, that Cassivellaunus at least came from an area within the later territory of the Catuvellauni. It may be that he led just one of a number of smaller groups that were later to form the classic Catuvellauni, but equally it is possible that he had already started the process of uniting them. Judging by his selection to lead the British resistance to Caesar and his ability to cause problems for the Trinovantes (noted by Caesar as one of the most powerful tribes) he was already a leader of some power and authority. It may even be that the name of Cassivellaunus and Catuvellauni are linked. Niblett suggests that the difference between the two names indicates different roots.[19] However, even if this is so, rather than representing an accident of transmission (if Caesar was really capable of mangling Iceni into Cenimagni, he could probably manage Catuvellaunus into Cassivellaunus) there still remains the possibility that one name inspired a very similar, but slightly different name. The naming of political entities after individual leaders is a recognised feature of post-Roman political geography in the British west (Brychan/Brycheiniog, Ceredig/Ceredigion, for instance). Equally Cassivellaunus may have been named after the Catuvellauni. The name Catuvellaunus, which means something like 'strong in battle', does go on to be a popular personal name in post-Roman times in the British form Cadwallon.

The origins of the Catuvellauni used to be thought to be connected to a passage in Caesar where he describes how, at some stage prior to his time, a group of Belgae had raided part of Britain and subsequently settled there, farming the land.[20] In the days when it was assumed that a change of culture automatically represented a wave of immigration, Caesar's immigration of Belgae used to be linked to the appearance in southern Britain of cremations and wheel-turned pottery. However, it now seems likely that these cultural developments largely post-date Caesar rather than pre-date him, making a link with his Belgic immigration less likely.

Cunliffe suggests that if such an immigration as described by Caesar did take place, then it was archaeologically invisible and took place in roughly the same area as the probable immigration of Commius and his Atrebates (see below), in the region later named the *civitas* of the Belgae by the Romans.[21] This is certainly possible, but the Atrebates in mainland Europe were also a Belgic tribe and it seems perhaps more likely that the Belgae referred to in the *civitas* of the Belgae were Commius and his Atrebates.

It is clear from ceramic evidence that eastern England had strong links with the continent going back at least as far as the third century BC,[22] and it is not inconceivable that the region constitutes an area particularly susceptible to foreign cultural influence because of previous Belgic immigration. It is even possible that Cassivellaunus might have been such an immigrant or a descendant of one and played a similar role with the Catuvellauni as Commius probably played with the Atrebates, founding a dynasty and making it a major political force in Britain.

There are a number of hillforts in Catuvellaunian territory. However, the *oppidum* form of settlement makes an appearance at Verulamium in the late first century BC. Other major pre-Roman sites within Catuvellaunian territory include Welwyn, Baldock, Braughing, Cambridge and Dorchester on Thames (site of another *oppidum*), all of which were to see subsequent Roman development.

The territory of the Trinovantes probably effectively covered the area of modern Essex. As mentioned earlier, by contrast to the Catuvellauni, Caesar does record the Trinovantes, referring to them as almost the most powerful tribe in Britain. 'Almost' is here the key word because, by Caesar's own account, the Trinovantes already at that stage seem to have been suffering from the impact of Cassivellaunus and his possible proto-Catuvellauni.

Later, as we shall see in the next chapter, the Trinovantes joined the Catuvellauni under joint rule.[23] However, this should probably not be seen as conquest but as more a process of confederation, even if possibly enforced confederation. The two tribes both show shared cultural influences and archaeologically they seem almost indistinguishable in the late first century BC and early first century AD. The Trinovantian capital of Camuludonum probably became the capital of both Trinovantes and Catuvellauni under Cunobelin[24] (which seems unlikely if this had been a simple case of the Catuvellauni lording it over the conquered Trinovantes) and, by the Roman invasion, Camulodunum was a sophisticated complex with separate areas for religion, inhabitation and industry. Catuvellaunian and Trinovantian territory included some excellent farmland, and, in the Roman period, about 130 villas are known in Catuvellaunian territory alone, with about another 100 probable villa sites recorded.[25] There were also a number of other significant sources of wealth.

In the Roman period, Catuvellaunian territory included at least three major pottery industries – one in Oxfordshire, one in the Nene Valley and one based in the area between London and Verulamium centred on Brockley Hill. In the north there was probably salt extraction along the fenland edges. Ptolemy names a site in the area which he attributes to the Catuvellauni and calls Salinas (clearly implying a connection with salt extraction) and, as will be discussed in Chapter 3, it is possible that the Catuvellauni acquired control over some previously Icenian fenland in the first century AD where salt extraction may also have taken place.[26] Salt extraction also seems to have been important along the Essex coast in Trinovantian territory. In addition, there was iron extraction at a number of locations in Catuvellaunian territory, starting in pre-Roman times and expanding in the Roman period. Ashton and Cow Roast near Northchurch are two sites which both show extensive evidence of iron extraction, as do a number of sites in the Water Newton area. Barnack Rag Stone was quarried in significant quantities to the north of Water Newton.[27]

Regni, Belgae, Atrebates

To the west of the Cantii, Ptolemy locates a tribe he calls the Regni. To the north and west of this tribe he has the Belgae. Then to the north of the territory of the Belgae, he places the Atrebates. There are, however, as with the Catuvellauni and Trinovantes, cultural and political reasons to treat these three entities as linked. Cunliffe argues that ceramic evidence suggests a single tribal grouping in this area may have been defined as early as the second or third centuries BC.[28] Certainly, the same coinage appears across the region in the first half of the first century BC.[29] The establishment of the core identity of this tribal grouping is probably, however, down to the arrival of Commius, a member of the Atrebates tribe of northern Gaul, with presumably a group of accompanying tribesmen, in the middle of the first century BC. Commius is an interesting character, extensively mentioned in Caesar's *Gallic Wars*, and is probably a fascinating example (even though many aspects of the story remain unclear) of how power and political identity could translate across the Channel in pre-Roman times.

After Commius (according to Caesar) had a spell as king of the continental Atrebates, he is recorded by Frontinus as fleeing to Britain.[30] Shortly afterwards, a Commius turns up on coins in the area we have been discussing, and it has been widely assumed that this is the same figure (*6*). Certainly, the existence by Ptolemy's time of Atrebates in this area, the reoccurrence of the name Commius, the fact that Caesar took Commius to Britain with him to negotiate with tribes there (suggesting he already had contacts and influence on the island) and the mention of Commius fleeing to Britain make it very plausible. Subsequent rulers in the area show their allegiance to the Commian dynasty by using the inscription COMF, standing for 'son of Commius', on their coins. Due to the probably central role of the Atrebatic Commius and the definite existence of Atrebates there by the time of Ptolemy, it has been traditional to use the term 'Atrebatic' for a pre-Roman political entity covering most of the Roman-period *civitates* of Atrebates, Regni and Belgae. I shall continue to use this name, rather

6   Coin of Commius

than a more neutral alternative, like 'southern kingdom', because, whatever the pre-Roman people of this area actually called themselves, Atrebates is at least one genuine possibility and it is a name with a real pedigree in the period and the area.

The *civitas* of the Regni seems to have been centred on West Sussex and the part of East Sussex up to the Pevensey area. It included the large pre-Roman *oppidum* at Selsey. Coastal erosion has removed much of the archeological evidence of the settlement itself, but the extensive network of linear defences protecting it and the richness of stray finds washed up on the beach suggest a significant pre-Roman site. Certainly, the new Roman capital of the Regni was built next to it, at Chichester, and not far away lay the great early Roman palace of Fishbourne which may have belonged to the king and ally of the Romans in the early post-invasion years, Togidubnus. Also nearby was the pre-Roman and Roman-period cult centre on Hayling Island which has been tentatively identified as the location of an Atrebatic ruler cult, perhaps incorporating a shrine of Commius,[31] or the mausoleum of the Atrebatic king at the time of the invasion of 43, Verica.[32]

West of the Regni, Ptolemy locates the territory of the Belgae which, according to him, included Winchester and a town he calls Aquae Calidae, which is probably Bath. If so, coin distributions and ceramic links suggest that the eastern half of the *civitas* of the Belgae was Atrebatic in pre-Roman times,[33] and coin distribution suggests the western half was Dobunnic. This is an unusual administrative arrangement by Roman standards and one which we will study in more depth later. Winchester itself, prior to its development as the Roman capital of the Belgae, was the location of a large *oppidum* where occupation began in the first century BC. By contrast to the territory of the Regni, with its strong coastal focus, the territory of the *civitas* of the Belgae was largely inland.

To the north of the *civitas* of the Belgae and the Regni, Ptolemy locates the *civitas* of the Atrebates. This area was centred on Calleva (*7*) and included eastern Berkshire. It also seems to have extended into eastern Wiltshire, probably (judging by the slight preponderance of Atrebatic over Dobunnic coins there) including the area around Marlborough and Mildenhall.[34] The distribution of Atrebatic coin finds also suggests the territory of the Atrebates may have originally stretched as far north as the Thames in this region but, if so, their dominance soon came under pressure from the southward expansion of Catuvellaunian influence. Earthworks at Calleva indicate the development of an *oppidum* here in the second half of the first century BC. It may represent the original base for Commius at a time when Atrebatic power was probably at its strongest in this region.

The three Atrebatic and partly Atrebatic *civitates* included much rich farmland. The coastal strip of the *civitas* of the Regni was heavily settled with villas in the Roman period, as were the *civitas* of the Atrebates and the eastern part of the *civitas* of the Belgae. By contrast, the part of the *civitas* of the Belgae in central and south Wiltshire shows a definite lack of villas (although 11 villages of pre-Roman and Roman date are known in the area[35]). It has been suggested that this was due to the area being an imperial estate, but there is little explicit evidence for that.

7   Coin of Eppillus proclaiming him king and referring to Calleva

On the far eastern border of Atrebatic territory lay the great iron-mining area of the Weald. Iron seems to have been extracted here in small quantities in the pre-Roman period, while, from the second century AD, large-scale extraction started at a number of sites, with an estimated 10,000 tons of iron being produced by the Bardown site alone.[36] Some of the major pottery industries of the Roman period were also based in the tribal territory of the Atrebates – in particular, the Alice Holt/Farnham Ware industry and the New Forest industry. In addition, there is evidence of commercial salt extraction, probably starting in the pre-Roman period and extending into the Roman period, along the creeks between Portsmouth and Chichester. The Atrebates seem to have formed the other great power block in southern Britain in pre-Roman times and we will examine their probable rivalry with the Catuvellauni in the next chapter.

Durotriges/Durotrages

To the south-west of the Atrebates lay the Durotriges, or possibly Durotrages (if the evidence of a building inscription from Hadrian's Wall is to be believed[37]). Their territory seems to have consisted of Dorset (a county name which in its original Anglo-Saxon form incorporates the Duro element of the tribal name) and part of Somerset to the north. The Durotriges appear to have had a distinctly different identity to their Atrebatic neighbours to the east. This unique identity seems to owe much to influences from across the channel. By 100 BC, at the latest, extensive trading links had been established between the Durotriges and ports in Armorica/Brittany across the Channel. Through their contacts with the Gauls of this region, the Durotriges had access to Atlantic trade routes that eventually linked all the way south into the Mediterranean trade networks. As a result, comparatively large quantities of Mediterranean goods seem to have reached the Durotrigan tribal area in the first half of the first century BC.

The idea that Britain was always a beer-drinking nation, until package tours started giving us a taste for wine, may be somewhat wide of the mark. Quantities of Dressel 1 Amphorae, for instance, which would originally have contained Italian wine, have been found in Durotrigan territory and there is also evidence of other exotic items, such as figs.[38]

With the trade came extensive continental influence. Significant numbers of coins from Armorica are found in the area and significant quantities of Armorican pottery too.[39] As already discussed, and it is a point we will return to later, the presence of large quantities of foreign goods does not necessarily imply the presence of large quantities of foreigners. However, it is unlikely that such a marked cultural influence could have been created without the presence of at least a reasonable number of Armoricans.

8 View of Maiden Castle showing proximity to Dorchester, the new Roman tribal capital

The extent of ethnic links in the pre-Roman period is unclear, but it is interesting to speculate on the nature of the movement in the opposite direction that created Brittany in the post-Roman period. Gildas is our main historical source for Britons fleeing overseas to avoid advancing Saxons and it has been argued that he may have been writing in the tribal area of the Durotriges.[40] It seems quite possible that Brittany became one of the main destinations for British emigration in the fifth century AD because of already existing long-standing ethnic links. The original main terminus for cross-Channel trade in Durotrigan territory was the site at Hengistbury Head but there are signs that, as the first century BC progressed, Poole Harbour took an increasing share of the trade.

Ultimately, however, the economic glory days of the Durotriges seem to have been relatively short-lived. In the second half of the first century BC, possibly as a result of Caesar's activities in Armorica, or perhaps as a result of the developing trade between Gaul and the east of Britain, cross-Channel trade in the Durotrigan area seems to have been curtailed dramatically. It is notable also that Durotrigan coinage, which had started as gold, subsequently became white metal and then finally bronze, perhaps reflecting the economic impact of the collapse of the tribe's cross-Channel trading.[41]

By contrast to the increasing appearance of *oppida* seen in tribal areas to the east, the Durotriges seem to have kept the hillfort as the mainstay of their

9   Hod Hill, a Durotrigan hillfort captured by the Romans in the period after the invasion

defended living space right up until Vespasian and his army arrived and started firing ballista bolts at them. In fact, many of the best known hillforts in England lie in Durotrigan territory, including the massive and spectacular Maiden Castle (located immediately outside the Roman-period Durotrigan capital, Dorchester) and the impressive Hod Hill, with its sweeping views and later Roman fort (*8, 9, 10, colour plates 3 & 4*).

Ilchester was the Roman town of Lindinis and is mentioned in conjunction with the *civitas* of the Durotriges on two Hadrian's Wall building stones.[42] It is possible, therefore, that Durotrigan territory included two sub-groups, one based around Dorchester and another centred on Ilchester. The Durotrigan economy was probably based largely on mixed farming and it has even been suggested that the area was already exporting food in the pre-Roman period. Grain appears to have been gathered at Hengistbury Head for export and there is also evidence of an unusual number of cattle bones, suggesting perhaps either live export or, possibly, the presence of a 'leather for export' industry.[43]

Durotrigan tribal territory also included some other valuable resources. In the north-west of their territory, on the border with the Dobunni, lay the silver and lead mines of the Mendips, exploited in both pre-Roman and Roman times.[44] It has been suggested from the evidence of coin patterns that the relationship

10 Badbury Hill, a Durotrigan hillfort and still an important feature of the landscape in Roman times. It sits at the junction of two major Roman roads

11 Coin of Durotriges. *Courtesy of David Shelley*

between the two tribes in the area may not always have been a peaceful one, and competing claims to the mineral resources of the area may have been one reason for this. On the coast around Poole Harbour lay reserves of excellent potting clay. There is evidence of a pottery industry here in pre-Roman times while in the Roman period this became the site of a huge Black Burnished Ware industry. Other natural resources exploited by the Durotriges include sea salt and Kimmeridge shale which was carved into a wide variety of items including jewellery and even furniture. Purbeck stone was also exported over long distances in the Roman period.[45]

Dobunni

To the north of the Durotriges, according to Ptolemy, lay the Dobunni, a large tribe probably controlling territory that stretched as far north as Worcester and as far west as the Upper Thames. The central position of the Dobunni, with powerful neighbours, may be reflected in the cultural development of the tribe. At an early period, there are strong suggestions of Atrebatic contacts and influence. For example, until about 35 BC, Atrebatic coinage appears in the area, and when separate coinage starts being issued, it appears to have been based on Atrebatic designs. However, later there are suggestions of increasing Catuvellaunian influence with, for instance, a coin of Bodvoc showing similarities to coins issued by Tasciovanus (*12*).[46] The most significant element of Dobunnic geography internally may be a cultural and perhaps, at times, political division between regional groupings north and south of the River Avon.

12   Coin of Bodvoc

Different styles of pottery were in use in territory north and south of the Avon. Equally, while coins carrying the name Corio appear throughout Dobunnic territory, those of Bodvoc occur almost entirely north of the Avon.[47] Moore and Reece question whether such a neat equation can be made between different artefact distribution and political/cultural differences in this area,[48] but although it cannot be proved, it does not seem improbable. As we shall see, the later history of the region certainly does suggest some significant difference between the two areas.

The main tribal centre north of the Avon may have been the *oppidum* at Bagendon (*13*), just a few miles from the later Roman capital of the Dobunnic *civitas* at Cirencester (*colour plate 10*). It is not clear where any major tribal centre might have been located in the part of Dobunnic territory lying on and south of the Avon (Camerton is one possibility) but it is known that the hot springs at Bath were already a religious site in pre-Roman times.

As already mentioned, Ptolemy lists Aquae Calidae (Hot Waters) as one of three towns in the *civitas* of the Belgae and Bath/Aquae Sulis seems the only likely location. The location of Winchester/Venta Belgarum also in the *civitas* of the Belgae indicates then that this would have been a *civitas* with an eastern Atrebatic half and a western Dobunnic half. Doubts have been expressed about whether the Romans would have done such a thing, but the apparently somewhat separate nature of this region south of the Avon does suggest that it could have been a feasible candidate for the Romans to have detached from the rest of Dobunnic territory.

As well as a more upland region north of Gloucester, the tribal area of the Dobunni included the rich farmlands to the south and east of Cirencester, where the Roman period saw the development of a number of large, affluent villa complexes such as at Woodchester and Chedworth.

In addition, there is extensive evidence of iron extraction in the Forest of Dean in the Roman period, while in the far south of Dobunnic territory, as already discussed, close to the border with the Durotriges lay the rich silver and lead mines of the Mendips. There was also quarrying on a significant commercial scale at Dundry Hill and The Tumps.

Cornovii

To the north of the Dobunni, Ptolemy places the territory of the Cornovii. The Cornovii never issued their own coinage so defining the extent of their territory is a matter of relying on Ptolemy and rather sparse archaeological evidence.

Ptolemy indicates that this tribal territory stretched as far as Chester in the north and included the Roman-period capital of the Cornovii at Viroconium/Wroxeter. A few miles from Wroxeter lies the hillfort on the great Wrekin Hill.

13 Ditch and bank at the Dobunnic *oppidum* at Bagendon, about four miles to the north of the Roman-period capital of the Dobunni at Cirencester

Wrekin is a name closely linked to Viroconium and the hillfort may have been a capital of the pre-Roman Cornovii.

A number of Dobunnic coins have been found in what appears to have been the territory of the Cornovii. However, the small numbers do not suggest extensive links. Certainly, from an archaeological point of view, the culture of the Cornovii seems almost entirely unaffected by the continental styles that spread west with Catuvellaunian contacts, influence and coinage.

In addition to farming, salt extraction was probably a major economic activity in the territory of the Cornovii. There was commercial salt extraction at both Salinae/Middlewich and Condate/Northwich. Trenches and the discovery of lead ingots at Linley also suggest lead mining there.[49]

TRIBES OF WESTERN BRITAIN

Dumnonii

To the west of the Durotriges, Ptolemy places the tribe of the Dumnonii. Like the Cornovii, the Dumnonii did not issue their own coins, so tribal territory and contacts cannot be determined in that way. However, with the Dobunni and Durotriges both issuing coins and the Dumnonii being the only tribal grouping mentioned by Ptolemy on the south-western peninsula at this stage, we can have at least some idea of their borders. Some have argued that there were separate tribes in Cornwall and Devon, with the tribe in Cornwall perhaps being called the Cornovii, probably the origin of the word Cornwall.[50] This is possible, but then it is equally possible that the Cornovii were a constituent sub-tribe of the Dumnonii.

We have already seen with, for instance, the Atrebates and the Durotriges that the idea of Britons as a separate island race until the advent of fast ferries, the Channel Tunnel and cheap flights was far from true. The Dumnonii seem to have had even more in common with Armorica than the Durotriges and it has been argued that culturally the Dumnonii had more in common with Armorica than with any of their British neighbours. Characteristic cliff castles and *fogous* (underground rooms) for instance, are found extensively in both areas but not in Durotrigan or Dobunnic territory to the east. The ceramic tradition in the area also seems to owe a lot to cross-Channel contacts, with the South-Western Decorated Ware style having particularly close similarities with Armorican traditions.[51]

Previously, it was common to argue that the area had seen extensive actual settlement from Armorica, including a possible invasion by the Veneti in the first century BC. Recently there has been much more of a tendency here, as elsewhere, to emphasise trading links over actual immigration. However, the kind of cross-Channel excursions probably seen in the case of Commius and the Atrebates and in the case of those carrying the Arras Culture to East Yorkshire to establish the Parisi brand there (see below) should certainly not be ruled out.

Cornwall, of course, had a number of valuable mineral resources. In particular, tin, essential to the making of bronze, brought foreign imported items along the Atlantic trade routes and into the territory of the Dumnonii. Copper and lead deposits were also exploited in the Roman period. The tribe, though, relied mainly on mixed farming and, in the most upland regions where agriculture was harder, pastoralism for economic survival.

In pre-Roman times, there seem to have been few if any substantial settlements in Dumnonian territory, with much of the population in Devon living in small hamlets surrounded by multiple ditches and in Cornwall, most living in the so-called Rounds, small farmsteads surrounded by an often round ditch. By Ptolemy's time, the Dumnonii had a Roman-style capital at Exeter. However, outside Exeter there seems to be little sign of adoption of Roman culture. There are very few villas in Dumnonian territory (as opposed to the large numbers in nearby Durotrigan and Dobunnic territory) and only one villa, in the far south-west at Magor Farm.[52] Many pre-Roman sites show evidence of occupation, with few signs of change, throughout the Roman period.

In post-Roman times the tribal area of the Dumnonii gave rise to the Kingdom of Dumnonia, and it is hard not to think that the Roman presence in this area had comparatively little impact.

THE TRIBES OF WALES

Ptolemy lists three tribes in the area of modern-day Wales. The Silures were located in the territory to the west of the Dobunni with a Roman-period capital at Caerwent. Beyond the Silures, further west, lay the land of the Demetae with a Roman capital at Carmarthen. In the central mountains, to the north, was the territory of the Ordovices. In addition, from accounts of the early Roman campaigns after the invasion of AD 43, we know of a tribe called the Deceangli living along the north coast of Wales.

Archaeological evidence for Wales in pre-Roman times is much more limited than that found in territories to the south and west. However, there are signs of trading networks and cultural influences from neighbouring tribes.

In the territory of the Demetae, for instance, there are a large number of cliff castles. These are very similar to examples in Armorica and the territory of the Dumnonii to the south.[53] In the eastern part of the territory of the Silures, by contrast, a number of hillforts bear quite close similarities with those to the south and west, in Durotrigan territory.[54]

In the central, more mountainous regions of Wales, food production in both pre-Roman and Roman times was probably mainly pastoral, but in the south and north, mixed farming seems to have been more common.

Wales was a highly important area for mineral extraction in the Roman period, with lead and silver mines in the south-east and north-east, copper mines in the north-west and gold extraction (with the mines complex at Dolaucothi) in the south-west.[55]

As in the territory of the Dumnonii, Roman culture seems to have been largely ignored in Wales. There are, however, areas, such as that around the large Roman sites at Caerwent and Caerleon, which show a degree of Romanisation comparable with that of tribal territories further east.

TRIBES OF EASTERN AND NORTHERN BRITAIN

Iceni/Eceni

Returning to the east coast, in the area to the north of the Trinovantes and to the east of the Catuvellauni lay the territory of the Iceni, probably covering modern Norfolk and much of Suffolk. Ptolemy locates their major Roman-period centre at Venta, Caistor by Norwich. It is possible that they should really be called the Eceni if, as is widely assumed, the inscription ECEN, on some coins from the area is a reference to the name of the tribe (*14*).

As has already been discussed, these may be the Cenimagni, 'the great Iceni', mentioned by Caesar. Certainly they seem to have been a powerful and affluent tribe. Two of the best known features of the pre-Roman archaeology of the region are the hoards of gold torcs and the large number of often elaborately decorated and enamelled horse fittings found. Both suggest a wealthy aristocracy. Notably though, the Iceni do not seem to have spent much of their disposable income on the trappings of Mediterranean culture that flowed into the territory of their southern and western neighbours in the late first century BC and the early first century AD, nor did they start using cremation. This may reflect a somewhat tense relationship between the Iceni and the growing power of the Catuvellaunian/Trinovantian confederation which, with the exception of access through the Fens to Corieltauvian lands, came to control all land approaches to Icenian territory.

The first linear earthwork protecting Icenian territory where it met Catuvellaunian territory on the important Icknield way corridor seems to date from the pre-Roman period,[56] and there is some evidence of conflict between Trinovantes and Iceni on the Iceni's southern border. The hillfort at Burgh by Woodbridge originally shows evidence of probably Icenian occupation but, after

14 Icenian coin showing distinctive double crescents

burning some time in the first two decades of the first century AD, artefacts similar to those in use further south appear.[57] Certainly, there is a marked advance of Catuvellaunian/Trinovantian coinage northwards into Icenian territory in this area under Cunobelin.

There are few defensive pre-Roman sites in Icenian territory. However, Thetford, Saham Toney and Caistor by Norwich (the latter both important centres in Roman times too) probably had significant concentrations of population.[58]

The wealth of the Iceni was based largely on farming, with their territory including much fertile agricultural land. However, in the north-west of their territory lay the Fens and it is likely that salt extraction here was also a source of wealth in pre-Roman times[59] (though one that, as discussed in Chapter 3, may no longer have been under Icenian control by Ptolemy's time). The area around Brampton also held a large number of pottery kilns in the Roman period.[60]

There is some possible evidence of regional sub-groupings among the Iceni or, at least, of regional cultural differences. Davies, for instance, draws attention to the distribution of different terret types, with lipped and knobbed terrets being found in the west of Icenian territory, simple terrets being found in the south, and mini terrets being found in the south and east.[61] It is also noticeable that, in the Roman period, villas are clustered in the west of Icenian territory and are much rarer in the east.

Corieltauvi

Further up the North Sea coast from the Iceni were the Corieltauvi. Ptolemy attributes Leicester and Lincoln to this tribe and it is probable that their territory roughly covered modern Warwickshire, Leicestershire and Lincolnshire. In contrast to a number of the tribes and tribal areas to the south, this tribal region makes very few appearances in Roman historical sources.

Like the Iceni, they made little use of defended population centres. However, Kirmington and Old Sleaford both seem to have been major pre-Roman population centres and there is also evidence for pre-Roman occupation at Leicester and Lincoln, the locations of the two major cities within the Roman-period *civitas* of the Corieltauvi. There is a sense of continuity in other parts of the *civitas* of the Corieltauvi too. Dragonby, for instance, seems to have been occupied from after the mid-first millennium BC right through the Roman period.[62]

The Corieltauvian countryside was heavily dotted with settlements practising mixed farming, in particular on the light soils of the river valleys and the on the limestone of the Jurassic Ridge.[63] There is also, however, evidence in the shape of numerous salterns, of extensive salt extraction along the Lincolnshire coast. Pottery found in association with the remains of evaporation vessels suggests that the industry was operating from at least the middle of the first millennium BC.[64] In addition, extraction of iron from the ironstone of the Jurassic Ridge was probably a major industry in both pre-Roman and Roman times. Production at Wakerley, at least, certainly seems to have started in the pre-Roman period.[65] Mancetter/Hartshill also saw the development of a considerable industry producing mortaria in the Roman period and large numbers of kilns were based around Lincoln.[66] There are none of the cremations found in the territory of the Catuvellauni and Trinovantes to the south but pottery forms in Corieltauvian territory do increasingly show southern influence in the second half of the first century BC and the first half of the first century AD.[67]

Conversely, the distribution of Corieltauvian coinage north of the Humber Estuary (in addition to probable Corieltauvian influence on the pottery styles of the Parisi) suggests extensive commercial and possibly even political links with the Parisi.[68] By contrast, the relative lack of Corieltauvian coinage territory to the west of the tribal territory suggests far fewer links with the Brigantes.

15 Corieltauvian coin showing one name, Volisios, on one side and another, Dumnocoveros, on the other. This might indicate joint rulers and possibly regional sub-groupings within Corieltauvian territory

There is, however, an unusual concentration of Corieltauvian coinage that has turned up deep inside the territory of the Brigantes.[69] It has been suggested that this might represent the savings of exiled Corieltauvi, though it is just as likely, and perhaps more likely, to represent the result of a Brigantian raid into Corieltauvian territory.

A feature of some Corieltauvian coins is the appearance of more than one name on them (*15*). It is possible that this may represent some form of joint leadership, like the two consuls in Rome. Alternatively it may suggest at least two regional sub-groupings within Corieltauvian territory. As already mentioned, there were two major Roman-period centres present in the territory. Leicester, in the south, was the Roman-period capital of the Corieltauvi. Lincoln, in the north, started life as a fortress, then turned into a colony for retired soldiers but clearly became a major centre for the surrounding Britons later in the Roman period. It is conceivable that the presence of these two major centres in different regions of Corieltauvian territory might represent a continuation of a pre-Roman territorial division, perhaps with one of the pairs of rulers in control of each.

Parisi

Across the Humber Estuary from the territory of the Corieltauvi were, according to Ptolemy, the lands of the Parisi. Here again, we move beyond the range of tribes issuing coinage. However, the territory of the Parisi is, most likely, broadly defined by the extent of cemeteries belonging to the so-called Arras Culture. Starting by, at the latest, the fourth century BC, East Yorkshire developed a number of cemeteries which feature burials where the person being buried is accompanied by a cart (either simply placed upright in the grave or with its wheels removed and laid by the side). This burial rite is, in Britain, restricted to this area of Yorkshire. However, it has close parallels in mainland Europe, Burgundy and in the area occupied by a continental tribe also called the Parisi or Parisii.

British artefacts from the so-called Arras Culture are mostly not exact matches for their continental counterparts, suggesting that those found in Yorkshire are not simple imports but British products derived from a continental tradition. However, an early Arras Culture burial from Cowlam does feature artefacts that may have come direct from the continent, including a bracelet and necklace of a very similar style to examples from Burgundy.[70]

The combination of these cultural links and the identical tribal name do strongly suggest that something happened with the Parisi similar to the process which probably occurred with Commius and the Atrebates in the south. However, while the arrival of Commius may have left little mark archaeologically, the extensive evidence of continental influence on Arras Culture suggests a rather larger immigration. Stead has demonstrated that most of what immigration did occur probably took place prior to the fifth or fourth centuries BC, with no signs of significant change between that period and the Roman occupation except increasing contacts with southern culture.[71] Certainly, it is an interesting archaeological prototype of how foreign immigrants could transform the culture of an area of Britain and create a new combined tribal identity.

As discussed above, there is evidence of Corieltauvian contacts in the territory of the Parisi in the pre-Roman period and it is interesting to note the discovery of a fourth-century AD buckle of Corieltauvian style north of the Humber, between Market Weighton and Beverley, suggesting a later continuation of such influence (whether of a friendly nature or otherwise).[72]

In Roman times the main town in the region was Malton, though the official capital of the *civitas* was probably the town of Petuaria which may be Brough on Humber. This lay close to a major north–south crossing point of the Humber Estuary in pre-Roman, Roman and post-Roman times. There is, however, little sign that Petuaria ever flourished in the same way that some other *civitas* capitals did.[73] In the Roman period there were major pottery industries based near the borders of the Parisi, including the Dales Ware and the Crambeck Ware industries.

Brigantes

According to Ptolemy, surrounding the land of the Parisi (except in the south) was the vast territory of the Brigantes. The Brigantes are described by Tacitus as being the most populous tribe in Britain.[74] Certainly they seem to have occupied the largest tribal area.

Their territory may have stretched as far south as the Peak District and, as the evidence of dedications to the tribal deity Brigantia suggests, tribal lands probably stretched beyond the Tyne Solway line in the north.[75] Ptolemy states that the Brigantes stretched from 'ocean to ocean',[76] though his probable attribution of Corbridge to the Votadini tribe suggests that Brigantes territory did not extend north of Hadrian's Wall at its eastern end. With such a large extent, and with so many natural boundaries included within Brigantian lands, it is highly likely that regional sub-groups existed. The Carvetti, who later formed their own *civitas* in the region of Carlisle are one obvious example. Others include the Setantii of the Fylde, perhaps the Gabrantovices in East Yorkshire, the Tectoverdi and Lopocares in the region of Hadrian's Wall and possibly the Latenses in the area around Leeds.[77] It is, in fact, possible that the Brigantes should be regarded as more of a confederation of tribes than a single tribe.

Without the coin evidence available in the centre and south of Britain, again it is hard to get much sense of contacts between the Brigantes and their neighbours in pre-Roman times, unless the Corieltauvian coin hoards do represent the proceeds of a Brigantian raid into Corieltauvian territory or of commercial activity. However, it is clear from the resistance put up by sections of the Brigantes to the Roman occupation (and other evidence, such as a category of sword that is distinctively Brigantian) that the Brigantes were well used to, and well equipped for, fighting.[78] There are a number of hillforts in Brigantian territory including those at Almondbury and Barwick in Elmet and the impressively high example at Ingleborough – less of a hillfort and more of a mountainfort (*16*).

Most settlements in the period immediately prior to the Roman occupation, though, seem to have consisted of, at most, small groups of huts.[79] The exception is the huge and impressive *oppidum* at Stanwick which appears to have been occupied from around AD 40-70. Massive earthworks enclose a large area, and a significant assemblage of luxury pottery from the south, as well as a hoard found in 1845 containing a sword and a wide variety of horse and chariot fittings, many beautifully worked, suggest the wealth of the Brigantian leadership. Ptolemy lists a number of settlements within the territory of the Brigantes, including the large Roman city of York, the Roman-period capital of the Brigantes at Aldborough, Catterick, Binchester, Ilkley and Camulodunum (possibly the auxiliary fort at Slack).

16 Ingleborough (723m/2373ft) which has a hillfort located right on top. Perhaps it should be more accurately described as a mountainfort

In terms of adoption of Roman culture, the *civitas* of the Brigantes is unusual, with evidence of a distinct difference between the two halves on either side of the Pennines. In the area to the east of the Pennines, there is extensive evidence from the Roman period of Roman-style culture. In the area to the west of the Pennines, by contrast, there is very little sign of the Brigantes adopting Roman ways.

Brigantian territory contained large upland areas and many farmsteads were located at between 200 and 300m above sea level, often on steep slopes, which suggests that herding was the primary activity in much of the area.[80] However, in lower-lying areas there is also plenty of evidence of arable farming with, for example, a large number of possibly pre-Roman beehive querns being found in north-eastern Yorkshire and with actual examples of crops coming from a number of sites including Stanwick.[81] In the Roman period a number of villas were built in Brigantian territory east of the Pennines, but none in the Pennines themselves or in the area to the west of them. Generally, a map of villa distribution shows a strong presence in both Corieltauvian and Parisian territory, petering out as we move further west and north into Brigantian territory.

The finding of a number of cast ingots of metal in Derbyshire demonstrates that lead was being mined there from around AD 70-80 by the latest and this may have continued a pre-Roman industry.[82] Lead mining also went on in the Roman period in the Yorkshire Dales and further north in the area around Alston.

In addition, Brigantian territory incorporated a number of significant pottery industries in the Roman period, including production in Derbyshire as well as at Aldborough and Rossington Bridge. Other industries included the quarrying and dressing of gritstone for querns and the carving of jet. This was even exported abroad and a factory for its manufacture was found under the railway station at York.[83]

THE TRIBES OF SCOTLAND

Ptolemy goes into some detail on the tribes he locates in what is modern-day Scotland. In the process, he includes a number of entities for which there is no evidence apart from his word. However, it should be remembered that Ptolemy was writing in the early second century AD, probably the time of maximum Roman knowledge of Scotland. The previous decades had seen Agricola's drive into Scotland as far north as the elusive Mons Graupius, and Roman naval units sailed even further north at this time. Moreover, despite the Roman retreat from Agricola's high water mark, the Roman Army still occupied territory as far north as the Forth-Clyde line during its mid second-century AD occupation of the Antonine Wall. Ptolemy's account should, therefore, be treated with some respect, at least insofar as it relates to the period about which he was writing. In the main part of Scotland, Ptolemy lists a large number of tribes. In the north and west of the area were the Epidii, the Creones, the Carnonacae, the Caereni, the Cornovii, the Smertae, the Lugi and the Decantae. In the centre lay the Caledoni and in the eastern coastal area were the territories of the Venicones, the Vacomagi and the Taezali. The area seems to have had relatively little access to iron. It did, however, have plentiful supplies of stone and the area sees stone-built brochs and wheel-house construction alongside other forms of settlement sites. Food production included agriculture in lower and coastal areas, with pastoralism on the higher ground. Ceramics were in extensive use, with a range of well-made types in a number of different distinctive styles.[84]

Despite the brief appearance of Agricola and his army in the area, and the occupation of the Antonine Wall for decades in the southern part of it, Roman cultural influence in the area seems mainly restricted to the occasional coin or fragment of pottery or glass.

In the area between the line of Hadrian's Wall in the south and the Antonine Wall in the north, lay the tribal territory of at least five other tribes. As discussed, a significant slice of land to the north of Hadrian's Wall probably lay in Brigantian territory. Beyond that, in the area of Galloway and Dumfriesshire were the tribal lands of the Novantes, with the Damnonii to their north.

17 Fragments of dragonesque brooches, an elaborate style of brooch probably with its origins in Brigantian territory

The central region to the north of the Brigantes was inhabited by the Selgovae and along the eastern coast was the tribal territory of the Votadini.

Occupation consists of a mix of hillforts, brochs (in coastal regions), stone-built huts and so-called 'scooped enclosures', with a small terrace scooped out of a hillside to allow space for a hut and surrounding yard.[85] As in many areas to the south, a number of the hillforts seem to have been going out of use in the first centuries BC and AD. However, occupation may have continued at a number of the larger hillforts, including possibly the great royal stronghold of the Votadini at Traprain Law.[86] This could have been occupied throughout the Roman period and certainly seems to have seen a renewed period of activity in the post-Roman period.[87]

Dragonesque brooches found at Traprain Law suggest contacts with the tribes to the south,[88] and a number of Roman-period items at sites such as Traprain Law indicate a very limited degree of Romanisation (*17*).

CHAPTER 2

The First of Rome

Judging by the evidence of the Arras Culture and other signs of foreign influence, the tribes of Britain may, by the first century BC, have been accustomed to the intermittent arrival of new players from abroad on the British political scene. The years between 55 BC and AD 43 were, however, to see the piecemeal appearance of a new arrival that eventually was to dominate British tribal politics for over 350 years – Rome. In a reversal of later developments, though, the first contact between the British tribes and the new player seems not to have been in the form of Roman intervention across the Channel but rather British intervention across the Channel.

Caesar states, and there is no reason to doubt him, that Britons fought in all the Gallic wars against him.[1] The precise context of this early British involvement in Gallic politics is not clear. There has been a suggestion that the Britons involved were well paid for their services, and the evidence of large quantities of Gallo-Belgic E staters flowing into Britain has been linked to payments for British mercenaries.[2] There is also the possibility that Britons fought in Gaul for less commercial reasons. As mentioned before, Caesar claims that Diviciacus, King of the Suessiones, exercised some form of political authority in parts of Britain. The third option and perhaps most likely is, of course, that British motivations were a combination of cash and loyalty. The interplay between Caesar and the British tribes was not, however, to remain on continental soil for long.

In 55 BC, after crushing resistance in Armorica, Caesar prepared to set sail for Britain.[3] In doing so, he made Rome's first foray into the arena of British tribal politics. It was not an entirely successful start. Ahead of him he sent Commius to try to persuade tribal leaders to ally themselves with Rome. It is likely that Commius would have offered Roman support in tribal conflicts in return for support for Rome against those who opposed it. For whatever reason, however, Commius seems not to have been successful in his mission and was taken prisoner, only later to be returned to Caesar. It is quite probable that Caesar's inability to play an effective role in inter-tribal politics at this stage guaranteed the failure of his first invasion. He set sail for Britain with 80 transports for two legions and 18 for his cavalry units. The cavalry, however, failed to arrive and, while Caesar claims some tribes sued for peace and offered hostages as a guarantee of good behaviour, there is no indication that any tribe decided to commit itself seriously to Caesar on this occasion. The first Roman invasion of Britain, therefore, was short-lived and ended with Caesar retreating back across the Channel to the safety of his bases in Gaul.

However, 55 BC probably had at least one positive effect for Caesar and Rome. It demonstrated to the tribes in Britain that there was a potential major new participant in British tribal politics, one that could prove a valuable ally. Certainly inter-tribal solidarity, if such a thing had existed in 55 BC, did not last long when Caesar returned to Britain with a bigger force, in 54 BC.[4] By this point Cassivellaunus, if he should in some sense be seen as a proto-Catuvellaunian figure, seems to have already started the later Catuvellaunian push into Trinovantian territory. Caesar states that Cassivellaunus had killed the King of the Trinovantes and driven the King's son, Mandubracius, into exile. When Caesar landed in 54 BC the Trinovantes initially lined up with Cassivellaunus against Caesar but rapidly switched sides, allying themselves with the Romans against Cassivellaunus.

Caesar's account suggests that this switch by the Trinovantes took place after initial military setbacks for Cassivellaunus. However, it seems equally plausible to suggest that significant elements of the Trinovantian leadership had been pro-Caesar from the start and may well, indeed, have invited Caesar across the Channel specifically to be an ally against Cassivellaunus. Certainly Mandubracius, on being forced into exile by Cassivellaunus, had fled to Caesar and duly returned with Caesar's forces.

A number of other tribes, including the Cenimagni (possibly the Iceni) now abandoned Cassivellaunus. Like the Trinovantes, these were likely to have been tribes who had a history of conflict with Cassivellaunus and his possible proto-Catuvellauni. Caesar says of Cassivellaunus that prior to the Roman invasion he had been in a state of constant war with other British tribes.[5] Certainly, as already discussed and as we will consider further in the next chapter, there was a possible tradition of hostility between the Catuvellauni and Iceni. The tribes now siding with Caesar pointed him in the direction of the stronghold of Cassivellaunus. Commius then took charge of negotiating a peace deal which included the handing over of hostages, an agreement to pay annual tribute and, significantly, a commitment by Cassivellaunus to leave Mandubracius and the Trinovantes in peace.

If one strips away the inevitable focus on Rome and himself in Caesar's historical account, it is perhaps possible to see Caesar's intervention in 54 BC as essentially a tribal conflict conducted by British tribal leaders, with Caesar, from a British perspective, serving as an ally of the Trinovantes and doing the work they needed him to do. Caesar does not mention warriors from any British tribe fighting alongside him but, bearing in mind the assistance offered by some Britons in locating Cassivellaunus, it is certainly not impossible.

One would not expect much archaeological sign of an incursion of the relatively small size and short timescale of Caesar's invasions. However, Rodwell has argued that a number of unretrieved hoards found in Kent which date from this period may be related to Caesar's invasion of the area.[6]

At the end of 54 BC Caesar took his forces and left Britain, never to return. The idea had now been firmly established, however, that there was a new player active on the British tribal scene. For the next decades, though, that player had other things on its mind, mainly civil war. It was not until the reign of Augustus that Rome was again to become involved in British inter-tribal rivalry. In the meantime, the tribes had not stood idly by. For a start, in the immediate years after Caesar's final withdrawal, Commius seems to have returned to Britain.

Judging by his biography in Caesar's writings, he appears to have been a long-term political wheeler-dealer and manipulator but in the end his luck ran out in Gaul. After initially siding with the Romans, he found himself fighting against them alongside Vercingetorix and then in a revolt by the Bellovaci. Finally, after leading a guerrilla war among his own people, the continental Atrebates, he was forced by the Romans to make peace, and agreed terms on the condition that he never had to meet another Roman. Frontinus describes him fleeing across the Channel to Britain.[7]

Shortly after, British coins in the name of Commius and successors claiming descent from him, appear across much of the territory covered by Ptolemy's *civitates* of the Atrebates, Regni and Belgae. It has been widely assumed, as discussed in the last chapter, that this is Caesar's Commius. At Westhampnett, near Chichester, cremations dating from around 90-50 BC show marked similarities with cremations from across the Channel in Normandy and neighbouring regions, suggesting a degree of cross-Channel influence on Atrebatic territory before Commius.[8] However, there is no sign of any major cultural changes in the archaeology of the Atrebatic tribal area at this stage, so it is likely that Commius (and presumably some supporters) took power effectively by a coup d'état (whether peaceful or violent) rather than by any form of mass immigration. It is even possible that the tribe were called the Atrebates before the arrival of Commius but it is more likely that just as the Parisi gave a new tribal name to East Yorkshire, so Commius and his Atrebates gave a new name to a formerly British tribe.

However, the main historical story in Britain in the decades after Caesar's brief intervention seems to have been the rise of the Catuvellauni under first Tasciovanus and then Cunobelin. It has been argued that leadership in this period was not always territorially based and that the rise of Tasciovanus and Cunobelin should not necessarily be seen, therefore, as the rise of the Catuvellauni. Certainly it is true that, as with the selection by the British tribes of Cassivellaunus as their leader against Caesar, leadership could in special circumstance stretch beyond single tribes. However, such war leadership was probably in most instances a very temporary and unstable situation (as it was with Cassivellaunus) with the leader probably exercising control, if at all, more by consensus than by real power. The spread of the coinage of Tasciovanus and Cunobelin, however, implies a much more long-lasting and permanent relationship.

Whatever the origins of the Catuvellauni, by about 30 BC Tasciovanus appears to have been issuing coinage from his capital (and the capital of the Catuvellauni in the Roman period) at Verulamium with a mintmark VER (*18*). However, his name also appears on a few coins minted at the Trinovantian capital Camulodunum, with the mintmark CAM and at this time Catuvellaunian coinage begins to spread more widely into Trinovantian territory.[9] The exact sequence

18 Beech Bottom Dyke, part of the pre-Roman network of linear earthworks that marked the Catuvellaunian capital at Verulamium

and method of the union between Catuvellaunian and Trinovantian territory remains controversial,[10] but it clearly seems to start under Tasciovanus (if it had not already started, in some sense, under Cassivellaunus). At around this time, Catuvellaunian and Atrebatic spheres of influence may have come into conflict in Kent. A limited number of coins of Tasciovanus appear south of the Thames, in this area. Then (after a development which sees the coins of Tincomarus appearing in the south of Atrebatic territory and those of the Atrebatic Eppillus in the north around Calleva) coins of Eppillus appear in Kent.

Dominance of Atrebatic influence in Kent may not have lasted long. When Cunobelin succeeded Tasciovanus as ruler of the Catuvellauni (marking his coins TASC FIL, 'son of Tasciovanus' whether that was meant literally or dynastically) his coins almost immediately appear to go into use across Kent, suggesting Kent became more firmly part of the area of expanding Catuvellaunian influence not long after about AD 10 (*19*).[11] Any rivalry between the Catuvellauni and Atrebates might certainly have had economic aspects and been at times a relatively peaceful competition for influence and control but, bearing in mind the evidence for a strong military side to British life in the period and Caesar's comments on the constant wars of Cassivellaunus and his neighbours, one certainly cannot discount the idea that the conflict was conducted in a rather more nakedly bellicose fashion. It is worth noting, for instance, the regular appearance on the gold coins of Tasciovanus of a man on horseback brandishing a *carnyx*, a Celtic war trumpet. Some may argue that this is merely a symbol of potential power but it is certainly feasible to see it as a statement of actual military muscle and, perhaps, conquest too. It has also been argued from the recurrence of the figure of Victory on the coinage of Eppillus that he took over Kent through some kind of military conquest.[12]

Under Cunobelin, the expansion of Catuvellaunian influence probably did not just continue to the south of the Thames. In the west, Bodvoc of the Dobunni had already issued coinage based stylistically on coins of Tasciovanus, perhaps suggesting some sort of political link during his reign, and Cunobelin's coins spread further west than those of Tasciovanus in the region north of the Thames. Cassius Dio, in his description of the events of AD 43, indicates that the Catuvellauni had political control of at least part of a tribe he calls the Bodunni, widely assumed to be a mangling, or variant, of the name Dobunni.[13] In the east, Cunobelin's coins spread significantly further into formerly Icenian territory than those of Tasciovanus. Ultimately Cunobelin seems to have had influence over a huge part of central and eastern Britain, to the extent that Suetonius could refer to Cunobelin simply as '*Britannorum rex*', 'King of the Britons'.[14]

It is at the time of Cunobelin, however, that Rome again begins to appear as a serious factor in British tribal politics. Two British leaders, probably Tincomarus of the Atrebates and Dubnovellaunus either of the Cantii or Trinovantes, seem

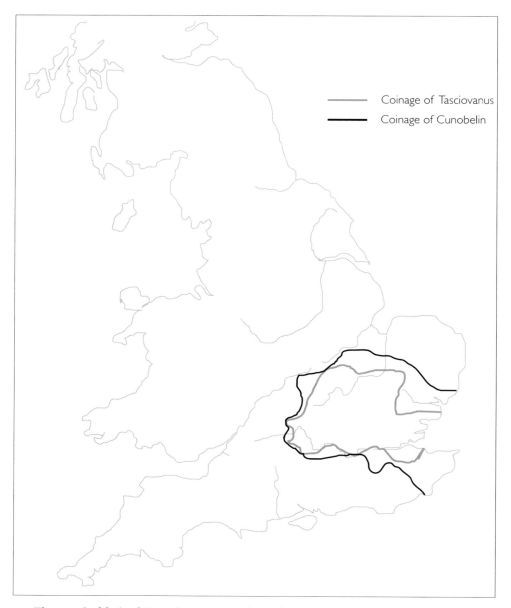

Coinage of Tasciovanus
Coinage of Cunobelin

19   The spread of finds of Catuvellaunian coins shows the spread of Catuvellaunian contacts and influence under first Tasciovanus and then Cunobelin. *After Cunliffe*

to have fled to the Emperor Augustus to seek his help. The circumstances of this flight are not at all clear and may be connected either with internal problems in the relevant kingdoms or with the expansion of Catuvellaunian power. Either way, it is another indication that British politics of the period was

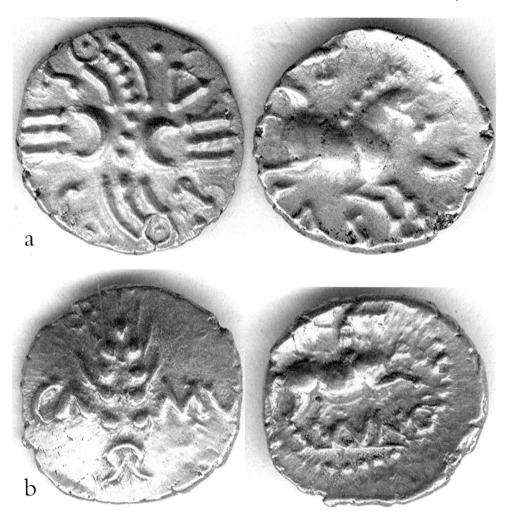

20 Coins of Tasciovanus (a) and Cunobelin (b). *With kind permission of David Shelley*

far from peaceful. It has been suggested that Rome played a role in the rise of the Catuvellauni in this period. Certainly the large quantities of Roman-style luxuries entering Catuvellaunian/Trinovantian territory and the increasingly Roman-style designs found on Catuvellaunian coinage do imply significant links with Rome (*20, colour plates 1 & 2*). However, Atrebatic coinage too shows an increasingly Roman-style repertoire and it is perhaps hard to imagine that Rome would have backed both sides in the rivalry which probably became the most prominent feature of politics in southern Britain in this period. Creighton suggests that the use of classical imagery may be specifically linked to the idea of British tribal leaders growing up as hostages in Rome.[15] The taking of hostages to ensure pro-Roman behaviour was standard Roman practice and Caesar certainly took British hostages, so the hostage idea may account for the use of some specific designs, as suggested by Creighton. However, the power and influence of Rome was so great in mainland Europe by this stage that, in those parts of Britain in close contact with the continent, the equation 'Rome = power and wealth' was almost certainly widely accepted. In that context, Roman imagery would be a natural choice to adorn any ambitious British leader's coinage both for the message of power it sent to Britons and for the message of friendship it sent to Rome. The presence of any returned hostages would only add to the reasons for 'going Roman' on coins.

Around AD 35, coins of Epaticcus appear in the northern part of Atrebatic territory, in the region of Calleva (*21*). It is not entirely clear who Epaticcus was. However, it is likely that his coins do represent a significant extension of Catuvellaunian influence into the heartland of Atrebatic territory. The reverses of his coinage continue Atrebatic traditions of design, but the obverses are based on Cunobelin's coinage, and on his coins Epaticcus styles himself, like Cunobelin, 'son of Tasciovanus'.[16]

At around the same stage, Adminius, a son this time of Cunobelin, may have attempted to separate Catuvellaunian-controlled territory in Kent from the main area of Catuvellaunian dominance to the north.[17] Certainly he seems to have issued coins in his name in Kent and then fled to the court of Caligula, perhaps in an attempt to persuade Caligula to intervene on behalf of his territory in Kent against the Catuvellauni, just as Caesar had helped the Trinovantes against the proto-Catuvellauni. The result seems to have been Caligula's strange 'conquest of the ocean' where, rather than actually invade Britain with reluctant soldiers, he is said to have told them to gather shells to celebrate a triumph over the waves.[18] It was not, however, to be long before another tribal leader made an attempt to bring Roman military muscle into British tribal politics on his side and this time the attempt was rather more successful.

Cunobelin died around AD 40 and was probably succeeded eventually by his sons Caratacus and Togodumnus. In the place of the coins of Epaticcus, in formerly northern Atrebatic territory, appear identical designs but marked CARA, which probably stands for Caratacus.[19] At around the same time, a certain Berikos is recorded as seeking the help of the new Emperor Claudius in regaining his kingdom.[20] This seems likely to be a reference to Verica, probably the last pre-Roman Atrebatic ruler, who may have been forced out of his territory by a new, aggressive Catuvellaunian leadership moving south. Certainly, when the Roman intervention did finally come, it seems to have been aimed squarely at the Catuvellaunian/Trinovantian confederation.

21   Coins of Epatticus (a) who issued coins with both Catuvellaunian and Atrebatic characteristics (suggesting the expansion of Catuvellaunian influence into Atrebatic territory) and of the Atrebatic ruler Verica (b), who refers to himself as COMF 'son of Commius' and who probably invited Claudius into Britain

For the actual invasion of 43, we are almost entirely reliant on a brief account in the works of Cassius Dio, writing some 170 years after the actual event. Among self-righteous outrage at the alleged sexual frivolities of the Empress Messalina, we find these passages. It is worth quoting them at some length, to show the flavour of Cassius Dio's approach:

> The invasion soldiers were sent over in three detachments, to prevent their landing being hindered, which might happen to a single force. At first they became demoralised while sailing, because they were being driven back, but then their courage picked up when they saw a flash of light rise in the east and shoot across to the west, where they were heading. They landed on the island unopposed, because the Britons had not expected them and had not therefore assembled. Even when they did assemble, they would not come to grips with the Romans, but hid in swamps and forests, hoping to wear the invaders down, so that, as happened with Julius Caesar, they would sail away without achieving anything.
>
> For this reason, Plautius had a lot of trouble finding them, but when he finally did, he defeated first Caratacus, and then Togodumnus, sons of the deceased Cunobelin. The Britons did not live freely, but were divided into groups under various kings. After routing these leaders, a part of the Bodunni, who were ruled by the Catuvellauni surrendered to Plautius. He placed a garrison and advanced further until he came to a river.
>
> Thinking that the Romans would not be able to cross the river without a bridge, the barbarians gathered on the opposite bank in a rather careless fashion. So Plautius sent across a unit of Germans, who were able easily to swim across the most raging torrents in full armour. The Germans surprised the enemy, but rather than shooting at the men, they attacked the chariot horses instead, and in the confusion, not even the mounted Britons could escape. At that point Plautius sent across Flavius Vespasianus, later emperor, and his brother Sabinus, as his lieutenant. They too, managed, in some way, to cross the river and surprised and killed many of the enemy,
>
> The survivors, however, did not flee, but came to grips again, the next day. The battle was indecisive, until Gnaeus Hosidius Geta, after almost being captured himself, beat the barbarians so decisively that he was awarded the ornamenta triumphalia, even though he had not been consul. From there, the Britons retreated to the River Thames, at a point near the sea and where it forms a lake at flood-tide. They crossed the river easily, because they knew where the ground was firm and where passage was simple. The Romans, trying to follow, had more trouble. However, again the Germans swam across and some others managed to cross a bridge a short way up-stream. After this they attacked the barbarians from a number of sides and killed many of them. Pursuing the

rest without due care, they got stuck in swamps where it was difficult to escape and so lost some men.

Soon after this, Togodumnus died, but instead of surrendering, the Britons united even more firmly to avenge his death. Due to this, and his trouble with the Thames, Plautius became nervous, and instead of advancing further, decided to guard the territory he had conquered and send for Claudius. He had been told to do this, if he met any particularly stubborn resistance, and large quantities of supplies, including elephants, had already been prepared for the expedition.

When the message reached him, Claudius handed over domestic affairs, including command of the army to his colleague Lucius Vitellius, whom he had arranged should stay in office, as he had, for half a year. He then headed for the war. He sailed along the river to Ostia, and then along the coast to Massilia. From there, he travelled partly by land and partly by river, until he reached the Ocean. After crossing to Britain, he joined the legions waiting for him near the Thames. Taking command, Claudius crossed the water and, after engaging the barbarians, who had gathered as he approached, he defeated them and captured the capital of Cunobelin, Camulodunum. He won over many tribes, some of whom surrendered and some of whom had to be forced. He was hailed as imperator a number of times, which is contrary to custom, because a man may only be hailed imperator once per war. He disarmed the conquered and told Plautius to conquer the remaining Britons. At this point, Claudius himself hurried back to Rome.

Cassius Dio, *Roman History* 60. 19-22

Particularly noteworthy is the long wait for the emperor to arrive before the capture of the capital of the Catuvellaunian/Trinovantian confederation at Camulodunum. Cassius Dio asserts that this was because the Romans in Britain were hard-pressed and badly needed the emperor to rescue the situation. It seems more likely, though, as others have pointed out, that the real reason for the wait was to allow Claudius to claim the victory in person. After all, if help was so badly needed by Plautius, it is hard to see why he did not ask for it from the Roman armies in Germany, just across the North Sea, rather than wait for the emperor to come all the way from Rome. If it is true that the delay was in fact to allow Claudius the credit, then it seems likely that Cassius Dio was basing his account on Claudian propaganda rather than solid history, which is significant in assessing the rest of his description.

It is interesting to note that after Dio's lovingly elaborated accounts of swimming across rivers and splashing around in swamps, his account of the final battle against the Britons, once Claudius had come all the way from Rome, is restricted to 'after engaging the barbarians, who had gathered as he approached, he defeated them.' It appears as if maybe even Claudian propaganda could have

22 Richborough – traditional landing place of some of the Roman forces in 43. Others, however, may have landed in friendly Atrebatic territory at Bosham Harbour

been struggling with the task of making Claudius look like a traditional Roman conqueror here. Support for this interpretation comes from one of the few other mentions of the invasion by a Roman historian. Suetonius, in his *Life of Claudius*, dismisses the invasion of 43 by saying that Claudius received the submission of part of the island without any fighting, and was back in Rome six months after leaving it.[21]

This sense of propaganda at work is increased by the apparent discrepancy between Dio's account, which has inspired numerous modern reconstructions of grim-faced legionaries stabbing their way across Britain, and the other evidence for the invasion which suggests an entirely different picture of 43. In this alternative scenario probably more of the Britons, and certainly more of the British leadership, in south-east and central Britain were supporting the arrival of the Romans than actually opposing it. They might even, on some level, have seen the Romans as liberators from domination by the Catuvellaunian/Trinovantian federation, from the heirs of Cunobelin 'king of the Britons', and while they may not have been throwing flowers at the arriving troops they certainly would not have fought them. In this scenario, the invasion of 43 is again as much an act of British politics as of Roman. Recent parallels might be the situation

23   Coins of Caligula (a), who may have been encouraged to invade Britain by Adminius, and Claudius (b) who did invade Britain, probably at the invitation of Verica

of the Kurds at the time of the Iraq invasion, or the Northern Alliance at the time of the Afghan occupation. Western forces went into both countries for their own reasons but, to the Kurds and the Northern Alliance, they were just new allies come to help them against their old enemies. For a start, if, as seems likely, Berikos is Verica, then most of the Atrebates were probably supporting the Roman intervention. In fact, it is now thought by some that at least one of the initial three landings described by Dio took place in Atrebatic territory, probably near Chichester. Cunliffe long ago suggested that timber buildings at Fishbourne represented a Roman military storage area dating from 43, or very shortly afterwards.[22] Recent work has also uncovered a Roman-style ditch, east of Fishbourne Palace, that seems to have been constructed even before 43.[23] If this is the case, and if this is a Roman military ditch rather than one just dug in a Roman style by a Romanised Atrebatic dynasty, then it might imply the presence here of at least some Roman soldiers prior to 43, perhaps to offer assistance to Verica. This landing spot may well then have been chosen in 43, both in order to take advantage of pro-Roman sentiment in the area and because it was already known to the Roman Army.

There is also little, if any, archaeological evidence of actual fighting connected with the initial Roman invasion of 43. Cunliffe draws attention to evidence of the refortification of hillforts on the eastern and western edges of Atrebatic territory around the time of the Roman invasion. He interpreted these as signs of the Atrebates in these areas abandoning Verica and possibly preparing to resist the Roman advance.[24] However, even if the refortification is connected with the invasion, rather than with any inter-tribal fighting that preceded it, it seems just as likely that the hillforts were being refitted in order to defend the flank of a Roman advance from Bosham Harbour rather than to resist it.

Support for the idea that the Atrebates were backing the arrival of Roman reinforcements for their quarrel with the Catuvellauni comes from the Roman treatment of the area after the invasion. Rather than being subjected to Roman military rule, much of the Atrebatic tribal area, perhaps all of it, was probably made into a kingdom for Rome's ally Togidubnus. Tacitus states that he was given several *civitates* to rule, and the inscription from Chichester that calls him 'great king of Britain' (*24*) both confirms his link to Atrebatic territory and indicates, again, his rule over an extensive area. If Togidubnus was in control of Chichester, a few miles from the major pre-Roman Atrebatic centre at Selsey, it seems reasonable to assume that the *civitates* in question may have been the *civitas* of the Atrebates, the *civitas* of the Atrebatic Regni (whose capital was at Chichester) and the semi-Atrebatic *civitas* of the Belgae.[25]

By the same token, it seems likely that the Iceni, probably long-term opponents of the Catuvellauni and for decades, surrounded on almost all their

24 Inscription from Chichester mentioning Togidubnus, 'great king of Britain'

land borders by the Catuvellaunian/Trinovantian confederation, would also have welcomed Roman assistance. That the Iceni were, like the Atrebates, permitted to continue in semi-independence as an allied kingdom after the invasion strongly suggests this was the case. The Cantii may or may not have fought for their Catuvellaunian masters. It is impossible to tell.

The Bodunni (widely assumed to be same as the Dobunni) seem to have ditched their Catuvellaunian links as soon as possible and allied themselves with the new power in Britain. In fact, from Dio's account, the only people we can be certain actually resisted the Romans were some Catuvellauni and some Trinovantes. Even here it seems likely that resistance was short-lived and that the Catuvellauni and Trinovantes rapidly realised they needed the Romans as tribal allies, reverting to their previous love affair with Roman culture and trappings.

There is no archaeological evidence of bitter fighting, or in fact any fighting, in the territory of the Trinovantes at any time around 43. At Camulodunum, which Dio says Claudius captured after a, presumably nearby, battle, there is little sign of disruption. Occupation at the royal compound at Gosbecks seems to continue uninterrupted through the invasion period, except for the positioning of a small Roman fort within the outer defences.[26] It has been argued that this represents a dramatic symbol of the new power in Britain,[27] but frankly burning Gosbecks would have been rather more dramatic, or just going to the trouble of evicting the occupants. It could even be argued that having a detachment of Roman troops acting as the palace guard at Gosbecks, might be seen as increasing the status of the Trinovantian leadership rather than diminishing it. Also, there is no sign of burning or devastation in Catuvellaunian territory in the period of the invasion. In fact, all the archaeological evidence suggests that the

Catuvellauni accepted the new political status quo in Britain with enthusiasm. In Catuvellaunian territory there is evidence for continuity between pre-Roman high-status habitation sites and Roman-period villas, suggesting some of the tribal aristocracy remained in place. Thus, for instance, at Gorhambury a high-status pre-Roman compound is succeeded by a Roman-style villa.[28] In addition, soon after the invasion, the Catuvellauni started on the construction of a new Roman-style capital at Verulamium. If Tacitus is to be believed, their capital may even have been granted privileged *municipium* status within about 15 years of the invasion.[29]

In terms of the takeover of the Catuvellaunian/Trinovantian confederation, the most apt model again seems to be the coup d'état. Once Togodumnus was dead and Caratacus had fled, the remaining Catuvellaunian aristocracy probably accepted pro-Roman or Roman leadership rapidly and willingly. It is even possible that Adminius, who had fled to Rome in the time of Caligula, may have returned with Plautius or Claudius and formed a new pro-Roman tribal leadership in Catuvellaunian/Trinovantian territory.[30]

In the centre, south and east of Britain, the story of 43 should, therefore, again probably been seen more as an intervention in tribal politics than as an invasion. To many of the Britons at the time, the arrival of the Romans might have seemed no more momentous than the arrival of the Parisi in East Yorkshire or even the arrival of Commius and some Atrebates in Hampshire. The Romans were probably seen as powerful allies in the fight for tribal advantage and, in return for the assistance of their military muscle, the tribes would offer the new player in the British tribal power game a measure of loyalty and accept a degree of Romanisation of culture and identity. One tribe, though, after initial enthusiasm for the Romans, was about to change its mind with dramatic consequences and bring about the first of three major convulsions that rocked Britain during the Roman period.

CHAPTER 3

60-61

By the end of the 50s AD, the situation for the Romans remained unstable both in the west and in the north of Britain. In Wales, where he had fled, Caratacus had been defeated in 51, and after hard fighting against the Silures in the south, Suetonius Paulinus (who had acquired a reputation for mountain warfare by being the first Roman general to cross the Atlas Mountains in Mauretania) had advanced north against the Ordovices and was poised to attack Anglesey. This was a major centre for the druids and was also probably crowded with refugees from the fighting further south.

25   The gateway of the Roman fort that sits within the Durotrigan hillfort at Hod Hill, marking the rapid expansion of Roman power westwards after the invasion

In the north of England, the hardest fighting for the Romans was yet to come. They had already had to step in once to assist their ally Cartimandua against her ex-husband Venutius and they would have to do so again in 69. This would eventually lead to bitter fighting and full annexation by Rome of the Brigantian kingdom in 71.

In the south and east of England, however, by the beginning of the 60s the Roman authorities presumably hoped that the Britons were becoming accustomed to the realities of their new status and would now settle down as peaceful and obedient members of the Roman Empire. If so, they were in for a severe shock, with one of the tribes set to reassert its independent identity in the most emphatic manner possible.

The evidence for Boudica's rebellion relies almost entirely on Tacitus[1] and, again, on Cassius Dio.[2] In this case, though, the accounts by Tacitus (in the *Agricola* and the *Annals*) seem to represent the more authoritative surviving record, being fuller and much closer in date to the actual events (having been written around the end of the first century and beginning of the second, as opposed to the section in Cassius Dio which dates from around 229). There seems no reason to doubt the broad outline of what Tacitus describes. His father-in-law, Agricola, served in Britain around this time and he may even have contributed first-hand information to his son-in-law's account of the revolt.

The main details of Boudica's rebellion are the familiar ones. According to Tacitus, Prasutagus, client king of the Iceni, had died leaving his two daughters and the emperor in Rome as joint heirs in his will, hoping thereby to ensure a smooth transition to another generation of client monarchy. Instead of allowing such a handover, however, some of the Romans in Britain had decided to take more direct control of Icenian territory, in the process abusing the locals and the royal family in particular.

> Both the kingdom and the household were treated like spoils of war, the one by Roman officers, the other by Roman slaves. His widow Boudica was beaten, to start with, and their daughters were raped. As if the Romans had been given the whole country, the Icenian chiefs had their estates taken away. Even the king's relatives were abused like slaves.
>
> Tacitus, *Annals* 14, 31

In response to brutal treatment by the Romans, the Iceni rose under the leadership of Boudica sometime in the years 60 or 61. From a Roman point of view, with Paulinus preoccupied with his campaign against Anglesey far away on the other side of Britain, they chose a particularly unfortunate moment to do so.

The rebel army headed south from Icenian territory into Trinovantian territory. Here, according to Tacitus, local Trinovantes, enraged both by mistreatment at the hands of veterans settled in the Roman colony at Colchester and by the expense and symbolism of the new temple of Claudius there, helped Boudica and her Iceni burn the new Roman town to the ground. The procurator Catus Decianus had only been able to spare 200 men for its defence and these, in collaboration with the veterans living there, were not sufficient to defend the unfortified colony.

Responding to the news from Colchester, Petilius Cerialis, then in command of the Ninth Legion, led his men south to confront the rebels. Somewhere en route, though, the two opposing forces clashed and Cerialis was forced back to his fortifications (which fortifications is not precisely clear) after suffering losses to his infantry.

Paulinus, in turn, then began a march back from Wales to London (at this stage a growing commercial settlement) intending to hold it against Boudica. It is probable, though, that he had only arrived with part of his forces, perhaps those forces capable of moving fastest like his cavalry, because he subsequently decided that he would abandon the town to Boudica. He retreated and her forces advanced, plundering London and slaughtering those they found remaining there. At some stage, Verulamium was also destroyed by Boudica. Tacitus mentions the destruction of Verulamium immediately after that of London in the *Annals*. It is unclear, however, from the context whether this is because the attack there actually took place chronologically after the sack of London, or merely because Tacitus adds the reference almost as an aside after his description of events at London.

At some stage after the destruction of London and Verulamium, Paulinus, presumably now with all his forces, managed to confront Boudica and inflict a crushing defeat on her, effectively ending the main part of the rebellion (*26, 27*). Tacitus gives no real indication of where this final battle took place. The only clue he supplies is that Paulinus is said to have drawn up his forces 'in a valley with woods behind them'.[3] Even if the account by Tacitus is accurate (and the sheer vagueness of the description raises questions about that) this could represent a large number of places within the possible range of Boudica's operations. Trying to tie it down without specific archaeological evidence of a battle from the right years, may remain impossible. Recent progress in identifying the location of the defeat of Varus by Arminius in Germany is encouraging, but the historical accounts of that incident give more geographical clues than are available for Boudica's defeat.

These, then, are the basic facts as presented in Tacitus and they are supported by evidence of burning from the right period at Colchester, London and Verulamium.

26   Panel from Adamclisi, from about 50 years after Boudica's revolt, showing a heavily armed Roman soldier fighting a lightly armed Dacian opponent. The final battle between Paulinus and Boudica would have seen many similar scenes

27 Tile showing the stamp of the Fourteenth Legion, a force which probably played a crucial role in the defeat of Boudica

This is not to say, however, that Tacitus does not have his own angle to impose on the material. It needs to be remembered that the primary goal of Tacitus was to present an account of history which was relevant and of interest to his Roman readership, not to historians in the twenty-first century. He is almost bound to make the Romans in the story the main area of focus alongside Boudica. Even more significantly, there is also a strong sense in his fuller account in the *Annals* of the writer intentionally contrasting what he sees as the iniquities of some contemporary Romans with a romanticised view of Boudica as a prototype 'lover of liberty' – a genre which would have been familiar to Romans from stories of their own Republican past.

The speech attributed by Tacitus to Boudica before the decisive final battle with Paulinus is a perfect example of this tendency, including, as it does passages such as this:

> The gods will support just vengeance. The legion which did fight, died. The rest
> of the Romans are skulking in their camp or thinking of fleeing. Even the noise

and shouts of our thousands will be too much for them, let alone the impact of our charge. Bear in mind the numbers fighting and the reasons, and you will see that you must conquer or die. This is what a woman will do. As for men, they may live as slaves if they choose.

Tacitus, *Annals* 14, 35

It seems highly unlikely that Tacitus would have had any idea what, if any, words were spoken by Boudica to her forces before the battle, but the business of ancient history writing demanded regular speeches from key figures at key moments to sum up the action. Tacitus has, therefore, composed a speech for her to emphasise her credentials as freedom fighter, using some particular facts relevant to her case and some general rhetorical comments on fighting for liberty. The 'those who don't want to fight for freedom may live in slavery' is a classic of the genre, as is 'conquer or die'.

It is also noticeable that Tacitus, while saying Boudica's forces massacred the inhabitants of various towns, does not go into great detail, perhaps because he does not want to spoil his freedom fighter's image. Cassius Dio, by contrast, details some particularly unpleasant practices that Boudica's rebels are supposed to have used in order to dispatch their prisoners (as bad as anything alleged in Bosnia or Iraq).[4]

It has long been recognised that Tacitus is putting a gloss on Boudica. Nonetheless, his romanticised view of 'female freedom fighter' still holds surprising power over the modern imagination when it comes to the Icenian queen. In an era even more liable than that of Tacitus to canonise freedom fighters, both the worthy and the unworthy, that should come as no surprise. In addition, it should be remembered that the female freedom fighter has always held a special mystique (particularly for a certain type of male) with long hair flowing freely, jaw jutting defiantly, sword or AK-47 in her hand, or as Cassius Dio puts it:

She stood very tall. She was terrifying to see, and had a fierce look in her eye. Her voice was harsh, and a great mass of tawny hair hung all the way down to her hips.

Cassius Dio, *Roman History* 62, 2

What we then need to explore in relation to 60/61 is to what extent this attempt by Tacitus to construct a compelling narrative of British freedom fighter battling against the Romans, his main preoccupation, may mask a more complex reality.

The reasons for the rising at first glance seem clear-cut. The Iceni rebelled in response to a brutal takeover by Rome. However, even on this point, the account by

Tacitus raises questions. The picture of pillage is a rather generalised one and, more importantly, there is no indication as to why the Romans should suddenly launch such a savage onslaught against an allied royal family, or on whose authority. It seems unlikely that anyone junior could organise such a radical change of policy.

Cassius Dio suggests that the sudden calling-in of Roman loans and quasi-loans to various Britons may have been a problem,[5] but this does not appear in Tacitus. It is just conceivable that the account by Tacitus could represent a rather exaggerated picture of Roman bailiffs at work. Again, however, it seems slightly unlikely that they would have treated the family of a client king in such a way without approval from someone high in the Roman administration. If such approval was granted then some kind of political calculation would presumably have been involved as well as purely commercial ones. Whether any political motivation was purely Roman or in some ways connected to the complications of British tribal conflicts is, unfortunately, unclear.

In his brief account in the *Agricola*, Tacitus suggests that Boudica led a large-scale rising of Britons against the Romans, and in the *Annals* there is mention of other unspecified tribes apart from the Iceni being involved.[6] If there was a general revolt against Rome across large sections of Britain, then this might justify a view of Boudica as a freedom fighter against Rome. Tacitus, however, only actually mentions the Iceni and Trinovantes by name in the *Annals* and there is no clear evidence, either historical or archaeological, for fighting connected with 60-61 south of the Southwark area of London or anywhere west of Catuvellaunian territory. Tacitus, for instance, says of Togidubnus that he had been loyal 'down to our times', suggesting that his kingdom (perhaps comprising the *civitates* of the Regni, Atrebates and Belgae) took no part in Boudica's revolt.[7] Tacitus does say that Paulinus reached London through the enemy. However, Tacitus gives no indication of who these enemies might have been (they might even have been enemies in Wales or just outside London) or how many there were of them. By contrast, the fact that Paulinus seems to have been able to march all the way across the country from Anglesey rapidly and without any specific recorded combat, does lend weight to the idea that Boudica's actions had little or no support beyond the Iceni and Trinovantes.

It has been suggested that the Second Legion did not initially move from its base in Exeter because of fears that the Durotriges and Dumnonii might rise in sympathy with Boudica. However, even if there was a possibility of trouble for the Romans from these tribes at this time, there is no specific reason to link it to Boudica. Their recently conquered status (in the case of the Durotriges, at least, a conquest that probably involved much death and destruction, including some or all of Vespasian's 30 battles and 20 towns captured as mentioned in Suetonius[8]) would be sufficient to account for it.

The probable geography of Boudica's rebellion raises questions about her status as a British freedom fighter and so do other elements of the historical account. The description offered by Tacitus of the techniques of Boudica's rebels, for instance, seems rather more consistent with traditional tribal border raiding than with freedom fighting.

In the *Annals* he writes:

> It is in the nature of a savage people always to be in search of booty. As a result, the Britons ignored places with strong defences and attacked with the most ferocity, wherever they expected little resistance and large plunder.
>
> Tacitus, *Annals* 14, 33

Here, the focus seems to be on taking revenge and riches from neighbours and their new ally, rather than on a serious attempt to throw Rome out of the island of Britain.[9]

28 The Roman walls of Colchester. The town was fortified with an earth rampart in the aftermath of 60/61 and with stone fortifications in the early second century, but was open to attack by Boudica

The strategy of Boudica's campaign too, to the extent that it can be reconstructed, in many ways seems to fit much more with a traditional border raid focused on the neighbouring tribes than with a war of liberation against Roman occupiers.

Her first move is to sack Colchester, admittedly a Roman colony by now, but still also in some sense the capital of the Trinovantes (for instance, the royal compound at Gosbecks continued in uninterrupted use during the initial building of the colony after 43[10]) (28). Boudica's next operations then are, in whichever order, to attack the other capital of the Catuvellaunian/Trinovantian confederation at Verulamium (29) and to attack, by then probably the third richest target in the former territory of Cunobelin north of the Thames, London.[11] After sacking these three towns and despite the fact that the rebellion seems to have gone on for some time, there is no evidence that Boudica moved beyond this relatively local area either to raise other tribes to join her or to search out the Roman occupiers. Instead, according to Tacitus, it is Paulinus not Boudica who ultimately forced the final battle.

29   The site of shops at Verulamium, capital of the Catuvellauni, burnt by Boudica

Since Boudica's strategy appears to be raiding rich targets in neighbouring tribal areas, not destroying Roman military forces or attempting to eject Roman political influence from Britain, it seems not unreasonable, therefore, to suggest that the Romans may have been only one focus, and perhaps not even the main focus, of Boudica's rebellion. Certainly, in terms of British tribal history, there were probably good reasons why Boudica would be at least as interested in attacking her British neighbours as in attacking the Romans. Tension between the Iceni and the Catuvellauni, in particular, may have had a long history.

To recap, if in Caesar's account of Britain the Cenimagni are the Iceni, then they did initially line up alongside Cassivellaunus and his possibly proto-Catuvellaunian army, but they also turned against it rapidly, possibly even playing a role in directing Caesar to the stronghold of Cassivellaunus. In the period following Caesar, as continental styles spread across Catuvellaunian and Trinovantian territory, the Iceni largely resisted them. The expansion of Catuvellaunian power under Cunobelin saw his coinage spreading into areas along the southern and south-western borders of Icenian territory, where Icenian currency had previously been dominant. As elsewhere, this may represent a spread of Catuvellaunian political as well as commercial power. Certainly by the time of Cunobelin, the Catuvellaunian/Trinovantian confederation effectively surrounded the Iceni on their land borders, with the exception of routes across the Fens to the Corieltauvi in the north. Such a situation could easily have bred a sense of extreme fear and resentment among the Iceni. As we have seen, there is also some possible evidence for actual conflict.

In the area on the Icknield Way corridor near Cambridge, which probably marks the border region between the Catuvellauni and Iceni, lie a number of ditches. The most significant of these are of late Roman or post-Roman date and will be discussed in later chapters. However, it is suggested that at least one, Mile Ditch, is likely to be pre-Roman.[12] In addition, in Suffolk an apparently Icenian hillfort at Burgh by Woodbridge seems to have been burnt some time in the first two decades of the first century AD and then reoccupied by people sharing the culture of the Catuvellauni and Trinovantes to the south.[13] Certainly, it is located in a border area that shows Icenian coinage and a subsequent intrusion of significant quantities of Catuvellaunian/Trinovantian coinage. A likely tradition of hostility between the tribes can only have been exacerbated by the marked difference in their attitudes to the new major player on the British political scene.

During the years after 43, the Iceni had kept their distance from Rome. They had managed to retain their independence as a client kingdom but there is evidence that they were resisting any close cultural and political embrace by their new ally. While Roman culture flowed freely into other parts of Britain, the Iceni seem to have been less enthusiastic about changing their lifestyle. The major Icenian religious and ceremonial site at Fison Way, Thetford, for instance shows a distinct lack of Roman imported goods.[14] Equally, in contrast to the established tradition among the Catuvellauni/Trinovantes and Atrebates of issuing coinage with Roman symbols, the Iceni continued to issue coins featuring British symbolism until 43 and possibly even after, depending on whether van Arsdell's or Creighton's dating is correct.[15]

What is more, some Iceni had, even before Boudica, expressed their lack of enthusiasm about the newcomers by reaching for their weapons. In 47, according to Tacitus, they had resisted efforts to disarm them by rising briefly in revolt.[16] It is unlikely that this was a major revolt, since the Iceni retained their independent status as a client kingdom, but it is clearly a sign that the Iceni viewed their alliance with Rome in a very mixed light.

The Catuvellauni, by contrast, once the period of the initial invasion was over, embraced the culture of their new Roman partners with enthusiasm. Not long before Boudica, around 55, a Catuvellaunian leader was buried with a wealth of Roman-style riches at Folly Lane outside Verulamium and by 60-61, construction was already well under way on a new Roman-style capital there. Tacitus even seems to suggest that this had already been accorded by the Romans the special honour of being granted *municipium* status.[17]

It is possible that the differences in the level of Romanisation between the two tribes point to some of the underlying reasons for the rising in 60-61. As discussed in the last chapter, the Iceni may have initially seen the Romans as liberators from domination by the Catuvellauni. Rome, however, seems to have done little after 43 to humble the Catuvellauni. In fact, the level of Romanisation in Catuvellaunian territory, the probable adoption by the Romans of the Catuvellaunian/Trinovantian capital of Camulodunum as the capital of all Britannia and the possible granting of *municipium* status to Verulamium, suggest quite the contrary. It may be that Boudica and her Iceni saw their supposed allies against Catuvellaunian domination rapidly changing into allies of Catuvellaunian domination and decided to act. Certainly the rebels left clear signs of their attack on Verulamium. That it took some 15 years to rebuild the workshops burnt at this time in *insula* XIV is suggestive of the impact Boudica had on Verulamium's early development.[18]

Evidence of destruction in the Catuvellaunian settlements around Verulamium is less clear-cut. It has been suggested that indications of burning at both Gorhambury and Park Street should be linked to Boudica,[19] but it has recently been questioned whether the burning can be tied to such a precise date.[20] Of course, while a lack of precisely datable burning evidence means it can't be proved such sites were raided by Boudica, it doesn't mean it can be proved that they weren't.

We tend to have a Hollywood picture of raiders torching settlements, but whether they take the time to burn as well as loot depends on a wide variety of factors. Is there fire handy? Is it raining? Is there a threat of interruption from an enemy? There was a lot of burning in Bosnia, but domestic gas, petrol and modern explosives make life a lot easier for the would-be arsonist. Pre-Roman-style houses would have contained less in the way of highly flammable furnishings, and soaked thatch, for instance, does not burn easily. Imagine trying to get a bonfire going on a cold, windless day, pouring with rain and with the fear that someone with a knife is about to creep up on you. Frankly, you wouldn't bother.

It is even possible that there were armed Catuvellauni around with knives and swords to deter some of the raiders. In the aftermath of the Roman invasion, the Catuvellauni are unlikely to have maintained their tribal battle-readiness (in contrast to the semi-independent Iceni who probably did). However, there is some evidence of Catuvellauni with Roman weapons at Verulamium in the first century AD. The Catuvellaunian leader buried at Folly Lane was buried with a Roman-style chainmail lorica and harness mounts of a type used by contemporary Roman cavalry.[21] What's more, even though there is no clear evidence of a Roman fort at Verulamium, quantities of first-century Roman military fittings have been found there. Niblett, at least, believes they may indicate the presence of Catuvellauni armed by the Romans.[22] These could be Catuvellauni recruited into the regular Roman Army. Alternatively, probably like the man at Folly Lane, they might be so equipped on a less formal basis. It is not impossible that, in the chaos of 60-61 or in the immediate aftermath, some Catuvellauni saw action against Boudica. There is the interesting discovery by fieldwalkers of a number of lead sling shots in association with first-century military strap ends at Windridge, about 1km south-west of Verulamium. These could, of course, be metalworking debris or relate to a battle connected to the Roman invasion. However, on the evidence of Suetonius (see previous chapter) it seems unlikely that there was much resistance to the invasion at Verulamium, and if this is a battle site it is perhaps more likely to be connected with an attempted defence of the town against Boudica.[23]

The Catuvellauni had, by 60-61, probably long been prime candidates for an attack by the Iceni, and Boudica duly obliged. The Catuvellauni had, however, up until 43 also been part of a confederation with the Trinovantes. One of the most interesting questions in relation to Boudica, despite being one that has hardly been touched upon by most writers, is the status of the Trinovantes in terms of the revolt. Tacitus states explicitly that the Trinovantes joined the Iceni in burning Colchester and this has usually been taken for granted as fact. There are, however, reasons for questioning whether we should be so certain.

Is it possible that Tacitus just assumed that the Trinovantes were involved because he knew the Roman colony at Colchester had been burnt, knew it was in Trinovantian territory, and thought the locals must have had something to do with it? If so, then that would remove the last plank supporting the idea of Boudica as British freedom fighter and show her revolt as, in many ways, a traditional border raid against other tribes, and, in this case, their Roman allies too. The Trinovantes do seem strange partners in an Icenian rebellion against Rome. For a start, there were significant cultural differences between the two tribes in the first century AD. The Trinovantes had, like the Catuvellauni, adopted a number of aspects of continental culture, including cremation burial. The Iceni by contrast were much more resistant to continental influence. One should probably not underestimate the ability of culture to divide as well as to unite. In Former Yugoslavia, for instance, there was a significant cultural divide between the Croats who clearly looked west culturally (with their strong connections with central Europe and the Adriatic, and with Roman Catholicism) and the Serbs who just as clearly looked east (with their strong connections with Russia and with the Orthodox Church). Even the alphabet became a battleground. Despite their languages being almost identical, the Croats used the western Roman script and the Croatian and Bosnian Serbs promoted the eastern Cyrillic script in their territories. For an ancient example of such cultural divides, consider the Athenians' view of themselves as sophisticated and humane compared to their competitor Sparta which they regarded as powerful, but dull, rustic, boorish and full of people speaking in a funny accent. In the 1990s, some Croats had almost exactly the same view of their more westernised, urban Croatian culture in comparison with the militarily strong, but more eastern and more agricultural Serbs (who also spoke the same language but with a different accent and slightly different vocabulary).

As members of the Catuvellaunian/Trinovantian confederation, the Trinovantes may, as discussed above, have benefited from expansion into Icenian territory on their northern border, around Burgh by Woodbridge. Then there are, again, the differences in their attitude towards Rome. The Trinovantes had been the first British tribe to make Rome a partner in their conflicts with another tribe. As discussed in Chapter 2, Caesar's second invasion of Britain may have been brought about by Mandubracius, and presumably other Trinovantes, needing Caesar's assistance against the Catuvellauni. Subsequently, in confederation with the Catuvellauni, they issued Roman-style coins, and the obviously significant local figure buried under the Lexden tumulus outside Colchester was interred with a medallion of Augustus and a number of other Roman luxury items. Clearly in 43 they found themselves in opposition to Rome, but this attitude does not seem to have lasted long, judging by the continuity of use of the royal compound at Gosbecks, Camuludonum, which suggests they had rapidly reconciled themselves to the new power.[24] By contrast, the Iceni, even if Prasutagus did cooperate with the Romans in 43, seem, as mentioned, to have been generally much less enthusiastic about Rome.

Most significantly, though, archaeology has provided a number of specific reasons for doubting whether the Trinovantes were really on the side of Boudica. For a start, it was not just Roman targets at Colchester that suffered in 60/61. The nearby British Sheepen site, for instance, also seems to have been burnt.[25] Equally, while the probable home of the Trinovantian tribal leadership at Gosbecks may have escaped burning at the time, there is no sign of it being abandoned in the aftermath of the revolt.[26] Tacitus talks of savage reprisals after the rebellion and, by contrast to the situation at Gosbecks, the Icenian ritual and probably royal site at Fison Way, Thetford, seems to have been systematically dismantled shortly after 60-61.[27] This differing treatment by the Romans of Trinovantian and Icenian high-status sites strongly suggests that the Trinovantian leadership, at least, did not join Boudica's revolt.

Then there is the question of fortifications. One would expect, in the period after Boudica, extensive signs of military reoccupation in those areas where the rebellion had started. Evidence of post-Boudican occupation has been suggested at a number of forts in the region and, interestingly, these seem to lie on the probable edge of Icenian territory, separating it from Catuvellaunian and Trinovantian territory. Thus post-Boudican Roman military occupation is suggested at Coddenham, Pakenham and Great Chesterford, running roughly in a line along the southern and south-western borders of the Iceni.[28] This might indicate an attempt to isolate the Iceni and defend Catuvellaunian and Trinovantian territory from future incursions from Icenian territory. Perhaps this suggests that the Romans did not view the Trinovantes as rebels.

Equally, the pre-Roman system of defensive dykes at Colchester seems to have been expanded after 55 (in the case of Gryme's Dyke) and probably after the burning of Colchester (in the case of a replacement for Sheepen Dyke). The earlier Sheepen Dyke had been filled in by around 60-61 and its replacement showed no evidence of burning, so Crummy believes that these extensions to the pre-Roman defensive system should be associated with the refortification of the colony after Boudica.[29] If so, it again suggests that the Trinovantes did not side with Boudica. It is hard to see that the Romans would spend time defending their colony with new walls on one hand, while on the other allowing former rebels to throw up their own defences just next door.

Finally, there is the strange case of the statue of Claudius. Tacitus cites the expense and the symbolism of the Temple of Claudius at Colchester as

30 Head of statue of Claudius torn from a life-size statue. Such a statue could well have been associated with the cult of Claudius at Colchester and it is interesting to note that it was found in Icenian, rather than Trinovantian, territory

one of the two major reasons for Trinovantian anger against Rome. A life-size head of Claudius wrenched from an equestrian statue (*30*) and part of a horse leg, possibly broken from the same statue, have indeed been found in East Anglia and it is widely assumed that these rare items were associated with the pre-Boudican cult of Claudius at Colchester. The head was found deposited, possibly ritually, in a river and the leg fragment was found in a British ritual site. If it was the Trinovantes who had broken up a hated statue in their midst, one might well expect the fragments of it to be found in Trinovantian territory. Instead, both fragments had been transported deep back inside Icenian territory, with the head being found in the River Alne and the leg fragment at Ashill.[30]

All in all it seems reasonable to suggest that in 60-61, rather than being Boudica's allies, the Trinovantes were more likely to have been her targets along with their confederate partners, the Catuvellauni. If so, that would undermine Boudica's last claim to be a wider British, rather than a purely Icenian, leader. In which case, as with the invasion of 43, it may be legitimate to see 60-61 primarily as an event thrown up by British tribal politics, with British tribes the key players on both sides and with Romans playing, if not exactly a subsidiary role, then joint lead at most. One might perhaps see parallels with the recent Sunni insurgency in Iraq.

While the US forces have been a target for the insurgents, the Shia became just as much, and in many ways, more of a target. Plus, in many ways, the US forces have remained a target because they have been seen as allies of the Shia majority and as defending a political status quo that enshrines Shia power.

Whatever the truth of Boudica's rebellion, one thing is certain. It damaged any chance of stability in a core part of Britain for years and is likely to have affected relations between the Iceni, Catuvellauni and the Trinovantes for generations. It stirred the pot and delayed any possibility of tribes merging into one ethnic identity under Rome. There is also the possibility that it may have helped create a whole new source of future conflict in the fenlands. In the pre-Roman period, finds of Icenian coins in the fenlands suggest that they and their lucrative salt-extraction industries were controlled by the Iceni. Around the middle of the first century AD, however, the planning of the Roman road network and pottery evidence suggests that the focus of the fenlands shifted dramatically to the west. It has been suggested that this represents a post-Boudican transfer by the Romans of the area from Icenian control to either Catuvellaunian or Corieltauvian control.[31] If so, as we will see in Chapter 6, it may well have been simply storing up trouble for the future.

In the decades after 60-61, Rome's blueprint for the civil administration of Britain becomes clear, and again it is one that, rather than erasing differences between the tribes and uniting them, seems instead to have cemented causes of conflict in place and even added some new ones. As elsewhere in the empire, the Romans introduced into Britain a civilian administration based on the *civitas*. This had its origins in the self-governing city states of the Mediterranean region and in the constitution of Rome itself, but in areas such as Britain, where city states had not developed, the Romans adapted the system to local circumstances. In the case of Britain, rather than giving *civitas* status to cities, they gave it to tribes.

The chronology of this process is far from clear. *Civitas* status was regarded as a privilege, so it is unlikely that, for instance, the Iceni received it any time soon after 61. However, probably by the end of the first century most, maybe all, of Ptolemy's tribes had become *civitates* (*32*). Some have questioned whether these *civitates* occupied all the pre-Roman tribal territories, suggesting that significant areas were retained under direct imperial control. However, there is little unambiguous evidence of large imperial estates being maintained over a long period in Britain, and it seems likely that the majority of tribal territories were transferred to the new *civitates*. By this gesture, the Romans helped ensure that, instead of Britons gradually losing their differences, separate individual identities were maintained throughout the years of Roman rule. Inscriptions from the Roman period, for instance, show Britons describing their identity

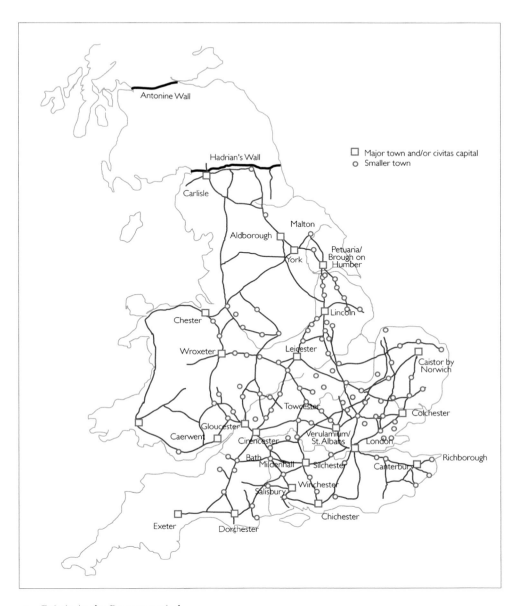

31 Britain in the Roman period

by their *civitas* or nation, in other words their tribe. Presumably, the inhabitants of a *civitas* did not feel the need to identify their nationality within their own home territory. Usually such inscriptions are, therefore, found in relation to individuals away from their own home territory. 'Away' for Britons, would have included being away from their own home *civitas* in another *civitas*, even

32 The *civitates* of Britain. The exact location of *civitas* boundaries is unclear, but it is most likely that they roughly followed the existing pre-Roman tribal boundaries

if it was another *civitas* in Britain. Thus a sandstone base at Colchester carries a dedication from *Similis Ci(vis) Cant(iacus)*, a citizen of the *civitas* of the Cantii to the south.[32] Similarly, the tombstone from South Shields of Regina, the wife of Barates the Palmyrene, records her nationality as '*natione Catvallauna*', 'of the Catuvellaunian nation'.[33] Again, one Aemilius, who had served with the *Classis*

Germanica, is recorded on a tombstone from Cologne where he is mentioned as '*civis Dumnonius*', 'a citizen of the Dumnonii'.[34]

A contrast between the Romans' simple description of the inhabitants of Britain as Britons and the Britons' own more complex view of their identity is suggested by a number of military diplomas. One from Pannonia and dating from the year 105 is issued to a member of '*Cohors I Britannica*'. He is named as '*Lucconi Treni F(ilio) Dobunn*'.[35] To the Romans, as evidenced by the name of his unit, he was a Briton but he still presumably described himself as Dobunnic. Another, dating from the year 110, is in the name of one M. Ulpius Longinus. He is described as being a member of '*Cohors I Brittonum*' but, again, he is also described as '*Belgus*', 'Belgic'.[36] Not every British veteran records his tribal origin but it is interesting that even after many years away from home serving in the Roman Army, and eventually becoming a Roman citizen, it was still thought important in the case of these two soldiers to record their tribal identity.

Not only did the *civitas* structure cement tribal identities in place, it is also likely to have cemented the tribal aristocracy in place as well. Though *civitas* constitutions did vary across the empire and we have few specific details of British *civitas* administration, the broad details are clear. The landowning classes controlled the *civitas* through the *ordo*, the senate of the *civitas*. This *ordo* elected the council or *curia* and also annual magistrates, usually two, like the Consuls in Rome, only these carried the name *duoviri*.

The likelihood is that much the same tribal aristocracy that had run the tribes before Rome took over, now ran the *civitates* under Rome. The archaeology lends support to this view. In a significant number of locations it has been shown that new Roman-style villas were built on top of, or very close to, pre-Roman dwellings, suggesting that these were the same families with the same power but now choosing to display their wealth in the new Roman style. Thus, for instance, at both Rockbourne in Hampshire (*33*) and at Gorhambury near Verulamium, pre-Roman farmsteads are succeeded by Roman-style villas.[37] Equally, at the other end of the villa zone in Roman Britain, in the territory of the Parisi, at Rudston and a number of other sites, British-style enclosed settlements precede the building of Roman-style villas.[38]

Religion also demonstrates a continuity both of identity and, quite possibly, of tribal structure as well. At least one tribe, the Brigantes, had a specifically tribal deity – Brigantia. Presumably her cult, linked so explicitly to the identity of the tribe, started in pre-Roman times, but it certainly existed in the Roman period with a number of dedications being recorded to her. It is possible that other tribes had similar tribal deities but due to the nature of Celtic religion, with its multiplicity of cult names, it has not been as easy to identify them. One such deity might be the focus of the cult at Uley. As with a good a number of

33 The outline of a pre-Roman roundhouse on the site same site as Rockbourne Villa, suggesting continuity among the British aristocracy here from pre-Roman into Roman times

religious sites, this shows continuity from pre-Roman times into the Roman period, with the central feature of a pit or tank surviving from the early first century AD right up until at least 380. After that a church was built on the site.[39] The site at Uley lies within a hillfort, which may suggest the shrine was a political as well as religious focus. Similarly at Maiden Castle, in the huge Durotrigan hillfort overlooking the Roman-period *civitas* capital of Dorchester, a Roman-period temple (*34*) lay near a hut, probably a circular shrine, which was built directly over, and in some sense was presumably intended to link to, a hut of the pre-Roman period.[40] Bearing in mind the probable tribal and political significance of Maiden Castle, the location here of a continuing cult is interesting.

In addition, in at least two cases it has been suggested that a cult focused on pre-Roman tribal leaders was maintained and extended during the Roman period. As mentioned previously, on Hayling Island there is some evidence for an Atrebatic dynastic cult, starting in pre-Roman times and extending into Roman times. A pre-Roman shrine here, with a central circular *cella*, constructed from wood in the late first century BC, was rebuilt after the invasion in exactly the

34 The Roman-period temple situated at the heart of the Durotrigan hillfort of Maiden Castle. Religion may have helped maintain a sense of tribal identity through the Roman period

same location and to the same design but in masonry. The development of the temple is thought to be linked to the activities of Togidubnus in his presumed capital, at Chichester, nearby. It has been argued by Creighton that coins of Verica suggest a shrine and a cult of Commius, the founder of the Atrebatic dynasty, and he suggests that this may be the Hayling Island site.[41] Others suggest that the shrine may be that of Verica himself.[42]

Perhaps the clearest example of a tribal dynastic cult flourishing in Roman times, though, is the Folly Lane site outside Verulamium. Here the burial site of a Catuvellaunian leader, probably buried shortly after the Roman invasion, became the centre of a major cult that survived long into the Roman period, connected by a processional way to the theatre and to the temple lying to the west of the forum.[43]

It is hard to know how closely the borders of the new Roman *civitates* followed those of pre-Roman tribal entities. It seems reasonable to assume that once the decision had been made to base the *civitas* system on tribes, efforts would be made to reduce friction with the local population by keeping to existing boundaries. However, in one instance at least, or two if, as discussed above, the fenlands were taken from the Iceni and given to the Corieltauvi or

Catuvellauni, the Romans seem to have stored up future trouble by fixing *civitas* borders that cut across tribal boundaries.

As discussed in previous chapters, Ptolemy indicates that the *civitas* of the Belgae contained the cities Aquae Calidae and Venta/Winchester (full name Venta Belgarum). It is hard to see how Aquae Calidae can be anything but an alternative name for Aquae Sulis/Bath. Judging from pre-Roman coin evidence the *civitas* of the Belgae, therefore, seems to have been carved by the Romans out of a section of Atrebatic territory in the east and a section of Dobunnic territory in the west.

Tacitus states that Togidubnus was given a number of *civitates* to rule and since he seems most likely to have been based in Atrebatic Chichester (where the inscription mentioning him was found) the most likely candidates for the *civitates* ruled by him are those of the Regni, the Atrebates and the Belgae, all except the western half of the *civitas* of the Belgae constituting the pre-Roman Atrebatic tribal territory.

What prompted the Romans to carve up Dobunnic territory in this way can only be guessed at, but Togidubnus was important to them, and no doubt he would have been grateful for the rich farming land taken from the Dobunni. The silver- and lead-mining area of the Mendips also lay on the southern edges of this territory. At the time of the invasion in 43, giving Togidubnus this area may have seemed like a good idea. As discussed in Chapter 6, though, it was a move that may have had huge ramifications later.

CHAPTER 4

155-211

If we are heavily reliant on historical sources as opposed to archaeological evidence for Boudica's revolt, with the next crisis to hit Britannia and put another few cracks in any prospect of tribal unity, the situation is almost exactly the reverse. There is significant archaeological evidence but almost nothing from Roman historical sources to explain what it all means.

In fact there is rather a gap in Roman historical sources on Britain for most of the second and third centuries AD. Tacitus gives a detailed account of the progress northwards of the Roman Army under Agricola in the late first century, culminating in the ultimately meaningless victory at Mons Graupius in 83 or 84. This was followed by a temporary occupation of southern Scotland and, judging by the archaeological evidence, a retreat to the Tyne-Solway line by the beginning of the second century (35).[1]

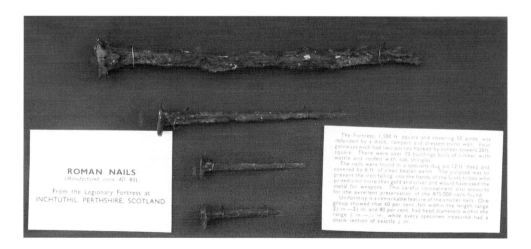

35 Roman nails from the Inchtuthil hoard, buried when the Romans left the fort there in around 86-7, abandoning territory occupied under Agricola

The original decision to withdraw from Agricola's high water mark may have been connected with the need to transfer one of four legions from Britain to deal with a crisis on the Danube.[2] However, the local inhabitants also seem to have been far from acquiescent about a Roman presence on their doorstep.

As opposed to the situation in the south, where Rome had been a major player in British tribal politics for over a century and had developed a network of alliances with tribes, in the north Rome was something of a newcomer. Through its cooperation with Cartimandua, queen of the Brigantes, Rome had some experience of the region, but its influence was probably much more limited than in the south. While early first-century Roman material is widespread on high-status British civilian sites to the south, in the north it is much less common.

Possibly starting under Domitian, and certainly under Trajan, a line of forts was developed along the Roman road, the Stanegate, that ran between the Solway and the Tyne. Presumably, this defensive system was developed in response to some form of military threat and certainly Hadrian's biographer states that, on his accession in 117, he found a situation where 'the Britons could not be kept under Roman authority'. This would tally with a fragment of tombstone which commemorates a centurion killed in war, who belonged to a unit stationed at Vindolanda in the reigns of Trajan and Hadrian. There is also the evidence of a coin issued by Hadrian in 119, featuring Britannia and usually assumed to refer to some kind of victory (or at least something that could be portrayed as a victory) in the island.[3] In this context, it is not surprising that in 122 Hadrian chose to solidify and strengthen the Tyne-Solway border with the construction of his world-famous wall (*36*). Not surprising, but perhaps not wise all the same.

The Tyne-Solway line has obvious advantages from a military point of view. It is the shortest line from sea to sea in this area. It also offers imposing crags in its centre which are natural defensive barriers in their own right, even before being topped by an impressive wall. However, it may have had one major drawback which the Roman military engineers either seem not to have been aware of, or thought unimportant. The line chosen for the Wall seems to have taken little notice of local tribal priorities, something which, as with the creation of the *civitas* of the Belgae and the possible reassignment of the fenlands, may have had serious long-term consequences.

In the area of the Tyne-Solway line[4] lay territory of the Brigantes, the largest tribe in the whole of Britain according to Tacitus. Ptolemy indicates that Epiacum/Whitley Castle, just to the south of Hadrian's Wall, was in Brigantian territory. However, the evidence of dedications to the tribal goddess Brigantia also suggests that the extent of Brigantian territory in the north is unlikely to have stopped at any neat line drawn by Roman military engineers (*37*). There is

36 Hadrian's Wall

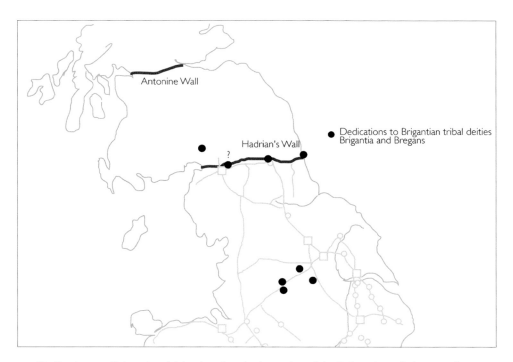

37 Dedications to Brigantian deities showing the huge size of the Brigantian tribal area and demonstrating a Brigantian presence in the area of Hadrian's Wall and to the north of the wall. *After Salway*

one cluster of inscriptions along the Wall, and, significantly, another beyond it at Birrens,[5] suggesting that the Wall would not only have occupied large stretches of Brigantian territory (there is evidence of pre-Roman ploughing and farmsteads under a number of the Stanegate and Hadrian's Wall forts[6]) but probably also separated one part of the tribe from the rest. Neither of these points is likely to have endeared the Wall to the Brigantes.

There is also no particular reason to think that the relationship of the Brigantes with any tribe immediately to their north was of a nature so hostile that they would welcome being permanently separated from them by a wall. A number of dragonesque brooches of probably Brigantian manufacture, for instance, have been found at sites north of Hadrian's wall, mainly on sites in Votadinian territory including the royal site at Traprain Law, but also in the territory of the Novantae to the west, suggesting either commercial or diplomatic contacts with both tribes.[7] It is highly unlikely that the Brigantes would appreciate having such links suddenly made conditional on permission from Roman soldiers. The evidence of occupations the world over is the same. Even if occupation troops commit no other offences, the presence of checkpoints, slowing traffic and humiliating locals simply by obliging them to obey orders from outsiders, is a huge irritant liable to turn them against occupation troops extremely fast. I can say from personal experience that it's bad enough being ordered around at checkpoints by foreign troops in foreign countries. In your own country, it is the sort of thing that can very rapidly lead to violence.

We have no evidence of how passage of Britons from north of the border across Hadrian's Wall might have been administered. However, it may be that, at least originally, the Romans would have attempted to organise such matters in the way they did along parts of the German frontier, where people from beyond the border were only allowed to pass into the empire unarmed, under guard and after paying a fee.[8] If the Romans did attempt to apply such measures to the Brigantes north of the Wall when attempting to visit other Brigantes south of the Wall, it would have caused extreme resentment. We mainly know about the German regulations in the context of complaints by locals about them. The Brigantes would doubtless have added their own complaints to the list.

Certainly, at the same time as the construction of the Wall, or very shortly afterwards, the builders decided it was necessary to construct along its course, a short way to the south, the *vallum*, a ditch 20 Roman feet wide and 10 deep with a mound 20 Roman feet wide on either side. Various explanations have been suggested for the *vallum*, but the most convincing explanation is that supported by Breeze & Dobson, that it was primarily defensive in purpose.[9] The arrangement with mounds on both sides of the ditch is unusual, but may have to do with the fact that the Wall remained the primary defensive platform in the area (being much taller than the northern mound and often towering over it on crags) and/or the necessity of protecting a communications route that seems to have run inside the *vallum* zone. Certainly building the *vallum* seems far too large an undertaking for some mere customs purpose (a function sometimes suggested for it). The ditch that ran north of the Wall, for instance, was in places left unfinished where cutting it would mean carving out solid rock. By contrast, the *vallum* was in some locations, as at the appropriately named Limestone Corner, taken straight through outcrops of rock. It is hard to see anything but pressing defensive reasons justifying such efforts.

However, while the *vallum* may have improved the situation from the point of view of the army on the Wall defending itself, it can only have worsened relations with the locals. For a start it would have taken considerably more land from the Brigantes. There is even evidence of one farmstead actually being sandwiched between the Wall and the *vallum*.[10] Futhermore, contrary to what has sometimes been thought, it now seems clear that there was no causeway across the *vallum* at most mile forts and that consequently the Wall and *vallum* offered only 14 places, all tightly controlled by the Roman military, where civilians could cross from north to south and vice versa.[11]

It is even possible that resentment of the Wall and *vallum* by the Brigantes lies behind the surprising decision by Hadrian's successor, Antoninus Pius, early in his reign, to abandon the huge investment made in Hadrian's Wall and advance the frontier to the Forth-Clyde isthmus and build a new frontier there – the Antonine Wall. Antoninus was, certainly by Roman standards, a well-liked and respected emperor who generally pursued cautious, moderate policies and it may be significant that the advance to the Forth-Clyde line is the only known example in his entire reign of expanding the empire through the expensive use of military force.

It seems possible that in some sense, therefore, even this advance may have been effectively defensive by nature. Antoninus may have thought that including the entire territory of the Brigantes and their northern neighbours within the empire would pacify the tribe. Certainly the abandonment of the Wall at this point seems to have been marked by an attempt to reduce the impediment it represented to civilian traffic. There is evidence at some fort sites of damage to the gate pivots at around this point, suggesting the gates may simply have been removed altogether (either by the Romans or by the Brigantes themselves) and it is likely the *vallum* was slighted, probably at this time, with, in some areas, the mounds being backfilled into the ditch to create causeways every 135ft.[12] Judging by an acclamation of Antoninus as imperator in 142 and the issuing of commemorative coins in 142-3, it is likely that by that time campaigning to take the area up to the new frontier was complete and construction of the Antonine Wall presumably started soon afterwards.

38 The Roman fort at Ilkley, reoccupied in the 160s, possibly in response to raiding by the Brigantes

Whatever the intention of the new border, however, it seems not to have been a success because it lasted an even shorter time than the previous frontier and by around 158 the archaeological evidence suggests that the new frontier was being abandoned and Hadrian's Wall was, instead, being recommissioned. At roughly the same time, or shortly afterwards, forts all over Brigantian territory as far south as the Peak District seem to have been reoccupied. Inscriptions suggesting rebuilding and reoccupation are found at Brough on Noe in 158, at Ribchester and Ilkley in the 160s and at Lanchester in the 170s (*38*). Analysis of the ceramic evidence also suggests that forts at Ambleside, Bainbridge, Binchester, Chester-le-Street, Ebchester, Lanchester, Manchester and Old Penrith may all have been reoccupied at around this time.[13]

So what's going on? The historical evidence is frustratingly unclear. In both 161 and 170-72 historical sources state that there is a danger of war in Britain without, unfortunately, giving any further details. Then concerning the early 180s Cassius Dio writes:

> The most serious war fought during the reign of Commodus took place in Britain. Tribes in the island crossed over the wall separating them from the Roman forts. In the process, they did great damage and slaughtered a general and his soldiers. Alarmed, Commodus sent Ulpius Marcellus against the barbarians and he ruthlessly suppressed them.
>
> Cassius Dio, *Roman History* 73, 8

In the 190s, Cassius Dio mentions the Caledonians and the Maeatae proving a problem for the Romans.[14] Ptolemy does not include the Maeatae among those he lists in Scotland, but it has been suggested that the name Dumyat Hill near Stirling is a derivation of the name Dun of the Maeatae, in which case the tribe might have been based in this area, just to the north of the Antonine Wall.

Subsequently, in 206, Herodian states that the governor wrote to the then-emperor, Septimius Severus, saying that:

> The barbarians had risen and the country was being overrun as they looted and ransacked. To counter the attacks effectively, either reinforcements or the presence of the emperor himself were needed.
>
> Herodian, *The Roman Histories*, 3.14

According to Cassius Dio, Septimius Severus then decided to conquer the whole of Britain.[15] Presumably, he had determined that this was possibly the only way to heal the open wound that Rome's northern frontier in Britain seemed to

39 Coin of Antoninus Pius from 154/5 showing Britannia and presumed to commemorate a Roman military action in Britain, possibly to be associated with the description by Pausanias of a Brigantian raid on 'the Genounian district'

have become. However, after some success against the tribes north of Hadrian's Wall, Severus fell ill in 211 and died, and his son Caracalla, anxious to move south and defend his claim to the throne, made peace with the tribes, abandoned their territory and headed for home.

Coins featuring Britannia seem to have been issued to commemorate both Ulpius Marcellus' victory and that of Septimius Severus. However, intriguingly, there is an additional coin issue featuring Britannia that appears in 154/5 and also presumably commemorated some kind of Roman military action (*39*). This is a coin of Antoninus Pius which refers to some military conflict in Britain about which we know nothing. It is possible, however, that it should be linked to a much-debated passage from Pausanias which states that Antoninus Pius deprived the Brigantes of part of their territory because they had launched an attack on a part of the empire known as 'the Genounian district.'[16] There is no known district in Britain that goes by that name and it has been suggested that Pausanias is confusing the British Brigantes with a tribe in Raetia, near the German frontier, called the Brigantii, who had neighbours called the Genauni.[17] This is certainly possible but there is no other evidence for trouble in Raetia around this date and the reoccupation of forts across Brigantian territory at about the same time can plausibly be explained by a serious revolt in the area which might tally with a raid by the Brigantes into neighbouring territory. The creation of the *civitas* of the Carvetii out of Brigantian territory along the border, at some stage before the mid-third century, would also match the description by Pausanias of Antoninus depriving the Brigantes of part of their territory.

One possible avenue to explore in the search for the elusive Genounian region is whether a British G, sometimes representing in British names a W sound, might have been retained by Pausanias or his sources in place of a Roman V which also represented a W sound. The tribe known in Roman texts as the Votadini, for instance, was known to the British by the sixth century as the 'Gododdin'. If G is replaced by V in this context, we get Venounian region. One area that might answer this description is the area around the Roman-period British settlement at Venonis/Venonae, modern-day High Cross. This lies a little way outside Brigantes territory, to the south-west of the Peak District. Certainly there are very strong reasons to believe that whatever did happen in the north between 155 and 211 had a huge impact beyond the borders of the Brigantes and, in fact, right across the *civitates* of central and eastern England.

One of the most mysterious aspects of the history of Roman Britain is the appearance of fortifications around a large number of towns and cities mainly in central and eastern England (mostly a long way from any military zones) in the second half of the second century and at the beginning of the third century. It is a phenomenon unparalleled elsewhere in the Roman Empire and must have a cause (and considering the expense of such constructions, it must have been a major cause) specific to Britain.

It has been suggested that this spate of fortification should be linked to the foray by Clodius Albinus into Europe in search of the imperial throne, the concept being that he ordered the defences built to protect the British civilian population while he took large sections of the army on his cross-Channel outing. However, there is, in fact, evidence that the spate of wall-building got under way significantly before Clodius (193-197) booked his ferry ticket. The lack of Nene Valley Colour-Coated Ware in the bank at Irchester, for instance, may suggest a date of around 160-180 and Gillam and Woodfield date the defences at Great Casterton to 170-180.[18]

It has been argued by others that these defences were purely prestige projects to mark the increasing size and affluence of British cities in the late second century. However, considering how British, Roman and other societies display prestige, it seems that town defences purely for the sake of display, rather than motivated by at least a perceived threat, are relatively low down on the list of desirable options. They are expensive, inconvenient in terms of blocked access and so on and there are more fun ways to spend money that will better confer prestige status. In Roman-British terms, theatres, baths and temples come to mind. That is not to say that impressive defences do not sometimes display a degree of ostentation but, like a prominent burglar alarm, such ostentation may also be an element of successful defence rather than a matter of simple status.

40 The walls of Silchester. Like many Roman-period towns in Britain, Silchester received its first defences in the late second century. Earthwork defences of about 160-190 were succeeded by stone defences in around 260-280

It is true that most *civitas* capitals and other large cities, if not already defended, did receive defences at this point (though note that Canterbury, for instance, did not) but it is likely that such sites would, in any event, have got priority in matters of defence if there was a threat (*40*). It is more interesting that a significant number of small towns also received fortifications in the late second century. It is hard to see anyone paying for the defence of such small towns except for fairly pressing reasons, presumably military ones. This view is supported by the fact that the defences, on occasion, clearly took precedence over the towns rather than merely being an adornment for them. At Towcester, for instance, as Woodfield points out, the construction of the defences must have done extensive damage to the town, cutting its way through probably at least eight major road frontages.[19] So what could be the cause of such extensive urban modifications?

Another much-discussed feature of late second-century archaeology in Britain is traces of destruction by fire (*41*). Such fires then, just as fires now, are, of course, not necessarily a sign of anything more sinister than a cooking accident. However, there are a good number of fires in Britain which seem to date from the late second century and there are some interesting clusters in their distribution. Unless one is going to argue that, for instance, the cooks in

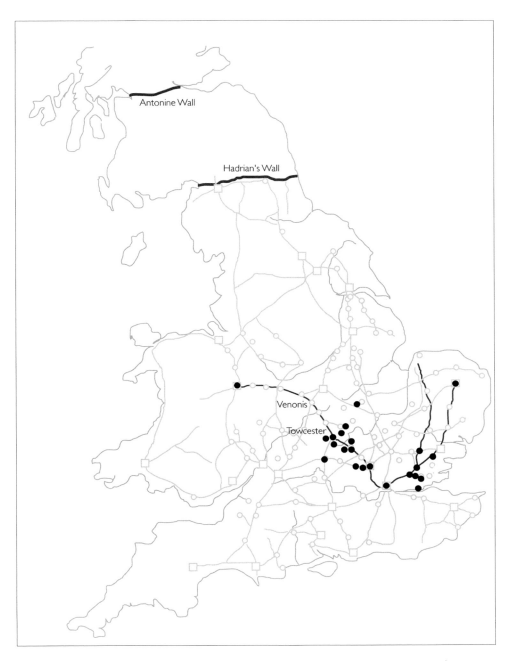

41 Clusters of late Antonine fires. Black dots denote fires and main relevant Roman roads are picked out in black

the area of these clusters were exceptionally careless, there is a need to search for another explanation. Apart from major fires at London in around 150-160 and Verulamium in around 155-160 or a bit later (with extensive burning at nearby Gorhambury in around 175) there are two areas that show significant concentrations of destruction by fire in the period we are examining. Woodfield has drawn attention to a group of fires on the northern and western borders of the Catuvellauni. The villa at Stanton Low, Milton Keynes, was destroyed by fire at around the time in question. The nearby villa at Bancroft was also destroyed around 170, judging by the Samian Ware evidence. The proto-villa at Wood Corner went the same way at about the same time, as did the villa at Piddington, Northamptonshire, and the villa at Easton Maudit, a few miles away. A villa at Great Weldon in east Northamptonshire has Samian Ware of 150-180 in ashy levels, while a villa at Mileoak, Towcester was burnt in the late Antonine period (though here probably before 170) and not far away there was a fire at Wood Burcote Villa that is dated to after 150 and before 200. In terms of the towns in this area, there is some evidence of late Antonine burning, dated probably after 160, at Towcester (where defences were built probably in around 170-175) and at Alchester a large fire pre-dates the building of defences not later than around 150-160.[20]

In the east of Britain, Rodwell drew attention to a series of fires in Trinovantian territory that also seem to date from this period. There appears to have been destruction by fire at Chelmsford, Billericay, Wickford, Gestingthorpe, Kelvedon, Mucking and Braintree.[21] Drury mentions human bone in the fire destruction areas at both Chelmsford and Wickford and dates the fires there on the evidence of the Samian Ware to 150-180.[22] Interestingly, these two towns were also among those equipped with defences in the late second century.

There is additional supporting archaeological evidence for something unusual happening in these and some other areas at this time. Very few coin hoards have been found from the period 96-138 (the reigns of Nerva, Trajan and Hadrian) south of the Humber. There are many reasons for someone to hoard money and many reasons for that hoard not to be subsequently collected. An uncollected hoard does not necessarily mean the owner is dead or fled but the scarcity of unretrieved hoards from this period must in some way represent the generally peaceful times seen by much of England in these years (*42*). Equally, as Robertson points out, unsettled times are at least one likely explanation for the rash of hoards that appears across central and eastern England in the second half of the second century.[23] The distribution of unretrieved hoards is certainly consistent with serious trouble in the territory of the Catuvellauni and in East Anglia but it also suggests problems a little further north, where Corieltauvian territory met that of the Brigantes.

Nerva, Trajan, Hadrian

Antoninus Pius, Marcus Aurelius, Commodus

Constantine

Constantius II - Julian

Valentinian I - Arcadius

Valentinian I - Honorius

42 Changing patterns of unretrieved hoards in different periods of Roman Britain. *After Robertson*

There are also signs of possible economic disruption around the same time. A survey of the amount of construction work being done on 78 random villa sites indicates a peak around 150, followed by a steady decline until around 225, followed by a steep rise in the second half of the third century.[24] Equally, a survey of three major pottery industries shows a decline in the number of pottery forms in use and a temporary suspension of new forms being introduced in the early years of the third century.[25] A recovery starts around 250, with a steep rise in both numbers of forms used and new forms introduced.

In the absence of clearer historical evidence, one explanation for at least some of these signs of trouble in central and eastern England is to link them to the fragmentary historical evidence that we do have – the mysterious Britannia coin issue suggesting conflict around 155, the indications from imperial biographers of imminent war in Britain in 161 and 170-2, the suggestion from Pausanias of raiding by the Brigantes under Antoninus Pius and the clearer evidence of war with the tribes of the north towards the end of the second century.

A look at the map (*41*) will confirm that it is quite conceivable that the concentration of fires and unretrieved hoards along the Catuvellaunian western and northern borders could have been caused by Brigantian raiders. If they had moved out of the Peak District and headed south along Watling Street, one of the first settlements of any size they would have come to would have been Towcester. Interestingly enough, if such an event had occurred, one of the first named locations the Brigantes would have reached would have been Venonis/Venonae, which, as discussed earlier, is at least one potential candidate for being the location of Pausanias' mysterious Genaunian district. Such attacks by Brigantian raiding parties could also explain the subsequent fortification of towns in the area.

There is no particular evidence for hostility between the Catuvellauni and the Brigantes in pre-Roman times, though that is not to say that it did not exist. Two such powerful political entities could well have had an uneasy relationship in the turbulent world of the early first century AD, particularly with the Catuvellauni espousing continental styles and the influence of Rome, while the Brigantes were almost entirely un-Romanised and mainly beyond the reach of Rome. A Brigantian attack on the Catuvellauni in the second half of the second century could be seen in the same light as the events of 60-61. Perhaps the Brigantes saw the Catuvellauni and Romans as allies and, therefore, equal targets. Equally, however, this could be a new tribal conflict, though one very much in the old Celtic tradition of cross-border tribal raiding. There is, however, only so much one can explain with Brigantian raiding. It is, for instance, inconceivable that Brigantian raiders, after torching villas in the area around Venonis/Venonae, would then have suddenly skipped over a large expanse of territory in between and started lighting fires again in Essex. Some other explanation must be found for these fires in the east.

A look at the map may again be instructive. Again it looks conceivably like the course of raiders, but if so then they are extremely unlikely to have been Brigantian and there are no particularly obvious overseas candidates for causing such destruction at this early date. In geographical terms, bearing in mind that the fires occur on a rough north–south axis and that, in the north, they start at Braintree not far from the northern border of Trinovantian territory, the most likely raiders would be the Iceni. This would fit with the significant signs of reconstruction from around this period that Woodfield notes in Suffolk villas.[26] If the Trinovantes were, in fact, largely victims of Boudica's rebellion rather than fellow rebels also, then this looks rather like a rerun of the initial stages of 60-61 (though, if so, in this case, the tribal raiding party understandably seems to have avoided attacking Colchester, strongly fortified after 61, or at least if they did they were not successful). Chelmsford, possibly by now some form of administrative capital of the Trinovantes (its name Caesaromagus, is a form associated in Gaul with tribal capitals[27]), is one of the sites in this area showing both evidence of burning and fortification in the late second century.

As we have seen recently in Iraq with Sunni and Shia, groups with a grudge will often use the cover and example offered by widespread chaos to settle their own scores. The probability that other tribes apart from the Brigantes were involved in the chaos of the later second century means we should look even more closely at the situation in the western half of Catuvellaunian territory because there is also evidence here that the inhabitants may have been under threat from another direction other than the north.

Woodfield has drawn attention to the apparent geographically specific nature of the destruction in the area. She has pointed out that there is no evidence of fires at this time in Leicestershire.[28] Effectively this means that the destruction was restricted to Catuvellaunian territory and the Corieltauvi did not suffer burning. As we have seen above, the evidence of coin hoards suggests that there may have been trouble along the Corieltauvian/Brigantian border at this time but it is the Catuvellauni who seem to have borne the full brunt. Equally, to the west, there is no evidence of fires in the rich territory of the Dobunni and interestingly, in this case, there are almost no coin hoards either. This raises the question of whether the Dobunni may in some way have become actively involved in creating the chaos in central England in the late second century.

Some of the fires in Catuvellaunian territory seem a long way south, even for a very adventurous Brigantian raiding party to have caused. Alchester, for instance, is a great distance from Brigantian territory but very close to that of the

Dobunni. The Gorhambury and Verulamium fires are also very unlikely to have been caused by Brigantes raiders and are much more accessible from Dobunnic territory. The two tribes certainly may have had grounds for conflict. As we have seen, the spread of Catuvellaunian coinage under Cunobelin may suggest Catuvellaunian expansion into formerly Dobunnic territory north of the Thames. In addition Cassius Dio says that a part of the Bodunni (probably meaning the Dobunni) were at one stage subject to the Catuvellauni. The strongest evidence for possible trouble between Dobunni and Catuvellauni in the late second century, however, comes from analysis of a map of town fortifications. It is also an exercise that throws a crucial light on the lack of integration between the tribes after over 100 years of Roman occupation.

As mentioned earlier, most *civitas* capitals and other major cities received defences in the late second century (if they had not already previously done so). However, it would be logical that major centres would receive priority treatment. If we are to know more about the nature of the threat we must look more specifically at the location of those more minor centres where it was thought worth the expense to erect defences.

When we do this, a fascinating picture emerges of the western and northern borders of the Catuvellaunian *civitas* (*43*). While small towns in the centre and east of the *civitas* remained without defences, as Woodfield has pointed out, almost all towns along the western and northern borders of the *civitas* were given defences in the late second century. Note that this includes the western border all the way down to Dorchester on Thames. It is difficult to see what other threat there could be to Dorchester on Thames in the late second century except one coming from Dobunnic territory.

Dating defences from the Roman period in Britain is not always easy and a significant number currently remain undated. However, including on the map later and undated fortifications gives an even more interesting insight into the planning of town defences in Roman Britain. Again, if we concentrate on the small towns that were given defences and those that were not, something particularly interesting emerges. The towns in the interior of the Catuvellaunian *civitas* still remain undefended but a line of defended small towns stretches roughly around the borders of the *civitates* of the Catuvellauni and Trinovantes linking them in one unit. When we remember the confederation of Catuvellauni and Trinovantes, this should not surprise us.

Equally interesting is the outline of other defensive networks which seem to run along and protect the borders of other *civitates*. In the west of England, a line of defended small towns runs roughly around sections of the borders of the Dobunnic *civitas* and in the north a line of three small fortified Corieltauvian towns defends the strategic road between the two major cities in the *civitas*,

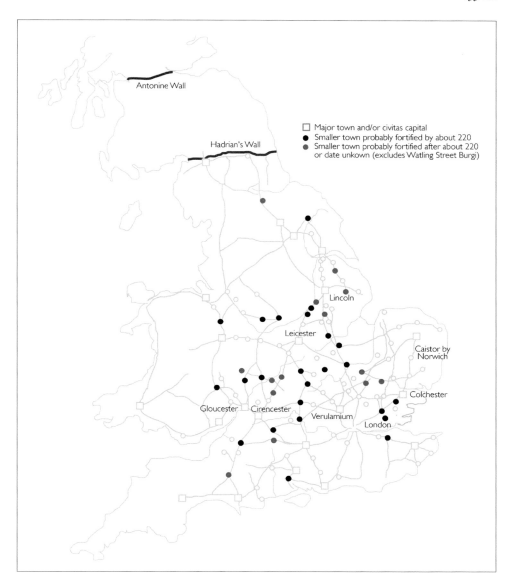

43   Distribution of fortified small towns showing lines of fortified small towns on some *civitas* borders, with unfortified small towns away from *civitas* borders. *After Jones & Mattingly, Millett and Woodfield*

Lincoln and Leicester, and also runs roughly along the probable border with Brigantian territory. As Millet points out, there is no evidence in the spate of fortification in the late second century that central Roman authorities were choosing which towns to defend and which not to.[29] The variability of design of the fortifications in question suggests that the towns, or, as the map suggests, more likely the *civitates*, were deciding what to defend and where. In other words, in the second century and later at least some of the *civitates* appear, in some way, to have been arranging their own defences. What is more, they seem to have been arranging them not against any external threat but against another British tribe or other British tribes. If this is the case, it is completely understandable in the light of pre-Roman tribal competition and disputed borders that must have left a legacy in Roman times. It is, however, a sledgehammer to any notion of Britannia under Rome as a united, peaceful part of the Roman Empire.

One question remains to be asked, though – who was manning these defences? Many assorted pieces of military kit from the second and third centuries have been found in civilian areas. Griffiths, for instance, lists 26 pieces of military kit of this date from Wilthsire,[30] and Bishop has reviewed the available second- to third-century evidence from towns both large and small.[31] This includes a wide variety of belt fittings and also more substantial pieces, such as scabbard chapes, and comes both from *civitas* capitals (including Colchester, Verulamium, Cirencester, Aldborough, Chichester, Wroxeter, Exeter, Dorchester, Canterbury and Silchester) and a number of smaller sites including, interestingly, three in East Anglia (Scole, Woodcock Hall and Wickford). As noted above, Wickford shows both evidence of fire and subsequent fortification in the late second century.

There seems little to distinguish the kit involved from that found on recognised Roman military sites and the quantities recovered might imply the presence of a significant number of troops. In addition, Bishop did not include military or military-inspired brooches from the second to fourth centuries in his survey. As with civilian brooches, military brooches seem to have had a higher rate of loss than other small artefacts. Considering the fact that most were cheap mass-produced items, constantly being opened and closed (and probably often being left in discarded items of clothing when not in use), this is hardly surprising. The two main types mapped in figure *45* are knee brooches dating from between the mid second and mid third centuries and crossbow brooches dating, in Britain, from the mid third to the beginning of the fifth century (*44, colour plate 12*).

It has been suggested that senior civilian officials also wore crossbow brooches in addition to the military. This is based on a few late depictions of senior officials with crossbow brooches. However, the distribution of crossbow brooches on the continent – thick along the imperial frontier and thin elsewhere – implies that only a few civilian officials can ever have worn crossbow brooche. In addition, it has to be said, the appearance of crossbow brooches among courtiers may be no more an indication of civilians regularly wearing military dress than the appearance of uniformed figures among courtiers in a nineteenth-century scene. Many courtiers at that time were military personnel or had some kind of role in

44   Crossbow brooch and knee brooches

the military and the same may well have been true of third- and fourth-century
Rome. It seems safe, therefore, to see the distribution of crossbow brooches
in Britain as primarily a military issue. As would be expected, military areas,
such as the region of the Saxon Shore forts and the Hadrian's Wall belt, feature
strongly on the distribution map. Much more interesting, however, are the small
clumps found inland away from any military areas. It is possible to pick out quite
distinctly a number of *civitas* capitals and major cities – Colchester, Verulamium,
London, Winchester, Silchester, Chichester. All of these had defences by around
the end of the second century/beginning of the third century, but the presence
of military-style brooches persists around *civitas* capitals from the late second
into the fourth century, suggesting a long-term presence rather than short-term
fortification construction missions. Equally the numbers of brooches found in
the *civitas* capitals are not out of line with those on some major military sites. This
looks, arguably, like specific armed garrisons placed in fortified *civitas* capitals.
Obviously it is impossible to tell whether those wearing these military brooches
were regular Roman soldiers or some kind of official *civitas* militia (such a force
would be extremely unusual at this stage, but then the mass fortification of towns

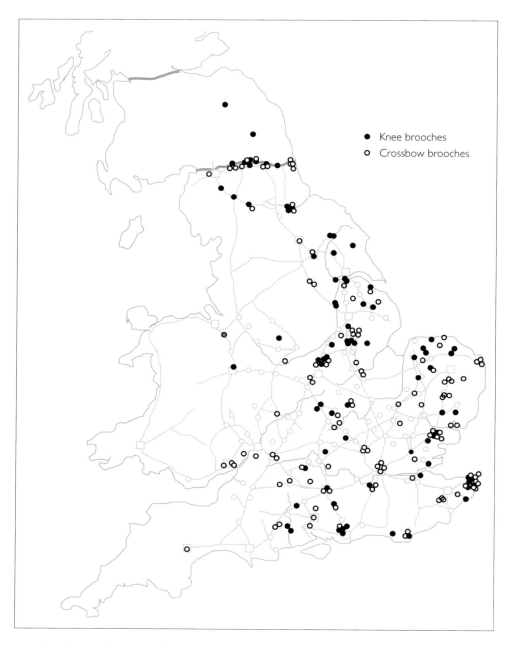

45 Distribution of knee brooches and crossbow brooches, suggesting a military presence in major towns and other key areas. For details of data, see Notes[32]

in Britain at this stage is also extremely unusual). Either way, it does seem more evident that in the second and third centuries, defence was being organised along *civitas* lines.

How such garrisons might relate to the smaller defended towns is less clear. Perhaps the *civitas* capital garrisons acted as a central reserve for the *civitas* as a whole, reacting as and when a specific threat developed. It is interesting to note the concentrations around Leicester and along Watling Street near Towcester, the two areas most exposed to any Brigantian raiding south from the Peak District. Note too (apart from at the *civitas* capital Verulamium) the lack of brooches in the interior of the Catuvellaunian *civitas* which also lacked towns with defences. Alternatively it may simply be that any soldiers or militiamen based in the smaller defended towns were just far fewer in numbers and would, therefore, have left far fewer brooches behind.

The picture of a divided Britannia suggested by the historical and archaeological evidence considered in this chapter is in striking contrast to the usual treatment given to the middle years of the Roman occupation. Often these years seem to be seen as a buffer period between the first and fourth centuries AD, as a time when nothing much of significance militarily and politically happened south of Hadrian's Wall. Nevertheless, in light of our analysis of the extent of tribal conflict and competition in pre-Roman central and south Britain, the idea of deep divisions in Britain in this period should come as no surprise. As demonstrated most recently in Bosnia and Iraq, the period between 43 and 155 would simply not be long enough to erase memories of conflicts and disputes from the pre-Roman period and create a unified Britannia. What's more, the events of the late second century would probably have served to reopen old wounds and renew old tensions (perhaps even adding some new ones) and give them new life for the next decades and centuries. Once again the pot had been stirred, delaying any possibility of the tribes merging into one ethnic identity.

Historical evidence for the third century in Britain is even thinner than for the second century. Little or nothing is known from the classical sources about the period between the death of Severus and the arrival of the forces of Constantius Chlorus in 296 to wind up the short-lived British empire of Carausius and Allectus. It is possible that, in the north, the Roman authorities effectively surrendered to the might of the Brigantes who, except in the area east of the Pennines, remained resolutely culturally un-Romanised throughout the years of Roman rule. Contrary to the popular impression of Rome smashing resistance wherever it found it, such an accommodation would certainly not be unknown. After his father's death, for instance, Caracalla hastily made peace with the tribes in Scotland on terms that included getting out of their territory and leaving them in peace so that he could concentrate on securing his position on the imperial throne.

In the late second century and early third century, there is evidence of gateways being narrowed and/or blocked at a number of milecastles and forts on Hadrian's Wall (*46*).[33] In light of the probable hostility of tribes both to the south and north of the Wall at this time, this measure is hardly surprising and more examples of blocking are found in the fourth century, when the situation in the north again became difficult for the Romans. The gateway blocking at the end of the second century and beginning of the third century is, however, accompanied by the abandonment of turrets between the milecastles and, along a central section of the Wall, the actual destruction of the turrets.[34] This rather suggests that the army was retreating into its bases and making patrolling the Wall itself less of a priority. After all, abandoning the turrets might be one thing but going to all the trouble of actually destroying them suggests there was a real possibility of unused and unvisited turrets being occupied by locals. This sense of the Wall itself (as opposed to the major forts) becoming less significant grows through the third century, as increasingly milecastles are also abandoned.[35] The *vallum* too was abandoned in the third century, with civilians even being allowed to fill it in and build over it.[36]

Such moves could have turned the formerly solid frontier into a more porous one which would have caused less resentment. Smuggling, for instance, across a wall perhaps only guarded in the vicinity of the main forts would become much easier. Moreover, such a development might have been aided by the changing nature of the garrison on Hadrian's Wall. Longer serving units on the Wall would increasingly have ties to the local community and, therefore, would have been less likely to have interfered with everyday traffic across the Wall. As soldiers at checkpoints all over the world will tell you, it's one thing to keep a complete stranger who doesn't even speak your language waiting for an hour and then to refuse him passage with a curt dismissal, it's an entirely different thing to do that to the father of your girlfriend or his relatives. Ammianus Marcellinus, in his reference to the disbandment of a Roman intelligence unit known as the *areani* for allegedly passing information to the tribes north of the border in the fourth century, may reflect the closeness of such military ties with the local population.[37]

However, there are suggestions that the military threat from the Brigantes to tribal areas south of them was not entirely over. Some time, probably towards the end of the third century or at the beginning of the fourth, a series of small fortifications, commonly referred to as *burgi*, was built along the line of Watling Street as it ran south of the Peak District. It is precisely the stretch of road that Brigantian raiders would have used in the late second century and it also leads, in the west, to the major city and capital of the Cornovii at Wroxeter.[38] It is hard to

46 A milecastle on Hadrian's Wall. A number of both turrets and milecastles were abandoned in the third century, suggesting that the Roman Army was concentrating its attention on the main forts in the Wall zone rather than the Wall itself

know what military threat might have prompted such fortifications at this stage and in a location so remote from any overseas danger, unless it was again raiding parties coming south from the Pennines.

In the centre and south of England, there is no evidence of anything that might represent another outbreak of tribal violence in the third century but, there again, with so few historical sources for this period in Britain, there is no proof that there was not. The brooch evidence certainly suggests that armed garrisons were maintained in *civitas* capitals and some other major towns throughout the third century and on into the fourth century. The Roman Army, as demonstrated in the north of England with its occasional abandonment of forts there, was perfectly capable of removing troops from areas where it did not see any reason for them remaining. Presumably, garrisons remained in the *civitas* capitals for a purpose.

There is also the strange instance of the large, probably early third-century forts built at Caister and Brancaster on the Norfolk coast. These (along with Reculver in Kent) form the first elements of what has become known as the Saxon Shore fort system. However, whatever the role of the later forts may have been, there is no question of Saxons, or probably anybody else, raiding these parts of Britain by sea at the beginning of the third century. It is possible that the forts could have fulfilled a general security function and certainly the fort at Reculver overlooked the Thames Estuary which was a vital strategic communications area. It is harder to see the function of Caister and Brancaster in isolated locations on the east and north coast of Norfolk. It is pure speculation but could it be that Caister and Brancaster were designed to face an internal rather than an external threat, perhaps as a response to any raids out of Icenian territory at the end of the second century. In Chapter 3 we noted the possible temporary positioning of Roman forts along Icenian borders after Boudica and, unlike in Brigantian territory, there were by the end of the second century no recently abandoned forts to be reoccupied. A strategy of control from coastal forts would have much to recommend it, including ease of resupply by sea. It is exactly the strategy pursued by Edward I in the thirteenth century when he established control over north-west Wales by building a line of coastal castles, including Caernarvon and Conwy.

CHAPTER 5

367-369

After the dearth of historical sources for Britain in the third century, the early fourth century sees a comparative glut. Almost a decade after his termination of Allectus' British regime, Constantius, newly made Augustus following the retirement of Diocletian and Maximian, returned to Britain in 305-306 to campaign against the Picts – the first time that this name appears in Roman histories. Picts, of course, is just an Anglicisation of Picti, 'the painted ones', referring to the common habit among British tribes of painting their bodies before combat. At the time of Constantius the name was used to refer to the Dicaledones (presumably linked to the Caledonii) and other tribes north of Hadrian's Wall, but it is perhaps worth considering whether it might also include some of the non-Romanised Brigantes in and west of the Pennines. After all, as noted in the last chapter, there is evidence of fortifications being built along the southern edge of the Pennines at about the time Constantius arrived in Britain to campaign against the Picts. The Romans were as capable as anybody else of using terms for foreigners loosely, and it is unlikely that a Roman soldier encountering a large number of painted warriors looking hostile would necessarily stop to enquire closely as to what tribe they belonged to.

The activities of Constantius in the north were, however, cut short by his death at York in 306. His son Constantine was thereupon acclaimed emperor in York and subsequently left Britain to pursue his imperial ambitions on the continent (though there is possible evidence of Constantine returning, with the London mint issuing coins of the *adventus* type in 307, 312 and 314[1]).

Later, in the 350s, Britain suffered disruption after the fall of the Gallic and British empire of Magnentius and Decentius. Ammianus records the activities of Paul Catena, sent to Britain by Constantius II to arrest supporters of Magnentius but taking his brief considerably too far, according to Ammianus, by arresting large numbers of completely innocent people as well.[2] We also have the reappearance of the Picts. In 360, Julian was informed that the Picts and Scots were plundering the area close to the Wall and responded by sending Lupicinus, his *magister equitum*, and four units of the field army to Britain. Sadly, apart from his wintering at London, the sources reveal little more about the expedition of Lupicinus and the situation in Britain at the time

The Picts, though, appear yet again at the centre of the controversial event which for many years dominated discussion of the late fourth century in Britain, and which is still arguably central to the last decades of Roman power in Britain. As with 60-61, the historical sources are key to any understanding of what may or may not have occurred in 367-369, so it is worth quoting the account by Ammianus at some length:

> After Valentinian had left Amiens and was hurrying to Trier, he received disastrous news that Britain was in severe difficulties due to the attacks of the united barbarians, that Nectaridus, the count of the sea-coast had been killed in battle and duke Fullofaudes had been ambushed and taken prisoner…
>
> It is enough to mention here that, at that point, the Picts, made up of two nations, Dicalidones and Vecturiones, along with the Attacotti, a very warlike tribe, and the Scots, were all ranging across various parts of Britain, plundering savagely.
>
> To prevent these disasters, the new, energetic general [Theodosius] took a chance and set out for that island which lies at the very ends of the earth…
>
> He crossed the straits from Boulogne in a relaxed manner and reached Richborough, a calm spot on the coast opposite.
>
> When the Batavi and Heruli and the Jovian and Victorian legions, coming from the same place, had arrived as well, he landed and, confident in the size and power of his forces, made for London, an old town recently named Augusta. Splitting his army up into several detachments, he attacked the roving bands of raiders who were weighed down with plunder. He quickly routed these groups with their prisoners and cattle, and he took off them what they had stolen from Rome's unfortunate subjects.
>
> He gave everything back to its rightful owners, except a small amount he kept for his own tired soldiers. Then, happy and victorious, he entered the city which had just previously been overwhelmed by disaster and was now rescued almost before it could have hoped.
>
> His victory spurred him onto even greater daring, but, after considering what the safest course of action might be, he hesitated, unsure of the future. He was convinced by information from prisoners and deserters that so many attackers, from a number of tribes, all very fierce, could only be beaten by secret stratagems and sudden attacks.
>
> Then he invited deserters and others spread across the country on leave to come to his camp, promising them impunity, in a number of edicts.
>
> Ammianus Marcellinus, *Roman History* 27, 8

He defeated and routed the various tribes, who had grown insolent in past security and so set out to attack territories inside the Empire. He entirely restored those cities and fortresses which had been damaged or destroyed in the catastrophes of the time.

Ammianus Marcellinus, *Roman History* 28, 3

The problems with interpreting the events of 367-369 can be summed up very quickly. Raids are said to be widespread yet archaeologists have had difficulty in finding specific evidence of any large-scale destruction that can be unequivocally linked to events in 367-369. The Picts, Scots and Attacotti are said to be the culprits yet the only action that Ammianus records is somewhere near London. Theodosius is said to restore the defences of the country but, again, archaeologists have struggled to find explicit evidence of this. Some defensive modifications previously attributed to him are now believed to have taken place at completely different times. For instance, the abandonment of forts north of Hadrian's Wall is now reckoned to have taken place much earlier in around 312.[3] Bearing in mind the difficulty of matching the description by Ammianus to an archaeologically and historically consistent scenario, a recent trend among historians has been to question if anything very significant at all happened in 367-369 and to wonder whether Ammianus was, instead, mainly attempting to flatter Theodosius by his account.

It is certainly true that Ammianus does appear keen to show Theodosius in a particularly heroic light. Bearing in mind that the son of Theodosius was emperor at the time Ammianus was writing, this is perhaps not surprising. However, writing off the events of 367-369 as some kind of fictitious panegyric is probably too easy. Ammianus Marcellinus is generally reckoned to be, by the standards of ancient historians, comparatively reliable and, however well inclined he may have been towards the central character, it seems unlikely that he would have deliberately fabricated the main elements of such an allegedly major incident so soon after the event. The death of such a senior figure as Nectaridus, for instance, would presumably have been a matter of record in late fourth-century Rome. It seems instead more feasible to accept that something major did happen in Britain in 367-369, but that we are getting a slightly distorted reflection of it through the lens of Ammianus.

The lack of damage may not be as significant as it seems at first. It is possible for a country to be thrown into panic and turmoil without large-scale destruction necessarily taking place. For instance, if, as suggested in the last chapter, Hadrian's Wall had become a largely porous frontier by the third century, raiders crossing it would not necessarily leave much evidence of destruction. Equally, the mere appearance of raiding bands where they had not been seen before, or had not been seen for a very long time, might have been enough to cause major panic.

The apparent collapse of at least a significant portion of the Roman military in Britain, implied by the attempts of Theodosius to rally deserters, would also have been likely to have spread public unease.

In addition, while evidence of actual destruction is thin, there is some evidence of unretrieved hoarding that may relate to 367-369. As discussed in the previous chapter, there are many reasons why someone might deposit a hoard of coins and then not retrieve it. It does not necessarily mean they are 'dead or fled'. The use of coin hoard evidence in the middle of the fourth century also unfortunately carries additional complexities, due to demonetisation in the mid 350s,[4] raising the possibility that some coin hoards may simply have been abandoned because the coins themselves had become worthless.

It is, though, questionable to what extent any emperor, particularly one ruling in uncertain times, could afford to wipe out people's savings. It is probable, therefore, that demonetisation was accompanied by exchange for new money, in which case the old money would not, effectively, be worthless. Equally, there is no reason to believe that demonetisation would affect just one region. In that context, concentrations of unretrieved hoards in areas where they did not exist in preceding decades and do not exist in succeeding decades and which do not correspond to the distribution of other fourth-century finds, are still likely to be significant. On this basis, the pattern of coin hoards from the years around 367-369 can be used to support the idea of significant problems in central southern England. A comparison with hoards from preceding and succeeding periods suggests an unusual concentration of hoards to the north and west of London. (*42*). This, it is true, is an area which features strongly on a map of all Portable Antiquities Scheme finds for the fourth century (*60*). However, a number of other similar concentrations on the PAS map do not produce similar levels of hoarding in this period. Some of the hoards to the north and west of London may relate to the earlier activities of Paul Catena already mentioned, but his target seems to have been mainly the rich and the eminent and many of these hoards consist of low-value coins with no apparent connection to high-status items or sites. It seems more feasible to connect the appearance of such a concentration of hoards, therefore, with the events described by Ammianus.

In terms of the geography of 367-369, it does seem unlikely that bands of Picts, Scots and Attacotti could have reached as far as London, but it is not inconceivable. Equally, it is perfectly possible that some of the raiders came from rather nearer to home. The coin hoard evidence suggests trouble in a rather similar area to that seemingly affected by events in the late second century. It raises the question of whether some of the same players may have been involved. Perhaps, as suggested earlier, some of the 'Painted Ones' were, in fact, painted Brigantes. If so, it might help explain the lack of coin hoards in the north around 367-369. An objection could be made that the network of forts across Brigantian territory in and to the west of the Pennines would have prevented such a move. However, while at many of these there is archaeological evidence of late fourth-century occupation, the situation in the years prior to 367-369 is much less clear. Many northern forts are known to have been abandoned in the late third century.[5]

Alternatively, the roving bands near London could have been composed of raiders from southern *civitates* taking advantage of a crisis originally created in the north, just as seems to have happened in 155. There is an interesting passage in Ammianus subsequent to his coverage of the main events of 367-369, in which he refers to one Valentinus allegedly trying to stir up some kind of rebellion among soldiers and exiles in Britain. Valentinus and a few other conspirators are executed but Theodosius refrains from carrying out a wider investigation, 'to avoid a situation where many became afraid of such an investigation, and new troubles revived in the province as a result.'[6] The implication that an investigation inside the Roman part of Britain might revive troubles there implies an internal element to the threat Theodosius faced in 367-369, in addition to any external one.

The difficulty of finding extensive evidence of reconstruction by Theodosius may also not be such a major barrier to accepting the importance of events in 367-369. While it is hard to find reconstruction that could only be attributed to Theodosius, there are some significant late Roman defensive features in Britain for which he could easily be responsible. In London, for instance, the site of Theodosius' triumphal entry, bastions are added to the Wall some time between 341 and 375.[7] Equally, on the northern frontier across which some of the raiders are supposed to have travelled, it is possible that a new style of construction using packed postholes, that appears at Ravenglass, Maryport and Bowness on Solway, should be dated to this period.[8]

Ultimately, though, the strongest evidence supporting Ammianus' assertion that something did occur in 367-369 that threw Britain into major turmoil, is what was to happen in the years immediately following. The tribes of central, southern and eastern Britain seem to have been rearmed. Military belt buckles where the loop is composed of two dolphins arching round to hold a ball or globe in their mouth appear in mainland Europe before 350. Their earliest appearance in Britain, however, seems to be in the graves of possible foreign soldiers at Lankhills, Winchester. Coin evidence, funerary rites and stratigraphic evidence date these graves to the period 350-370.[9] They would, in fact, be perfect in date for soldiers from the army of Theodosius.

Starting in around 370, however, these distinctive late Roman military buckles (and their associated belt fittings, mostly amphora-shaped strap ends and propeller-shaped belt stiffeners which were worn in numbers along the belt, both as decoration and to lend stiffness to the leather of the belt) begin to appear widely across Britain (*47, 48*). Dated examples of the buckles have been

47 Late Roman belt fittings, including dolphin buckles, propeller belt stiffeners and amphora strap ends. Similar styles of strap end and belt stiffener are widely found on both sides of the Channel, but British buckles rapidly become stylistically distinct

found with Valentinianic or later coins at Lullingstone, Lydney, Verulamium, Wye in Kent and the Cathedral Green site in Winchester.[10] A small percentage are imports, stylistically identical to those found in mainland Europe.[11] Most, however, judging by stylistic elements that are unique to Britain, seem to have been manufactured here (*colour plate 13*). They are found, as would be expected, in some military areas but they also appear on civilian sites too, leading to debate over who exactly was wearing these buckles and belt fittings.

The belt was not a normal piece of Roman civilian clothing and, though it was worn by civilians of both sexes in Germanic culture, there is no clear evidence that it was widely worn by civilians in Britain at any time before the arrival of Germanic immigrants in significant numbers in the fifth century. Some of the buckles seem relatively small, by modern standards, for military belts but third-century buckles which are undoubtedly military are often no bigger and even the smallest of fourth-century buckles are no narrower than, for instance, the slender shoulder belts being worn by Roman soldiers on Trajan's Column. The unusually long, narrow buckle plates attached to some of the smallest buckles would probably be uncomfortable on a belt round the waist and, in fact, seem more appropriate for shoulder belts.

It has been claimed that military belts were also worn by civilian officials. This is based on the fact that some late Roman civilian officials were, technically, soldiers and that the phrase 'to take the *cingulum*' (a Roman military belt) is

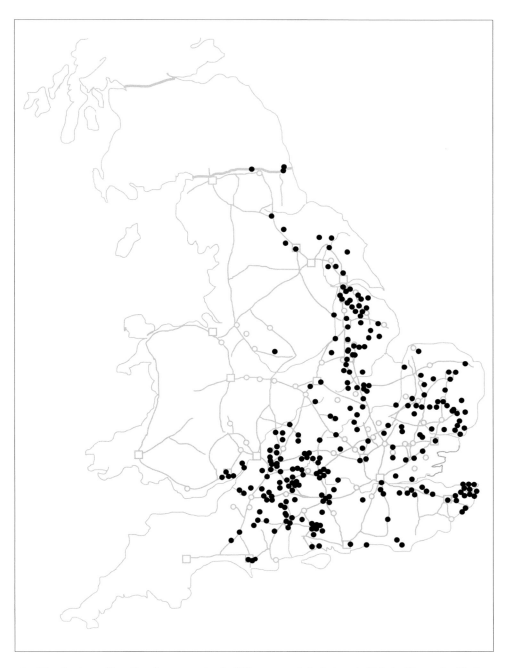

48 Distribution of late fourth-century/early fifth-century belt fittings in Britain (shown by black dots). For details of data see Notes[12]

sometimes used to denote joining government service. However, the distribution of finds of these military buckles and belt fittings thickly along the frontier, the *limes*, in continental Europe and thinly elsewhere, even in areas where there must have been large numbers of civilian officials, is a strong indication that these particular items were of a strictly military nature.[13] Whichever belt the civilian officials may have 'taken', it does not seem to have been these, and it is perhaps unlikely in a society not used to wearing belts that civilian officials would want to wear something as cumbersome as a leather and metal belt set. Maybe the *cingulum* of the civilian officials was a cloth band, like the item referred to by Catholic priests as a *cingulum*, or perhaps 'taking the belt' was metaphorical, like 'taking the king's shilling.'

Equally, though, it does not seem likely that these buckles and belt fittings were being worn, as the knee and crossbow brooches discussed in Chapter 4 probably were, by soldiers garrisoned in major towns. Considering that the brooches in question were being worn over a period of perhaps 250 years, while the buckles and belt fittings in question were being worn over a period of perhaps 50 years, the rate of loss of buckles and belt fittings is much, much higher, suggesting many more men wearing the items. In addition, there is less evidence of the buckles being concentrated in major towns, as the brooches often are.

Though the implications are huge, it is hard to see the sudden appearance in the years after 370 of large numbers of buckles and belt fittings on both military and civilian sites in Britain as anything but an indication that large numbers of British men had been armed or had armed themselves. The carrying of weapons by private individuals was, in any event, a growing trend in the late Roman Empire, with the appearance of the *bucellarii*, private armed retainers, paid for by rich individuals.[14] More specifically, there is in Spain an interesting parallel to the situation in Britain. Here, in the mid to late fourth century also, buckles of a similar style to those found in Britain start appearing on civilian sites. Here too, as in Britain, a percentage of the buckles are stylistically identical to buckles from the rest of mainland Europe and are likely to be imports, while most of the buckles have stylistic characteristics that are unique to Spain, indicating that they were made there. In this case, though, we are fortunate enough also to have a number of burials which explain how and why the belts were being adopted. The Spanish graves indicate that these late Roman belts were being worn by men to carry knives of a military style, and Aurrecochea Fernandez thinks that the buckles and belt fittings should definitely be seen as military or paramilitary equipment rather than as civilian accoutrements.[15] Significantly these buckles are never found in female graves,[16] unlike in Germanic areas, where buckles regularly are. Knives are also a feature of the Lankhills burials,[17] and while

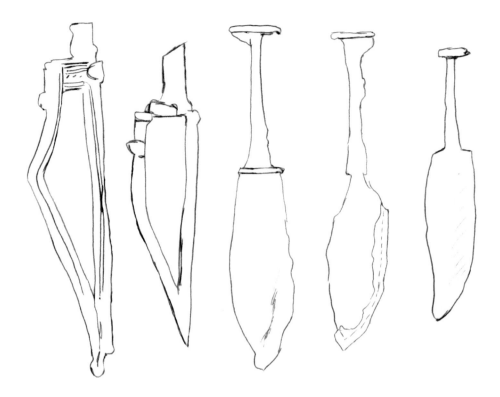

49   Late Roman knives of a probably military or paramilitary nature found in association with belt sets, from Spain (left two) and Britain (right three). Not to scale. *After Aurrecochea Fernandez and Clarke*

the disappearance of grave goods from most late fourth-century burial rites in Britain makes it impossible to assess the extent of knife-carrying at the time, it has been suggested that the proportion of knives found on Roman sites in Britain, as opposed to other tools, does increase noticeably in the late fourth century (*49*).[18]

When looking for evidence of rearmed tribes, we should not be too concerned about the lack of appearance of large numbers of other weapons on British sites in the period. Unlike copper alloy, iron does not survive well in the British environment, and most weapons that survive both from pre-Roman and post-Roman times do so either because they were ritually deposited or because they were buried as grave goods, methods of survival that would not apply to this period. In addition, as with the early Anglo-Saxon period, swords would probably be rare and prized possessions. These were not something that the average local blacksmith could knock up between making nails and hoes. Very few Anglo-Saxon graves contained a sword.

The Spanish burials feature some spears alongside buckles and knives and it is likely that most armed Britons of the late fourth century would have been similarly equipped. No specifically British spearheads have been identified from the end of the Roman period but two factors have probably limited such identification. Again, almost all Anglo-Saxon spearheads that have survived have done so due to ritual deposition or as burial goods. Equally, it is possible that British spearheads of this period are being wrongly identified as Anglo-Saxon. Swanton's early 'Anglo-Saxon' Type C1, for instance, with small leaf-shaped blades and a stronger distribution in western England than many other types, has no obvious parallels in Scandinavia or continental Europe where longer, more slender profiles were in vogue.[19] A pre-Roman spearhead from Llyn Fawr, however, is effectively identical to the type.[20]

Of equal significance to the actual appearance of these buckles in Britain are the styles that were developed. Most significantly, different tribes eventually seem to have developed different styles, with distinctive buckles appearing in a number of regions alongside the more generic examples.[21] When one considers that, in the third century, almost identical pieces of Roman military equipment could be found across large parts of the empire, the appearance of distinctively different styles of buckles within small and sometimes neighbouring regions of Britain is striking (*50, 51*).

In the previous chapter, we examined the evidence of fortified small towns which suggested that some of the *civitates* were organising defences along their own *civitas* borders in the second and third centuries. Interestingly, the same *civitates* involved in this process, the Dobunni, the Catuvellauni/ Trinovantes and the Corieltauvi, constitute three of the four groups which also seem to develop distinctive buckle styles in the late fourth century. The fourth *civitas* to do so is the *civitas* of the Iceni, a tribe who were eager to display their military prowess in 60-61 and may have done so again in the years after 155. The most distinctive stylistic element that defines specifically Icenian buckles and buckle plates is the use of human heads, often with Celtic-style flat mouths and staring eyes appearing at the top of the buckle loop (*50d*). Some of the dolphins on Icenian buckles also become transformed so that they more closely resemble Celtic-style boar heads (the boar was a major symbol on pre-Roman Icenian coinage) and even *carnyx* (Celtic war trumpet) heads (*52*).[23]

In Corieltauvian territory (with a scattering further south in Icenian territory, in a rather similar manner to the distribution of Corieltauvian coins in Icenian territory[24]) is found a group of buckles and buckle plates distinguished by small birds and a range of other, often zoomorphic, protrusions (*50c*).[25] Catuvellaunian/Trinovantian buckles and belt fittings feature, as the main focus of decoration, rows of dots or circles (this

50a-d　Examples of British buckles from the late Roman period showing tribal design elements
Above:　*50a*　Examples linked stylistically to Dobunnic areas

Above:　*50b*　Examples linked stylistically to Catuvellaunian/Trinovantian areas

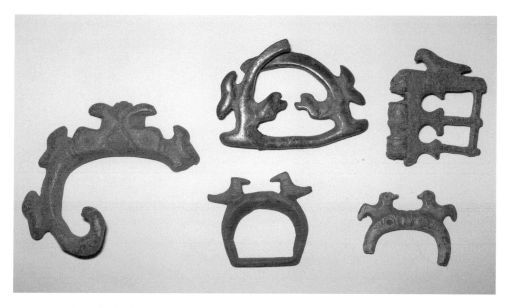

50c   Examples linked stylistically to Corieltauvian areas

50d   Examples linked stylistically to Icenian areas

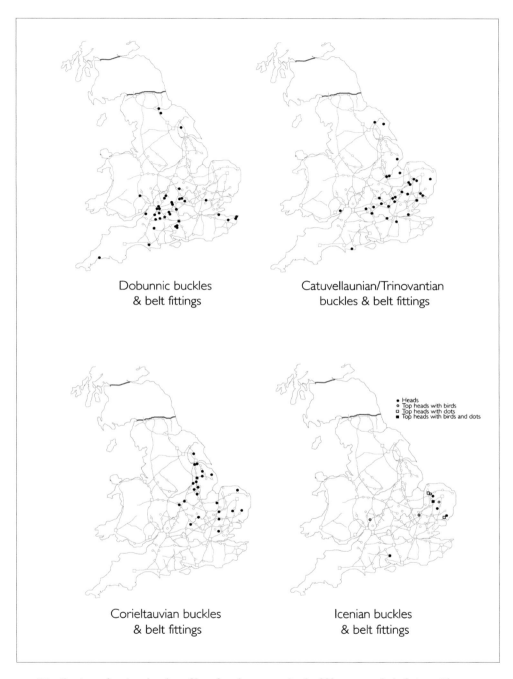

51 Distribution of regional styles of late fourth-century/early fifth-century belt fittings. The pattern of distribution suggests that the styles should be seen as tribal. For details of data see Notes[22]

does not include patterns made of a dot in a circle which was in much more general use as a decorative element, or minor use of dots). In their most distinctive form, these rows of dots or circles appear along the buckle loop (*50b*).[26]

Buckle plates linked to the probable territory of the Dobunnic *civitas* feature abstract geometric incised patterns (*50a*). The rows of roundels and associated features are often reminiscent of designs on pre-Roman metalwork, as is the extensive use of incised work and, in particular, the use of cross-hatching to fill spaces.[27] It is also noticeable that the Dobunni made extensive use of a variant of the dolphin buckles which featured horseheads sprouting from the tops of the dolphins. These do appear in other *civitates* as well but they only show a clear predominance over the more usual dolphin type in Dobunnic areas. The horse was, of course, a major symbol on pre-Roman British coinage and appeared extensively on Dobunnic coins (as well as on those of other tribes). Horsehead buckles found in Dobunnic territory show a tendency towards the type where the gap beneath the horse's chin disappears and the horsehead sinks more into the buckle frame, giving it a rectangular appearance. One of only two examples where a Dobunnic-style buckle plate has been found, still with its original horsehead buckle,[28] appears to confirm that this type should be seen as specifically Dobunnic. This is supported by the appearance on the Wickhambreaux buckle of cross-hatching, which is a distinctive feature of Dobunnic buckle plates, and by the appearance of similar heads on strap ends with Dobunnic-style designs, such as the example from Tortworth.[29]

Intriguingly, an understanding of the possible significance of incised designs featuring geometric shapes and cross-hatching suggests that there may even be

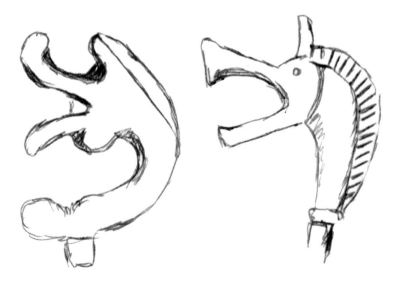

52 'Dolphin' from an Icenian-style buckle, compared with a *carnyx* from a Gundestrup cauldron

a surviving Dobunnic dagger of the period. It has already been recognised that the knife found in Grave 22 in a sixth-century cemetery at Brighthampton is, in terms of decoration, more closely linked to British designs of the Roman period than to Anglo-Saxon styles.[30] However, the incised triangular shapes filled with cross-hatching that form the main decorative device on the knife sling suggest this item should be seen as specifically Dobunnic; it dates from the same period as Dobunnic horsehead buckles and other belt fittings, and is linked to their use. The find-spot at Brighthampton, right on the edge of probable Dobunnic territory is certainly consistent with this interpretation. This said, the dagger was probably, by the standards of the late fourth and early fifth century, an exceptionally flamboyant piece. With its intricately decorated fittings it is a long, long way from the simple daggers found at Lankhills which appear to have had only fittings made of organic materials. These must have been much more characteristic of the period. The exceptional nature of the Brighthampton dagger probably goes a long way towards explaining why it was still treasured over 100 years after the date of its probable manufacture.

It is also perhaps briefly worth mentioning here a number of buckles from the south-east which have been classified together under the Quoit Brooch Style label, named after a number of spectacularly decorated so-called Quoit Brooches. These seem to date from the fifth century and appear to be a regional style from Kent.[31] We shall return to the question of the Quoit Brooches themselves later, but in terms of the majority of Quoit Brooch-Style buckles, it should be pointed out that they have very strong links with late Roman buckles. The Bishopstone, Mitcham, Orpington, Portway and Amiens buckles are,[32] in form, all clearly derived from a late Roman type.[33] Their decoration incorporates dragon heads also derived from late Roman buckles. Most of the known examples have come from Anglo-Saxon graves so it has been assumed that they are of specifically post-Roman date. However, late Roman buckles are regularly found in Anglo-Saxon graves and the apparent links of the style to Kent (the Quoit Brooches seem clearly Kentish in distribution, even if the buckles are more widespread) may suggest the Cantii also developed their own style of belt fittings at the end of the Roman period.

To what extent these buckle styles should be seen as tribal symbols or simply as regional styles is open to debate. Early in the Roman occupation, regional styles of metalwork did exist. Two-piece Colchester brooches, for instance, are found most frequently in eastern England,[34] while the Polden Hill type of brooch occurs most regularly in Dobunnic and Cornovian territory.[35] In the north, the Dragonesque style may have been Brigantian and Parisian in origin.[36] Later in the occupation, though, there is less evidence of such differences in small portable items. Attention has been drawn to regional styles in mosaics in the fourth century that appear to be related to different *civitates*.[37] On one level, this is interesting in reinforcing the idea that the *civitates* were still central to the running of Britain in the fourth century. On the other hand mosaics could hardly be traded from merchant to merchant across Britain in quite the same way as brooches or buckles (though the mosaicists themselves could, of course, have travelled).

In terms of the buckles and belt fittings it is worth pointing out that apart from the features specific to each *civitas* (the dots or the human heads or the birds/protrusions or the geometric decoration) individual buckles and belt fittings from a *civitas* often have little in common. It is, for instance, extremely rare to find two buckles that are so similar they have to be from the same craftsman or workshop.[38] This rather suggests we are looking at *civitas* symbols utilised by a number of different people on different designs in small workshops, rather than the stylistically homogenous product of large regional workshops. It is also quite notable that buckles and belt fittings which feature design elements associated with more than one *civitas*/tribe are rare and, in a phenomenon we shall return to in the next chapter, almost all are associated with the areas where Icenian meets Catuvellaunian or Corieltauvian territory and influence. The generally exclusive nature of the use of these symbols could indicate they had more importance than mere decoration.

It may even be that these symbols should be seen specifically as some form of tribal identification system. In the recent Bosnian conflict, for instance, where militiamen of all sides wore a similar combination of assorted civilian and military clothing, small pieces of coloured ribbon were often tied onto the uniforms to enable recognition. Soldiers would recognise people on their side by the colour of their ribbon. If the ribbon was a different colour, the soldier was on a different side, or at least in a different unit. If there were tribal militias in the fourth century, it is quite likely that a military belt and a knife would be all (apart from a spear and perhaps a shield) that would distinguish them from civilians. Having different symbols on the buckles and belt fittings (and quite possibly all over the belts too, which may well also have been highly decorated[39]) could, therefore, be quite a significant form of identification.

In themselves the birds/protrusions, the heads, the dots and the geometric designs may not seem significant enough to carry the weight of tribal identity. However, the differences between the designs of different tribes on some pre-Roman coins can often seem small to the inexperienced eye, with a wide range of variations on the basic horse design, for instance. Again, there is an interesting parallel from Bosnia. A huge number of badges were designed and printed for the myriad small units that fought the war. Many of these units were so small and insignificant that nobody outside a small area would actually have heard of them. The units, therefore, needed some shorthand for identifying which side they were on. They did this by incorporating into the design an element of the relevant national symbol. Thus Croat unit badges almost always had a small element somewhere of the distinctive red and white Croat chequerboard design. Serb unit badges would almost always feature within the design, the red, blue and white of the Serbian tricolour. Bosniak badges, if they did not simply feature the entire Bosnian flag, would have either the fleur de lys that appeared on the flag or, if the unit was expressing a distinctively Muslim identity, the star and crescent. Due to shared culture and geography there were different units named 'Wolves' fighting for three different sides, for the Croats, for the Bosniaks and for the Serbs. Each carried badges in which wolves, not surprisingly, feature as the most prominent design element. However, in each case, the relevant national symbol also appears as a more minor design element to make it clear which side each particular lot of 'Wolves' was on. To archaeologists, in 1500 years time, examining any of these badges that have survived, the wolf design might initially seem the most prominent and they might be tempted to assume that all wolf units were on the same side. It would take distribution maps and an understanding of other badges to understand that the wolf element was politically much less significant than the much smaller national symbol elements.

It is impossible to know whether rearming of the tribes was done with or without Roman cooperation. It might be that the events of 367 had been sufficient to demonstrate to the tribes/*civitates* that they could no longer rely on Rome's protection and that it was time for every man to have a knife and belt hanging in his home, just as many Bosnian men ended up in the 1990s with an AK-47 hanging in theirs. Equally, one should not be too surprised if the events of 367 added to pressures for the tribes to assert an independent identity more strongly. As demonstrated most recently in Iraq after the invasion, the military defeat of a central power is often a spur for regional fragmentation. However, there is evidence that there may, at the very least, have been a degree of Roman involvement in the rearming. For a start, there is the direct statement by the sixth-century British writer Gildas that, before the Romans left Britain, they armed the Britons, giving them '*exemplaria armorum*'.[40] Bearing in mind some of the inaccuracies in Gildas' account, one need not necessarily take this as irrefutable testimony but it is interesting nonetheless.

More concretely, there is significant evidence from the buckles themselves. The only type of late Roman buckle commonly found in Britain, apart from dolphin buckles and their derivatives, features a plain loop attached to a triangular solid or openwork plate (53). These buckles are found across Britain on much the same types of sites as the dolphin buckles (54). They are also found in quantity along the *limes* in mainland Europe and, as with dolphin buckles,

53   Triangular plate, plain loop buckles from Britain and from mainland Europe

are rare in areas at a distance from the *limes*, clearly suggesting their military character.[41] Unlike other buckles of the late Roman period found in Britain, though, which show great variation, these buckles are mostly of a very standard, simple design and construction. It is arguable, therefore, that these buckles are likely to be the product of one of the state arms factories – the *fabricae*, listed in the *Notitia Dignitatum*. No metalworking *fabrica* is listed in Britain, so the buckles

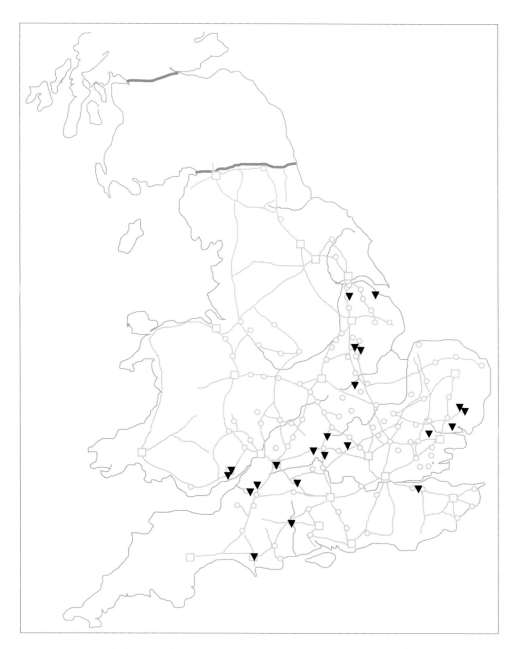

54 Distribution of triangular plate, plain loop buckles in Britain (shown by black triangles). These are of a type probably mass-produced for military use in mainland Europe. Their distribution in Britain across a wide range of civilian areas may suggest official participation in the arming of Britain. For details of data see Notes[42]

would have to have been imported from mainland Europe. Their extensive appearance on British civilian sites could be explained, just possibly, as the result of widespread desertions in 367 or of looting of Roman military stores at that time. Perhaps more likely, though, is that the appearance of the triangular plate buckles in Britain is the result of an official distribution by Roman authorities (maybe even on the orders of Theodosius himself). This probability is supported by other evidence possibly indicating an official role for the militias.

There is the intriguing case of the depiction of the office of the *Vicarius* of Britain in the *Notitia Dignitatum*. This essentially civilian official's position is, unlike those of other comparable officials, designated with a crenellated crown. Frere theorised that this might indicate that he had command over military personnel,[43] and it has been suggested that these units might have been some kind of civilian militia. It is also interesting that the excavator of the Saxon Shore fort at Portchester Castle identified the period 354-364 as representing 'ordered occupation', with the period from 364-400+ representing 'disordered occupation' (55).[44] It seems conceivable that this later period, therefore, might

55   The interior of Portchester Castle. Signs of 'disordered occupation' here in the period 364-400+ may represent the presence of British militiamen

1 Coins of Tasciovanus and Cunobelin showing a mix of British and Roman motifs. *With kind permission of David Shelley*

2 Coins of Tasciovanus and Cunobelin showing a mix of British and Roman motifs. *With kind permission of David Shelley*

3   The earthwork ramparts of Badbury Rings

4   The ramparts on the multivallate Durotrigan hillfort of Maiden Castle

5   Mosaic at Chedworth. The British aristocracy adopted Roman styles and customs and became, in archaeological terms, largely Roman

6   Hypocaust at Chedworth

7   The Roman theatre at Verulamium – just one of the trappings of a Roman lifestyle in the capital of the Catuvellauni

8 Projecting bastion on the third-century town walls at Verulamium

9   One of the best-preserved Roman gateways in Britain, the Balkerne Gate at Colchester

10 Remains of the circuit of walls at Cirencester, Roman-period capital of the Dobunni

11 Third-century belt fitting showing mounted figure hunting. Second- and third-century military fittings are found in a number of towns, suggesting a military presence

12 A range of fourth- to fifth-century crossbow brooches. Similar styles are found in military and paramilitary burials

13 Late fourth- or early fifth-century buckles from Britain, showing both dolphin and horsehead types

14   Wansdyke, running across the Downs to the west of Mildenhall

15   The north gate at Silchester. Part of a skull, probably dating from the fifth century, was found in the ditch outside

16   Post-Roman Latin inscription from Slaughterbridge, Cornwall, commemorating someone called Latinus, a sign of continuing Roman culture in the British west

17   Tintagel, site of a fifth- and sixth-century site linked into Atlantic trade routes connecting to the Mediterranean, just as sites in western Britain had done in pre-Roman times

18 Excavated early Anglo–Saxon urns at Cleatham. *With kind permission of Kevin Leahy*

19 Urns from Cleatham. *With kind permission of Kevin Leahy*

20 Devil's Dyke near Cambridge, showing how formidable an obstacle a post-Roman linear earthwork could be

21 Anglo-Saxon button brooch

22 Fragments of post-Roman enamelled metalwork. Celtic-style designs appear on bowl fittings often found in Anglo-Saxon contexts. Booty or signs of more peaceful contact?

23 Post-Roman Class 1 penannular brooch from Caxton, Cambridgeshire. Of a type found widely in British areas of the west and north, but also in Catuvellaunian/Trinovantian areas and Lindsey

24   The Saxon church at Bradford on Avon, near Bath, showing the spread of Saxon culture into formerly British areas of western England

25   A symbol of continuity. The pre-Roman hillfort at Old Sarum, location, according to the *Anglo-Saxon Chronicle*, of a battle between Cynric and Britons in 552, and later the site of a Norman castle and cathedral

represent occupation by some form of local militia either instead of, or as well as, a unit of the regular Roman Army. It is, again, interesting to note that Gildas links Rome giving arms to the Britons, prior to the final Roman departure, with the construction of defended towers along the south coast.[45] This passage probably refers to the Saxon Shore forts, so the combination might reflect some memory of British militiamen armed by the Romans manning such forts as Portchester.

There is also written evidence of tribal involvement in the official Roman defensive structures of Britain in the late fourth century. The *Notitia Dignitatum* refers to a unit drawn from the Cornovii tribe, the *Cohors I Cornoviorum*, being based at Pons Aelius/Newcastle in the late fourth century and there are a number of building inscriptions from Hadrian's Wall (56), usually dated to the fourth century, that record work by men from the *civitates* of the Dumnonii, the Durotriges and the Catuvellauni.[46] It has conventionally been assumed that these represent forced labour of some description but it is hard to see why forced labour should have been transported to the Wall from as far away as southern tribes like these. True, coming from areas where stone is the common building material, the Dumnonii and Durotriges tribes would have presumably had plentiful supplies of men skilled in using stone. However, the same would apply to tribes much closer to Hadrian's Wall and there is no special reason to associate the Catuvellauni with outstanding expertise in stonework. In light of the evidence about the arming of the tribes, it perhaps makes more sense to see these inscriptions as evidence of tribal militia units serving and working on the Wall, just as regular Roman Army units also served and worked on the Wall and also left inscriptions to record the work they had done. Troops on Hadrian's Wall, perhaps because of their remoteness from mainland Europe, do not seem to have adopted the styles of late Roman buckles and belt fittings found there. A small number of such items, however, have been discovered in the Wall area and the finding of a smattering of Dobunnic and Catuvellaunian/Trinovantian buckles and belt fittings in Yorkshire, a long way from their core distribution areas, supports the idea of at least some tribal units operating in the north. Again, Gildas is interesting in this context. Along with the giving of arms and the building of the Saxon Shore forts, the last thing he said the Romans did before their final departure was build a stone wall in the north, running from sea to sea. This wall, presumably Hadrian's Wall, Gildas says was built by 'public and private contributions' and was intended to be manned by the Britons.[47] Again it seems quite possible that this could be a memory of the *civitates* paying to send tribal militiamen to work on, and help defend, the Wall in the last decades of Roman rule. There is even some evidence that might suggest that elements of tribal militias were involved in at least one of the late fourth-century attempts by the Roman Army in Britain to seize power on the continent. Magnus Maximus

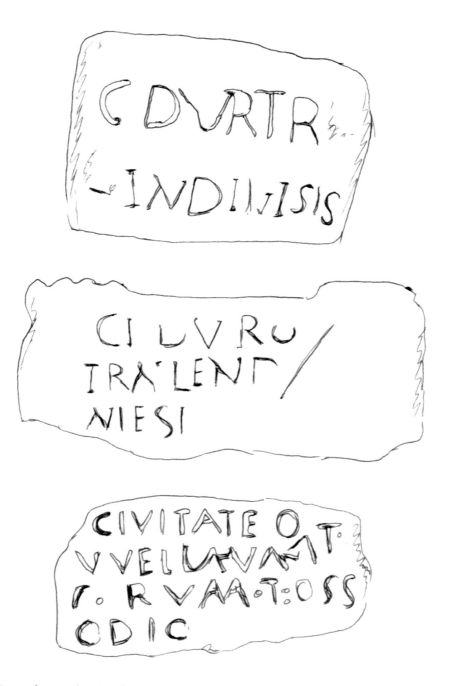

56 Stones from Hadrian's Wall indicating the presence of construction units sent by the *civitas* of the Durotriges (top two) and mentioning the *civitas* of the Catuvellauni (bottom). Roman Army units both fought and did construction work on the wall. It is possible that the units commemorated on these stones were also fighting units

made his ill-fated bid for the imperial throne in 383, while Constantine III set off on the same journey (with ultimately the same end) in 407.

There is a concentration of late fourth-century buckles and belt fittings in the area of Richborough, the most likely departure point for military expeditions to the continent, which includes two specifically British horsehead buckles.[48] In addition, a buckle plate and at least two buckles of distinctively late fourth-century British type have been found on the continent in locations that might link them to these ventures. An openwork buckle plate, featuring half a propeller belt stiffener, has been found at Aquileia, site of the final defeat of Magnus Maximus in 388. Buckle plates incorporating propeller belt stiffeners do appear on the continent but the type with only half a propeller seems to be purely British, with most examples coming from near the border between the Catuvellauni and the Corieltauvi.[49] Equally, a British horsehead buckle has been found at Iruna in northern Spain,[50] while a dolphin buckle that features Catuvellaunian/Trinovantian dots and a distinctively round British shape to the loop (as opposed to continental buckles which are mainly flatter and more lozenge-shaped) was found at Argeliers in southern France. Both locations fall well within the sphere of operations of Constantine III who set up the capital of his short-lived administration at Arles (57). Two late fourth-century buckles from southern France have also been found which show similar use of dot decoration to that which appears on Catuvellaunian/Trinovantian buckles.[51] Other stylistic elements about the buckles make it unlikely they are British but it is possible that they represent stylistic influence from the Catuvellauni/Trinovantes in Constantine III's ranks on local buckle manufacture.

There is also the fascinating instance of the Cervianus disc (58). Where it was originally found is unknown but it was published in France as long ago as 1698 and is now located in the Treasury of the *Bibliothèque Nationale*, Paris. This intriguing metal disc shows, above a scene of wildlife, soldiers identified in an inscription as being from the *Legio II Augusta* and the *Legio XX Valeria Victrix*. The disc is marked in the name of one Aurelius Cervianus and there is the usual good luck message '*utere felix*'. There has been much speculation about the date of the piece and what the presence of the two legions on it might indicate. A date as early as the third century has been suggested but it has also been argued, from the appearance of the two legions together on the piece, that it might date from the period of the final departure of these two legions from Britain.[52] The thinking behind this is that perhaps only at that date in the late Roman period might these two legions have been located together. *Legio XX Valeria Victrix* was at Chester until the late fourth century, while *Legio II Augusta* is listed at Richborough in the *Notitia Dignitatum*. If they were both brought together by Constantine III for his expedition, this

57 The Roman walls of Arles, capital of Constantine III at the beginning of the fifth century. Local buckle evidence suggests some British militiamen may have accompanied him on his venture into mainland Europe

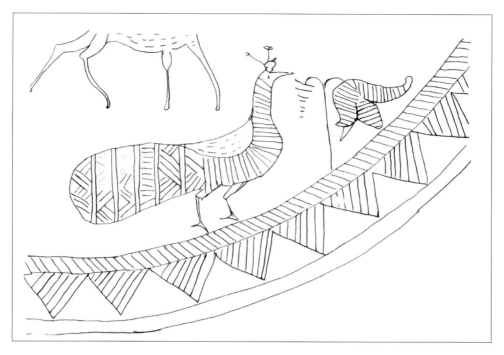

58 Detail of Cervianus disc, showing use of incised geometric decoration, similar to that seen on Dobunnic buckle plates. Shown as well, one of the two peacocks on the disc and the 'Tree of Life' which also regularly feature on late fourth-century British buckle plates. Note the basketwork effect on the tail which is similar to work seen on pre-Roman British metalwork

could account for the creation of the disc and for its (probable) finding in France.

The style of the decoration of the disc certainly suggests a date in the late fourth century. Even more interestingly, it indicates that the disc was probably created by a craftsmen accustomed to making British horsehead buckles. The style of incised work is typical of horsehead buckle plates and the cross-hatched triangle pattern is also characteristic of fourth-century Dobunnic buckle plates (as well as being very reminiscent of pre-Roman British designs). In addition, the two peacocks with a 'Tree of Life' motif which features at the bottom of the Cervianus disc also appears on a number of horsehead buckle plates (though on these the peacocks are usually facing each other with the tree between them). Horsehead buckles are not regular finds on military sites in Britain, so the Cervianus disc probably does not indicate that this was a military craftsman who turned out the disc in between decorating horsehead buckles. Rather it suggests that Aurelius Cervianus, a man associated in some way with the two legions, was also associated with a manufacturer of buckles for British militiamen.

All in all there is a mounting body of evidence for tribal militias being active in late fourth-century Britain. As mentioned earlier, archaeologists have struggled to come up with proof of Theodosius reorganising the defences of Britain and making towns and cities safer, as Ammianus Marcellinus claims he did. Maybe, though, by looking for evidence of refortification, they have been looking in the wrong place. Perhaps they should have been looking at buckles instead. It is possible the arming of tribal militias was Theodosius' main contribution to the defences of Britannia. If so, it does not seem to have had entirely the intended effect.

CHAPTER 6

The Last of Rome

Whatever may or may not have happened in 367-369, the account by Ammianus of the so-called 'Barbarian Conspiracy' is significant in another way. It marks pretty much the end of any detailed information from Roman writers about events inside Britain. There is a reference in Claudian to unspecified measures taken by Stilicho to fortify Britain against Scots, Picts and Saxons.[1] There is also coverage of the rebellions by Magnus Maximus and Constantine III, but the latter concentrates almost entirely on events once Maximus and Constantine reached the continent. Otherwise, there is virtually nothing until the final days of Roman rule. In 410 we have the famous Rescript of Honorius that has conventionally marked the end of Roman Britain. In this (if he is indeed referring to Britain, rather than a region in southern Italy, as sometimes suggested) he told the *civitates* of the island to look after their own defences. This is something that, as we have seen, at least a number of them had probably already been doing on some level since the late second century. It is even possible that the ending of Roman rule itself may have been the choice of the *civitates*, asserting their independence even more starkly, rather than of the Roman authorities. In a much-discussed passage Zosimus seems to claim that the British rose up and threw out the Romans:

> The barbarians above the Rhine, attacking without being stopped, forced those living in Britain and some of the Celtic peoples to abandon Roman control and live their lives independent of Roman laws. So the Britons armed themselves and, running their own risks, set their cities free from the barbarian danger.
>
> Zosimus, *Historia Nova* 6, 5.2-3

Here we have, presumably, the Saxons causing trouble and the *civitates* organising their own defences. In many ways it is similar to the probable situation after 367-369 (although with different raiders involved) but here the implication is that, rather than just arming themselves, the *civitates* went the whole way and took political as well as military power. This tantalisingly brief mention by Zosimus may offer an explanation of how Roman power in Britain ends. It does nothing, however, to explain *why* Roman Britain ends. No other Roman historical source offers any fuller explanation for the collapse of Roman Britain, so, for the crucial last 40 years of the Roman presence in Britain, we have to rely almost entirely on archaeological evidence. The picture presented by this source of the last decades of the fourth century is mixed, but, while some sites continue to flourish into the early fifth century, there is a broad sense of decline from about 370 onwards, leading to catastrophic collapse at the beginning of the fifth century.

In the countryside, for instance, Newman's work on the number of occupied rooms in villas, shows it peaking in the period 300-350, with a marked decline by 375 and then a continuing decline towards 400 and collapse in the fifth century.[2] A very similar picture emerges from a study of the pottery industry in Britain. Looking at the number of forms in production and the number of new forms being introduced in any one period is one way of assessing the vitality of the industry. Almost exactly like villa occupation, this graph shows a peak between the period 300-350, followed by a decline by 375, which continues steadily to 400, before collapse in the fifth century.[3] In the towns there is also evidence of decline in the late fourth century. (This is prior to the appearance of 'dark earth' deposits and widespread abandonment in the early fifth century.) The survey by Brooks demonstrates a decline in public activity in the towns in the late fourth century.[4]

What is puzzling, however, is that there seems no obvious reason why the beginning of the decline in Roman Britain should start as early as 375. Arguments about the disruption caused by the ending of a money-based economy do not apply this early, and while the revolt of Magnus Maximus between 383 and 388 may well have interrupted any flow of funds from central government in Rome, it is hard to see why it would have had any significantly more destructive impact than the interruption presumably caused by the rebellion of, for instance, Magnentius in the 350s.

The years 367-369 may well have been a major shock and clearly raids from Picts, Scots and Saxons continued to be a problem. However, there is no evidence of settlement by any of the attackers at this stage and it seems hard to believe that what can only have been comparatively small numbers of raiders could have had a serious impact on the economy of Roman Britain as a whole. There is a limited amount of evidence, near coasts, of destruction that may have been caused by the raids. It has, for instance, been suggested that Duncan's Gate at Colchester may have been burnt at this time. However, the only dating evidence for the two fires in the area is a coin associated with the earlier fire which from the description of it, probably dates from before 330.[5]

Although they must have been a menace in coastal and border regions, there is little evidence that the Scots, Picts and Saxons ever moved deep inland on a regular basis in the late fourth century. Indeed, with a British population of millions, much of it probably now armed, and with almost all cities and many towns strongly fortified, it is difficult to see how they could practically have done so.

To have a chance of understanding what may have caused the general malaise in Britain in the late fourth century, we need to look at an area that in the early fourth century had become one of the more affluent parts of Britain. In the rich agricultural territory to the south of Cirencester, the early decades of the fourth century had been a period of prosperity (*59, colour plates 5 & 6*). However, things began to change very significantly here in the second half of the fourth century. A glance at the map of unretrieved coin hoards for the period after 370 shows a contrast with the coin hoard map relevant to 367-369 (*42*). There, hoards were more spread across the country, including the group of hoards to the north and west of London. By contrast, a map of unretrieved coin hoards from after 370 shows a swathe of coin

59 Mosaic at Chedworth Villa. The early fourth century had been a period of prosperity in the west, but the second half of the fourth century shows evidence of serious disruption in territory to the south of Cirencester

hoards stretching across in a band from the Avon and the north Somerset coast to the area around Southampton. This strange concentration of hoards in the west (and an accompanying high rate of loose coin loss for the period 364-378 in the north of the area) has been noted before,[6] but there is little agreement on the causes.

When interpreting base metal hoards right at the end of this period there is the complicating factor that at some stage the coins may have become worthless (though they would still have had value across remaining parts of the Roman world). There were also variations in the supply of coinage in the second half of the fourth century.[7] However, these hoards stretch through the period from 370, well before any loss of value, and there is no particular reason why variations in the supply of coinage should so disproportionately have affected just this area in the west of England. It is the broad patterns we are looking at here and the broad movements of hoarding concentrations when compared with population distribution of the time. Such an unparalleled concentration of unretrieved hoards must have significance for an understanding of the development of Britain in its last years under Rome.

In addition, hoards containing just base metal coins represent only a proportion of the hoards in question. The large numbers of unretrieved gold and silver coins from hoards in Britain of this period have no parallel in mainland Europe.[8] For instance, no less than 80 per cent of all known Roman silver coin hoards, where the latest coin dates from between 388 and 410, are from Britain.[9] So what caused it all?

It has been suggested that the phenomenon may derive from a sudden development of extreme wealth in the area.[10] However, while the region under discussion was clearly an affluent one in the early fourth century, site finds[11] and the overall location of fourth-century Portable Antiquities Scheme finds (*60*) (even taking into account the slightly variable levels of reporting up to now across England) simply do not suggest this area was any wealthier than many other parts of Romanised Britain. Plus, if we are considering the exceptional amounts of unretrieved gold and silver, there is certainly nothing to suggest that this region was uniquely wealthy in terms of the empire as a whole. In fact, to the contrary, this area shows signs of increasing economic weakness in the late fourth century.

The Cirencester, South/Central and Dorchester mosaic schools of the early fourth century, for instance, did not continue to flourish long after 370[12] and there are extensive signs of what used to be called 'squatter occupation' (occupation which suggests a much less affluent lifestyle than previously customary) in villas here.[13] Moreover it is not even particularly clear that a great increase in wealth would lead to an equivalent rise in the number of unretrieved hoards. In settled times, even if someone were to bury a hoard for reasons totally unconnected with political instability and conflict, it would presumably not generally go

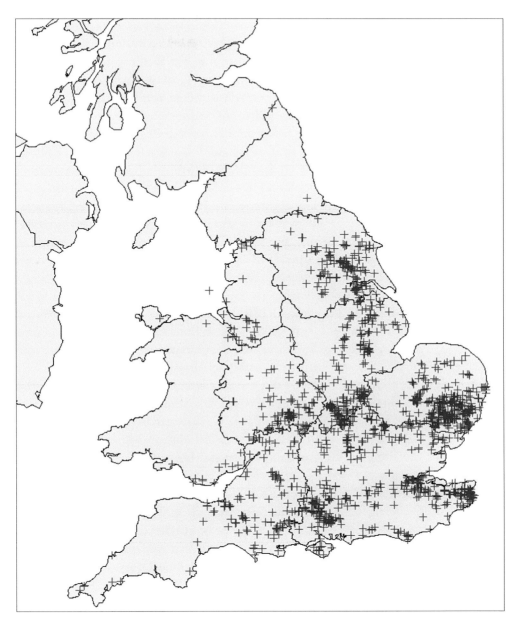

60   All fourth-century finds recorded by Portable Antiquities Scheme

uncollected. In a much more socially interdependent society than our own, even if the owner of a hoard died, it must have been comparatively rare that nobody else, not a single person, within the extended family and social networks of that person knew of the existence and at least rough whereabouts of the buried hoard. Presumably people in mainland Europe in the fourth and fifth centuries occasionally buried gold and silver for safekeeping but in these cases somebody usually seems to have come back to collect them.

It seems much more likely that, as previously, this concentration of hoards suggests disruption. The high rate of loss of loose coins is not inconsistent with this. Types of disruption, for instance, that involve displacement of people, changes of occupants and looting are likely to lead to a much higher rate of coin loss than normal. The context of what used to be called squatter occupation is controversial but one explanation would be refugee occupation or occupation by members of a poorer economic group who had supplanted the original owners.

There is also interesting evidence about this area in the late fourth century from the pottery industry. During the period of Roman occupation, a number of large pottery industries developed in Britain, exporting their wares often over very long distances. The New Forest Pottery industry was huge in the early fourth century, with much of its distribution in the same area as the concentration of western hoards. Most late Romano-British pottery industries seem to expire in the first years of the fifth century. The large New Forest industry was in decline in the second half of the fourth century and seems to have ceased production before the end of the fourth century, possibly as early as the 370s.[14]

Another feature of this period in this area, to which attention has previously been drawn, is a line of villas running through the northern part of the region that show signs of having been burnt. The west wing at King's Weston Villa was burnt sometime between about 335 and 380. Brislington Villa shows signs of burning and the bones of humans and cattle had been tipped into the well at some stage between 337 and around 370. At Keynsham Villa, there was a large fire sometime before 375 and a skeleton was found beneath a collapsed wall. At Box, two rooms were burnt and the coin series ends with a coin of Valens (364-78). At Atworth another two rooms were burnt between 340 and 375. At North Wraxall, the bones of three skeletons were dumped in a well, probably sometime in the fourth century. There was also burning at Combe Down and Wellow II. Neither fire can be dated but occupation at Combe Down seems to have been mainly fourth century, probably finishing some time around 370 or a little later. Finally, there is a group of four villas all located in a single valley and within five kilometres of each other. Bowood House produced evidence of burning and six skeletons. A villa at Calne with evidence of fourth-century occupation produced more signs of fire and bones. The villa at West Park Field produced burnt bones and a coin series ending with Constantius II (324-361). At Nuthills Villa, the excavator thought the villa had been attacked, and a series of 13 coins ends with Magnentius (350-353).[15] It cannot be proved that all these burnings are contemporary, but it is definitely possible that they all took place at roughly the same time. Certainly, as we have seen with the events of 155, unusual groups of burnt villas can potentially throw important light on the history of a period. Branigan suggested that these fires were the result of an Irish raid. This is possible but there seems little to support the idea. There is evidence of Irish visitors to the west of England in the period following the end of Roman rule, in the shape of a series of inscriptions in Irish Ogham script. However, apart from the single example at Silchester, all these lie much further down the coastline in Cornwall and Devon.[16] Equally, it is difficult to see how Irish raiders on the River Avon, whatever they were up to, could cause hoards to be deposited in such numbers all the way across as far as Southampton. Another explanation needs to be sought, and it may be linked to an intermittent stretch of linear bank and ditch (linked by a Roman road which itself originally probably ran along a substantial bank) known as Wansdyke. This lies almost exactly along the same line as the villa fires (*61*). The area with the largest number of sites showing high loose coin loss in the period 364-378 also lies in very much the same area (*62*).

61 Wansdyke and villas in the area showing signs of possible burning in the late fourth century. Black dots represent villas. Parallel lines mark Wansdyke

62 Wansdyke and area show a concentration of sites with exceptionally high loose coin loss between 364-378. After Moorhead

There has been much debate over the precise date and function of Wansdyke, but it is definitely late Roman or post-Roman (*63, colour plate 14*). The much stronger tradition of linear earthwork defences in Britain as opposed to the continental homelands of the Anglo-Saxons, the inclusion of hillforts into the design, and the naming by the Anglo-Saxons of the dyke after a non-human figure, Woden, rather than a person (common with pre-Anglo-Saxon earthworks, whether of a pre-Roman or post-Roman origin and implying they did not know its real origins) all suggest that Wansdyke is likely to be of British origin.[17] Dark has convincingly argued, on the basis of cultural differences visible on each side of Wansdyke in the post-Roman period, that this represented the border at that time between Durotrigan and Dobunnic political entities. South of Wansdyke, for instance, hillforts are reoccupied and there is the appearance of pottery imported from the Mediterranean. Neither of these are significant features of post-Roman culture north of Wansdyke where, by contrast, grass-tempered pottery, that rarely appears south of the linear earthwork, is comparatively common.[18] So the burnt villas lie along the line of a border that the Durotriges at some stage thought

63 Wansdyke, to the west of Marlborough

needed defending from northern attacks (or at the very least clearly delineating, in order to help deter incursions from the north). Perhaps even more to the point, they lie along a border that takes no account of the *civitas* of the Belgae.

In Chapter 3 we saw how the Romans, after 43, seem to have carved out the *civitas* of the Belgae, probably for their client king Togidubnus, from a chunk of Atrebatic territory in the east and a chunk of Dobunnic territory in the west. It has been demonstrated time and time again, particularly in the history of post-colonial Africa, that political borders drawn on a map with no reference to the ethnic realities on the ground are a recipe for conflict. It seems possible that the *civitas* of the Belgae may provide yet another example of this. Perhaps the hoards, the burnt and abandoned villas and the signs of economic collapse could be linked to the breakup and disappearance of the *civitas* of the Belgae.

If we compare the concentration of western coin hoards with the probable boundaries of the *civitas* of the Belgae, we see that there is a clear possible correlation, with the *civitas* too stretching across from around the north Somerset coast to the Southampton region (*32, 34*). To the south, where the *civitas* of the Durotriges lay, there are comparatively few coin hoards. To the east, where the *civitas* of the Regni lay, there are also few coin hoards. There are some coin hoards to the north in the *civitas* of the Atrebates, but with the eastern half of the *civitas* of the Belgae being Atrebatic, it would be surprising if the Atrebates here were not, in some way, involved in any trouble in the area.

Some people may feel that an ethnic conflict with its roots in the first century could not possibly have resumed 300 years later in the fourth century, but this is to fail to understand the often deep-seated nature of tribal identities and tensions.

As noted in the introduction, the nations of the Balkans were held together within the Ottoman Empire for over 400 years, yet when Ottoman power weakened, the nations attempted to reassert their identities and the result was a long period of changing borders and conflict. The memories of Serbia's identity and pre-Ottoman existence remained alive through the Turkish occupation, in the medium of oral poetry and through religion in the shape of the Serbian Orthodox Church. It is quite possible that memories of tribal identity and pre-Roman history were maintained through the Roman occupation in a similar way. The early Irish epics, of cattle-raiding and tribal battles, give a picture of the kind of poetry that might have been recited in the Roman period keeping ancient enmities alive, and in Chapter 3 we noted examples of possible links between tribal and dynastic identity and tribal and dynastic religion. Recently too, Daubney has explored interesting evidence of what seems to be a specifically Corieltauvian cult flourishing in the second to fourth centuries. Two types of ring have been found, almost exclusively in Corieltauvian territory, marked with a dedication to a god TOT (which may be an abbreviated form of the name of the god Toutatis). Dedications to Toutatis do appear elsewhere but this form of dedication seems to be specifically Corieltauvian.[19] Equally, in Durotrigan territory, Davey draws attention to the continuity of ritual practice from pre-Roman through into post-Roman times, near the pre-Roman and post-Roman stronghold of Cadbury Castle. In pre-Roman times, bovine mandibles and limestones burnt red were ritually deposited near Cadbury Castle, and in the Roman and post-Roman periods, bovine mandibles were also deposited with large red stones (*64*).[20] Christianity was undoubtedly a growing force in Britain in the late fourth century but it is unlikely that it would have erased memories of tribal religions before the end of the fourth century.

If one is looking for examples of long-lived cultural and political differences rather closer to home, then a number of examples come to mind. It is almost 200 years since we last fought the French and we have had extensive commercial and political links with them for most of that time, but there is still a measure of distrust and dislike towards them shown by many Britons which is readily exploitable by any journalist or politician who chooses to do so. Even closer to home is the relationship between England and Scotland. The two have been united by a common monarch for over 400 years and have been officially united

64 Cadbury Castle, famously reoccupied in the post-Roman period. Such reuse of hillforts is one of the cultural distinctions that Dark sees distinguishing territory to the south of Wansdyke from territory to the north

for over 300 years. Nonetheless, there is no question of English and Scottish identities merging, and the relationship remains a delicate one, with both sides capable of feeling sensitive about past injuries and present slights. Then, of course, there is Ireland. Hopefully now, at last, armed conflict there is becoming a thing of the past, but it has produced ample evidence of how grievances over land and culture can survive for centuries and flare up hundreds of years after the original events that caused them.

So how would we get from the *civitas* of the Belgae to Wansdyke? One possible scenario would be an attempt by the Dobunni to reassert their authority in the previously Dobunnic territory that made up the western half of the *civitas* of the Belgae. If such a move had occurred, it could easily have led to conflict with the Atrebates in the eastern half of the *civitas* of the Belgae and by extension with the Atrebates themselves. At some stage then, during such a conflict, the Durotriges could have moved north to occupy the territory coveted by the Dobunni, possibly coming into conflict with both Dobunni and Atrebates. Ceramic evidence from the pre-Roman period suggests links between the people in Dobunnic territory south of the Avon and the people in Durotrigan territory further south.[21] It would not, therefore, seem inconceivable that the

Durotriges might have taken an opportunity presented by conflict in the area to annexe it. Outlining such a conflict is, of course, hugely speculative, but there are reasons, in addition to those discussed, for supposing that something broadly similar to this may have happened. For a start, an overlapping coin distribution in the pre-Roman period might suggest an unstable border between Dobunni and Durotriges.[22] The area of the lead and silver mines in the Mendip Hills, exploited both in pre-Roman and Roman times, could also have been a cause of conflict between the Dobunni and Durotriges. In the east, early Dobunnic coinage is found in the area to the west of Marlborough but then seems to disappear,[23] to be replaced by Atrebatic coinage, perhaps also suggesting a change of control. There is also another dyke, apart from Wansdyke, in the area – the Bokerley Dyke (65). This linear defence, however, was built to protect the Durotriges from any threat from the direction of the Atrebatic half of the *civitas* of the Belgae. The dyke is either late Roman or post-Roman.[24]

Another puzzle of late Roman archaeology in the western part of Britain has been the massive defences applied to the small town of Mildenhall/Cunetio sometime around 370. Mildenhall lies a significant way from the sea and is of little obvious economic importance. There have been attempts to argue that Mildenhall was a logistical and financial centre for cereal production for the late Roman Army, but there is little hard evidence for this and generally there seems no obvious reason for such heavy fortification.

Mildenhall, however, lies along the same line as Wansdyke. More to the point, the evidence of pre-Roman coinage in the area (with more Atrebatic coins, but also a significant number of Dobunnic coins) suggests that Mildenhall may have been the nearest Atrebatic town to Dobunnic territory.[25] If there was violence or the threat of it from the Dobunni aimed at the Atrebates in the *civitas* of the Belgae, then there would be a good reason for the sudden appearance of heavy fortifications here. Interestingly when we consider Mildenhall's walls, we can see that they blocked most pre-existing roads and possibly only one road exit was left out of the town, on the south side, heading away from Dobunnic territory.[26]

Griffiths has also mapped the discovery of late fourth-century buckles and belt fittings in Wiltshire and, in light of the possible scenario we are considering, his findings make interesting reading. In contrast to a scatter of second- to third-century military material which is found more generally across the county, late fourth-century buckles and belt fittings are found in a cluster just north of Mildenhall (around roads leading from the Dobunnic capital at Cirencester) and along the line of Wansdyke and the road connecting its two main sections. The late fourth-century material then forms a line running approximately south through the centre of Wiltshire to Salisbury. It therefore roughly follows the probable boundary of the Atrebates in pre-Roman times.[27] It is also worth

65 Bokerley Dyke near Woodyates, helping protect Durotrigan territory from any advance from the territory of the *civitas* of the Belgae

noting the discovery of a late fourth-century dolphin buckle at the burnt villa of North Wraxall.[28]

In addition, there is the interesting case of Bedwyn Dyke. While not on the scale of Bokerley Dyke or Wansdyke, this linear earthwork appears to link the Roman villa at Castle Copse to the hillfort at Chisbury Castle.[29] Again this earthwork lies in the area of the Atrebatic boundary in pre-Roman times and faces west towards pre-Roman Dobunnic territory. Hostetter, Howe and Allison believe it is most likely to be post-Roman in date and not merely a boundary marker.

At Silchester itself, the capital of the *civitas* of the Atrebates, there are again possible signs of fortification against a threat from the direction of Dobunnic territory. A series of linear earthwork defences lies to the north of Silchester and is thought to be post-Roman. Much attention has been paid to the point where the earthworks meet the Roman road to Dorchester on Thames, and it has been suggested that the defences may have been dug to defend against a threat from early Anglo-Saxon settlers there. Less attention has been paid to the fact that the earthworks also stretch across to meet the road west to Cirencester, the capital of the Dobunnic *civitas*,[30] and that there were probably Dobunni to the north of Silchester as well as early Anglo-Saxon settlers. If these were, in fact, Atrebatic defences against the Dobunni, then there are also indications that they may not have been entirely effective. As indicated earlier, the number of hoards in Atrebatic territory suggests serious trouble there and in addition it is even possible that the Silchester area itself was attacked towards the end of the Roman period. Part of a skull probably dating from the fifth century was found in the town ditch by the north gate[31] (*colour plate 15*) and four Dobunnic-style belt fittings have been found in a group some way east of their main distribution area, including one at Silchester itself.[32] Obviously, these could have arrived there in a number of ways, but one way would be an attack on Silchester and the surrounding area by Dobunnic militiamen.

Clearly if there was a Dobunnic/Atrebatic confrontation in one of the wealthier areas of Britain in the last years of Roman rule, then it would be of major importance in its own right. Perhaps even more significantly though, it could have been a catalyst for more widespread fighting among the tribes. As discussed in the introduction, many historical parallels indicate that where a central force, that has been holding together culturally and/or ethnically diverse areas with a history of conflict, is suddenly removed, the result is often conflict over disputed resources and population centres as the areas reassert their independence. The disruption caused by the creation of the *civitas* of the Belgae is only one of a significant number of potential disputes that could have re-ignited as Roman power weakened. As we have also seen in a number of parallel historical situations, most recently including Former Yugoslavia, once one dispute re-ignites, it can lead to other disputes in a region re-igniting as well. Certainly there is evidence to suggest that the *civitas* of the Belgae may not have been the only part of Britain in chaos as Roman power faded.

In Chapter 4, the possibility was raised of conflict between the Dobunni and the Catuvellauni in the late second century. The two tribes probably had a history of competing for territory around the Upper Thames stretching back to the era of Tasciovanus and Cunobelin, and Limbrick has drawn attention to the concentration of pre-Roman fortifications here, attributing it to the meeting of tribal boundaries.[33] Concentrations of coin hoards in this area in the last decades of Roman rule (not matched by any concentration of fourth-century Portable Antiquities Scheme finds) suggest that competition for land here may have resumed at this point. In particular, there is an interesting eruption of hoarding near Cirencester at the end of the Roman period which might relate to conflict in the Upper Thames area, unless it is to be associated with the problems to the south of Wansdyke. The area between Dorchester on Thames and Cirencester is also rich in belt buckles and belt fittings, including Dobunnic, Catuvellaunian/Trinovantian and general late Roman and late Roman British types. If there was confrontation here, it presumably came later than that further south because the Oxfordshire potteries continue production up to the beginning of the fifth century. However, when and if confrontation did occur, that industry, situated as it was near *civitas* borders and with a distribution that spread over many different *civitates*, would have been doubly vulnerable.

Another probably long-running tribal dispute that may have re-ignited in the last decades of the fourth century is that between the Iceni on one hand and the Catuvellauni and Trinovantes on the other. Near the probably pre-Roman Mile Ditch, cutting the Icknield Way near Cambridge and presumably marking the Catuvellaunian/Icenian border at that point, a new linear defence, the Fleam Dyke, was dug, with radiocarbon dates of 330–510 for the first phase of construction, and a V-shaped ditch (*66*).[34] Again there is a concentration of hoards in this area, with a particularly significant number of precious metal collections (including the Thetford and Hoxne treasures) that runs roughly along the Icenian border with the Catuvellauni and the Trinovantes. Again there is a concentration of buckles and belt fittings in this area, including a line that also lies approximately along the Icenian border with the Trinovantes. The Portable Antiquities Scheme has produced many finds from this area too, but this concentration stretches across Suffolk to the south. It is not restricted to the border area, as the hoards, buckles and belt fittings mainly are. Interestingly, along this same border there is also possible evidence of most of the Roman roads that

66   Fleam Dyke, dating in its original form from 330–510, but one in a series of linear earthworks, roughly in the same area, which probably marked the shifting boundary between the Catuvellauni and Iceni (and their successors) from pre-Roman to post-Roman times

cross it going out of use in the post-Roman period, again suggesting this might be an area of conflict.[35]

Another area which may be significant in terms of coin hoards (including those containing gold or silver) and buckles is northern Kent and Surrey. Concentrations of both here do appear to be matched by other Portable Antiquities Scheme finds, but it is noticeable that there are few hoards in this area in the preceding periods. There is also a probably post-Roman ditch here, the Faesten Ditch, which cuts the main Canterbury to London road near Bexley.[36] In pre-Roman times, north-west Kent was an area of tribal dispute being controlled at different times by Cantii, Atrebates and Catuvellauni. Some of this tribal rivalry may have re-ignited towards the end of Roman rule.

The question of London is also an interesting one. Ptolemy makes it a city of the Cantii, but the area was well within the territory controlled by Cunobelin and, of course, only a short distance from the Catuvellaunian capital at Verulamium. Capital cities often have a bad time when ethnic divisions explode into actual conflict because they tend to have some of the most ethnically mixed populations, plus they usually have concentrations of wealth and are symbolically important, so that all sides want them. This was the fate of Sarajevo during the Bosnian War and has been the fate of Baghdad more recently.

Grim's Dyke, a pre-Roman earthwork north of London, seems to have been extended in late or post-Roman times, possibly to cut Watling Street and potentially to defend against an advance from Catuvellaunian territory (*67*).[37] However, the concentration of buildings over the archaeology in London makes it difficult to say too much more than that about its political position in the last years of Roman rule.

Another area that could have featured in a dislocation of Britain at the end of the Roman period is the area of Norfolk immediately to the east of the fenlands. There is an interesting situation here where two sets of linear fortifications appear to confront each other. Beecham Ditch and the post-Roman Foss Ditch seem to protect the Fens. Launditch and and Panworth Ditch seem to protect Icenian territory. Launditch and Panworth Ditch are both bigger and stronger where the Roman road crosses and, therefore, likely to be post-Roman in their final form.[38] In pre-Roman times the fenlands appear, judging by the coin evidence, to have been controlled by the Iceni. As discussed in Chapter 3, however, pottery evidence and the layout of the Roman road structure imply that, by the end of the first century, the fenlands were looking west rather than east. It has been suggested that this might represent a move by the Romans, after 60-61, to remove the lucrative salt industries of the fenlands from Icenian control and give them either to the Corieltauvi or Catuvellauni.[39] If so, it is a grievance that could still have been an issue much later.

Though there is little evidence of hoarding in this area, there is an unusually high rate of loose coin loss,[40] as also seen near Wansdyke, which is markedly out of line with Portable Antiquities Scheme finds of other fourth-century material in the area. Another interesting fact is that West Norfolk has produced some of the very few late Roman buckles where different tribal buckle styles are mixed. From East Winch, for instance, comes an Icenian head buckle with Catuvellaunian/Trinovantian-style dots on the buckle loop.[41] There are five examples, though, of buckles with an Icenian-style head on the top of the loop but also featuring Corieltauvian birds.[42] Three of these come from the West Norfolk/Cambridgeshire border area. To add to the stylistic confusion, one of the buckles from this region has Catuvellaunian/Trinovantian dots as well, making it a currently unique example of a buckle featuring symbols linked to three tribal territories (*68*).

It is probable that the Corieltauvian birds on head buckles from Icenian territory represent Corieltauvian influence in the area. A small number of Corieltauvian-style bird/protrusion buckles (without heads) have also been found in Norfolk and Suffolk (*51*). Their distribution matches a trickle of Corieltauvian coinage

67   Grim's Dyke, to the north of London

68 Buckle from Watton, Norfolk, showing a unique stylistic combination of head on top of loop, birds on side of loop and dots on the loop. Such stylistic mingling is a feature of the area and is reminiscent of mixed Corieltauvian and Trinovantian influence on pre-Roman Icenian coinage. It could also represent political chaos or even a break-away political entity

into the same areas in pre-Roman times, which may be a part of wider pre-Roman cultural/political links. At one stage, for instance, the Iceni were issuing silver coinage based on designs of the Corieltauvi while using Trinovantian gold coinage as well,[43] a stylistic mix which seems to reflect almost exactly the situation with buckles in Icenian territory in the late fourth century. Equally the stylistic connections might reflect some late Roman administrative arrangement. Were the Iceni and Corieltauvi, for instance, part of the same province? Or could it be that the stylistic mix just reflects political chaos in the area at the end of Roman rule?

The unusual use of different tribal symbols on individual buckles might suggest some kind of break-away political entity in the area, perhaps one emphasising links to more than one *civitas*. In Bosnia, for example, early in the war, before the fighting between Croats and Bosniaks, some Croats wore badges that, alongside the red and white chequerboard of Croatia, also featured the blue and white fleur de lys design of the central government in Sarajevo. The mixing of tribal styles is also rather similar to that noted on the coins of Epaticcus in Chapter 1, a ruler who claimed to be a 'son of Tasciovanus' but ruled in Atrebatic Calleva and issued coins with a Catuvellaunian-style design on one side and an Atrebatic-style design on the other. It is a reminder that along with inter-tribal warfare, the end of Roman Britain probably also saw chronic political instability within individual *civitates*. Gildas suggests as much when he writes of a slightly later period:

> Kings were anointed, not according to God's law, but because they had proved themselves more ruthless than the rest. Very quickly, though, they were then executed by those who had selected them, not because of an investigation into their merits, but because even more ruthless successors had been found.
>
> Gildas, *On the Ruin of Britain* 21

Hopefully, further finds of buckles and belt fittings will clarify the position.

One other area is worth considering at this point. This is the region where Brigantian, Corieltauvian and Catuvellaunian territory came close. It is an area that we have seen suffered greatly in the late second century and may have suffered again in 367-369. At the end of the period, there are also signs of trouble, with more coin hoards, including those containing gold or silver, and concentrations of buckles and belt fittings which do not seem warranted by the level of general fourth-century Portable Antiquities Scheme finds in the area. In addition, towards the end of the fourth century, the forum, basilica and market hall at Leicester were burnt and not rebuilt.[44] There are two possible tribal reasons for this. One could be a resumption of raiding by the Brigantes. The other, which would apply particularly on the Corieltauvian/Catuvellaunian border, is a further question of disputed territory. Judging from pre-Roman coin evidence, the Nene Valley area was very close to the Catuvellaunian border with the Corieltauvi. During the period of Roman rule, the area had grown wealthy, partly as a result of the huge and successful Nene Valley pottery industry, and it is perfectly conceivable that the Corieltauvi might have wished to attempt to claim land here. It is even possible that the Nene Valley had, at some stage in pre-Roman and pre-coinage times, been Corieltauvian territory. While the coins of Tasciovanus and Cunobelin far outnumber Corieltauvian coins here, it is noticeable that there are few of the pre-Roman cremation burials which are such a feature of most Catuvellaunian territory to the south, suggesting this as one possible area of Catuvellaunian expansion. As mentioned before, there are a number of Corieltauvian buckles found south of the Fens. Mostly this applies to Icenian territory but a few bird buckles have also been found in what was probably Catuvellaunian territory (*51*). This includes one found at Little Downham which is almost identical to another from Colsterworth in Lincolnshire, site of a major pre-Roman and Roman-period Corietauvian settlement. Fourth-century British buckles show huge variation and it is extremely rare to find two examples so similar, suggesting that the Little Downham buckle came south from Corieltauvian territory, quite possibly from Colsterworth.[45]

There are, of course, other areas where tribal conflict might have taken place. In particular in western areas where use of Roman currency was rarer and buckles were never adopted, it is hard to have any idea of what may have been happening at this stage. Dark has done valuable work in analysing how the region broke up into separate political entities based mostly on the old tribal territories (see Chapter 8). However, it is impossible to know to what extent this fragmentation occurred peacefully or otherwise. It is unlikely to have been entirely peaceful. The numerous parallel situations throughout history, with the recent wars in Bosnia and Iraq being just the latest, demonstrate that. Gildas, again is interesting on the subject. In his listing of the crimes of western British rulers in the early sixth century, he repeatedly accuses them of attacking other Britons. Referring to British kings, he writes, '… they fight wars, but they fight wars against their own countrymen, unjust wars …' (Gildas, *On the Ruin of Britain* 27). Of Aurelius Caninus, he says 'Have you not shut against your soul the gates of heavenly peace and rest, by hating the peace of your country, like a deadly snake, and hungering unjustly after civil wars and constant plunder?' (Gildas, *On the Ruin of Britain* 30). Of Cuneglasus, he writes, 'Why have you made such great wars, both against men and God – against men, your own countrymen, with deadly weapons, and against God with endless crimes?' (Gildas, *On the Ruin of Britain* 32). Maglocunus, he addresses in these terms, 'And you too, Dragon of the island, who have taken the kingdoms of many tyrants and taken their lives as well…' (Gildas, *On the Ruin of Britain* 33). If this was the situation at the beginning of the sixth century, it is quite possible that there was extensive conflict among British political entities in the area at the beginning of the fifth century as well.

An interesting footnote to the question of late Roman and post-Roman linear earthworks is the question of hillforts. Hadrian's Wall and the Antonine Wall were, of course, linear defences, but the location and style of linear defences in late and post-Roman Britain clearly suggest the phenomenon is more likely to be a re-adoption of pre-Roman forms of defence than a continuation of Roman types. Something similar happens with hillforts.

A well-known phenomenon of the post-Roman period in the west of Britain is the refortification and reuse of hillforts. South Cadbury and Cadbury Congresbury are the two best-known examples where pre-Roman hillforts were restored and put back into use in the post-Roman period. However, there is evidence to suggest that hillforts may have been put back into use both earlier and on a wider scale. Buckles dating from the late fourth century have been found at a number of hillforts, including Stanwick in Yorkshire, Penycorddyn in North Wales and Blewburton Hill in Berkshire.[46] There is currently no evidence for reoccupation of these hillforts at the end of the Roman period, but the number of hillforts thoroughly investigated archaeologically is low and signs of post-Roman occupation were notoriously difficult for previous generations of excavators to spot. Recent work on Irthlingborough hillfort near Northampton, however, may demonstrate post-Roman reoccupation and refortification,[47] and it could well be that more examples of such reuse will be discovered in central and eastern England in coming years.

So, if what we might be seeing here is the widespread dislocation of Britain by tribal disputes at the end of the Roman period, what impact would it have had on the economy? For a start, the large numbers of silver and gold coins hoarded in the years around the end of Roman rule clearly suggest that Britain did not simply run out of cash. That much seems evident, whatever some would suggest. However, the phenomenon of clipping (where the edges of many of these coins have been trimmed, sometimes quite severely, to produce spare silver) is so familiar that it is worth examining again, because it suggests something very specific about the end of Roman rule in Britain (*69*). It suggests a clearly delineated two-stage process. The first stage, the clipping, demonstrates a breakdown of Roman authority. Clipping was a serious offence punishable under Roman law by death, so for it to become such a widespread practice starkly illustrates an absence of Roman authority.

More interestingly, though, the survival of large numbers of clipped *siliquae* suggests a second stage. It suggests a period in which either large numbers of people were unable to retrieve precious metals they had buried (which means death or flight on a large scale) and/or it suggests a period in which precious metal lost its value, at least in some areas. The second is a particularly extraordinary proposition and the comparative lack of examples of very heavily worn clipped *siliquae* (which might suggest they stayed in use for some time) may indicate that this was indeed the situation in a number of regions.

Currencies which have an assigned value, but no intrinsic value, can quickly

69   Clipped silver *siliquae*. Their continued discovery in significant quantities suggests that Britain did not simply run out of cash at the end of the Roman period

become worthless in a range of situations. It would be understandable if Roman bronze currency became rapidly valueless at the end of Roman rule – though even that should probably be taken as symbol of extreme dislocation. Major currencies like dollars after all retain their value even in war zones and Roman bronze currency would still have been valid in much of Europe. Some post-Roman kings like the Vandals in Africa issued base metal currency in Roman style which shows that the credibility of Roman bronze coinage could often survive even big, sudden transformations of society. It would, however, be quite extraordinary for good-quality silver to lose its value. It is a well-known phenomenon that the value of precious metals usually tends to go up during crises, specifically because they have a universal value, not linked to the fluctuations of currency values. You cannot, however, eat silver or gold and if trade routes are cut so that goods for sale cannot be brought in and precious metals cannot be taken out, you could get a situation where silver and gold become effectively worthless. The only situation that could account for something like that would be very large-scale dislocation of society in the relevant regions. It is hard to know what, apart from the slicing up of the country by extensive tribal warfare, could create such a situation.

There is interesting evidence from the coins of Constantine III on the probable timing of this dislocation. The coins of the short-lived Emperor Eugenius (392-4) minted in mainland Europe managed, before the end of coin circulation in Britain, to reach most parts of Roman Britain.[48] By contrast, the coins of Constantine III (407-411), also minted in mainland Europe, are largely only found in Middlesex and Suffolk,[49] and fifth-century gold coins in general are found almost exclusively in the south-east (with a small group on, and especially to the east of, the Isle of Wight).[50] Without full details, of course, of comparative production of the coins of the two would-be emperors, it is hard to be 100 per cent sure what this indicates, but broadly the strongly contrasting distributions might suggest a fairly abrupt interruption of the free flow of coinage around the country around the time Constantine III's coins were minted.

When we look at manufacturing and trade, the picture is also consistent with a slicing up of territory some time near the end of the fourth century. It is hard to identify precisely what happened and when, in the collapse of much of the British economy. However, the clearest picture we can probably get is by looking at the pottery industries, which offer the most plentiful evidence of any of the sectors of the British economy in the Roman period. We have already seen how the collapse of the New Forest industry might reflect a collapse of the *civitas* of the Belgae. At the end of the Roman period, there is a mass extinction of the pottery industries.

This would hardly be surprising in the tribal wars scenario. Although, in pre-Roman times and in the earlier Roman period many pottery industries had supplied customers inside a single tribal area or *civitas*, by 400 only a few pottery industries (that of the Dumnonii in the far west being one example) seem to have been still supplying pottery exclusively to one tribal area. All the others supplied their wares across *civitas* boundaries. In fact, it has been argued that most of them were specifically sited near *civitas* boundaries in order to take advantage of the market in more than one *civitas*.[51] As mentioned, the Oxfordshire pottery industry is the perfect example of this, lying close to the border between the Catuvellaunian and Dobunnic *civitates*. In peaceful times, it would have been an excellent strategy and the Oxfordshire pottery industry became highly successful. If, however, the *civitas* boundary in question became a confrontation line then the industry would almost inevitably be in serious trouble very rapidly.

Most pottery production in Britain seems to have ceased around 410, or fairly shortly afterwards. Various sites show that the closure of the potteries was a

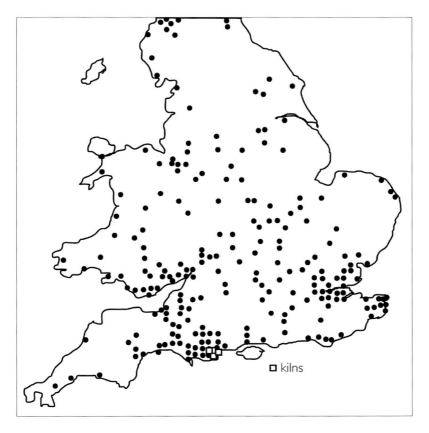

70 Distribution of South-East Dorset Black Burnished 1 Ware. Such a sophisticated and extensive distribution network would have been highly vulnerable to a closing of *civitas* borders. *After Tyers*

sequential event, presumably as different borders closed and different areas were affected by economic collapse. The villa at Orton Hall Farm, for instance, was originally supplied by the Nene Valley industry, located in the northern border region of the Catuvellaunian *civitas*, but when that collapsed, it received pottery from the Oxfordshire industries, located in the western border region of the Catuvellaunian *civitas*. When supply from there failed, the inhabitants seem to have taken to making their own pottery.[52]

There is evidence that some pottery industries did continue for a while after 410. However, they continued, as one would expect in the tribal war scenario, on a small scale and, crucially, mostly operating within the territory of one tribe. Thus, there is evidence that suggests the Black Burnished Ware industry based around Poole, which, at its height exported pottery across Britain as far north as Hadrian's Wall, may have limped on through much of the fifth century, but only selling its wares within Durotrigan territory (*70*).[53] In the east, Shell-Tempered Ware is found almost exclusively in the territory of the Catuvellauni and that of their confederation partners, the Trinovantes. South of the Thames, Surrey Buff Ware is found mainly in Atrebatic territory, as is Hampshire and Kent Grog-Tempered Ware (a few pieces of this have, as its name suggests, been found in Kent but by far the majority of pieces have been found in territory that was Atrebatic in pre-Roman times[54]). Interestingly while Hampshire and Kent Ware is present in the Atrebatic half of the *civitas* of the Belgae, it is entirely absent from the Dobunnic half (as well as from the territory of the *civitates* of the Dobunni and the Durotriges). It is yet more evidence that pre-Roman tribal boundaries were being reasserted at the end of Roman rule.

Compare this situation with what happened to the pottery industries in Gaul and the Rhineland at the end of Roman rule. Here, new incoming Germanic rulers took over large parts of the Roman Empire, keeping their economies more intact and preventing any fragmentation into *civitates*. As Tyers points out, across much of France and the Rhineland, pottery styles and pottery industries continued to flourish throughout the fifth and sixth centuries and beyond. At Mayen, for instance, pottery production continued through to the seventh century to become a major source of Rhineland pottery in the eighth century, while styles of pottery descended from the '*terra sigillata*' industries of the empire continued to be widely distributed across southern and western France during the fifth, sixth and seventh centuries.[55] The same withdrawal of imperial financing that affected post-Roman Britain also affected post-Roman Gaul, suggesting that this was not, as some have suggested, the crucial factor in destroying the British economy. The big difference does seem to be that Gaul did not fragment into small parts.

The pottery industry is the sector of the British economy in the Roman period that we know most about. However, it is probable that much of what happened to the pottery industry also happened to other areas of the economy. Commerce in late Roman Britain seems in many ways to have been remarkably complex, with many raw materials and goods, in addition to pottery, being transported over long distances. From Dutrotrigan territory, for instance, Purbeck marble travelled as far as London, Verulamium and Chester, while Kimmeridge shale and products made from Kimmeridge shale are also found widely across Britain.[56] From Brigantian territory, objects carved of jet, and possibly unworked jet were exported to the Midlands and southern England.[57] Such long-distance trade would, of course, be highly vulnerable to the kind of scenarios we are discussing, where *civitas* borders became, within a short period of time, impassable. Imagine if, for instance, every county boundary in modern Britain was suddenly closed. Chaos would ensue. Manufacturers would not be able to get access to raw materials and would no longer be able to reach customers with their finished products. Consumers would suddenly find almost everything in short supply, if supplied at all. Something rather similar happened in Former Yugoslavia and Bosnia as new, but closed, borders and confrontation lines sliced up the old integrated economy of Tito's Yugoslavia. As a result, the economy crashed in a short time from something comparable in sophistication and affluence with parts of Western Europe to, in many places, little more than subsistence farming and small workshops.

The question of what happened in the towns while the economy was collapsing is a contentious one. There is only evidence for continuation of a comparatively small number of buildings significantly into the fifth century. The structure in Verulamium *insula* XXVII constructed around 420-430 and then cut by a water pipe some 20 years later is among the most well-known examples.[58] Many fourth-century buildings, though, seem to fall out of use fairly quickly in the fifth century.

This brings us to the problem of so-called 'dark earth'. These deposits are a long-acknowledged feature of the latest levels of many British towns of the Roman period, overlying buildings abandoned in the later fourth and early fifth centuries. They are found at Canterbury, Gloucester, Lincoln, London, Southwark and Winchester, while similar earth deposits have also been found at Cirencester and Exeter, and there may, of course, be other examples yet to be found beneath modern cities.

It used to be thought that these represented the transformation of urban areas into arable farming areas and indeed some deposits do show evidence of ploughing at some stage. This would not be unexpected at a time when the towns were safer than the countryside. In Bosnia, for instance, open spaces in the city centre were planted with vegetables and I have seen sheep grazing happily outside closed and abandoned banks and shops.

However, investigation of dark earth from London has suggested a rather different picture. The analysis revealed clayey earth, with plentiful evidence of Roman pottery and other Roman artefacts, plus bone, shell and charcoal. Pollen in the sample was distinctive of plants that grow on abandoned sites. From this and other evidence it is increasingly being suggested that what dark earth represents is the collapsed debris of large numbers of wattle and daub buildings.[59] Such buildings were common in late Roman times but usually rested on stone sill-walls. Presumably, since there is no evidence of stone sill-walls connected to the dark earth deposits, the buildings that would have produced them must have been of the simplest kind, maybe even temporary buildings.

One thing that most tribal wars produce in plenty is refugees seeking shelter and protection. Is it possible that the dark earth deposits are the remains of, effectively, refugee camps – slum towns constructed by people fleeing from fighting and raiding to the most obvious sources of safety, the large towns? Certainly there are signs in a number of towns that at the end of the Roman period the organised city planning of earlier centuries was breaking down. In Canterbury, for instance, timber-framed houses have been found which were built on a road some time after 388,[60] while at Chichester hearths and wattle partitions are constructed over the floors of Roman-period town houses.[61] Interestingly, also, one of the very few instances where dark earth seems to appear in previous centuries is in London from the late second century.[62] At the time, London was the largest, most thriving city in Britain. In this context, one could therefore view dark earth as the product of the kind of slum towns that often grow up around large cities in areas where planning control is weak. Alternatively, if dark earth should always be connected to refugee occupation, then perhaps these deposits could be linked to the troubles in Britain in the late second century considered in Chapter 4.

Ultimately, however, as the pollen of plants associated with abandonment indicates, whoever was living where dark earth was later to form, eventually left. This, again, would not be surprising in the scenario we are exploring. While the immediate need for protection and food might have driven refugees to the cities in the first place, with the economy collapsing and trading over distances becoming impossible, there would be no way that the cities could sustain large numbers of refugees. Ultimately, there would have to have been a move back to somewhere in the countryside. This at least could offer access to food and wood for cooking-fires. It is interesting that in a city such as Cirencester, some of the latest occupation was probably in the amphitheatre which appears to have been transformed into a kind of fortress (*71*).[63] In other words, the last remaining reason for staying in the cities may have been defensive, their economic function already having almost entirely ceased.

The evidence of what was going on in the countryside while the economy was collapsing and the cities were being filled by dark earth, is also not inconsistent with a tribal war scenario. There is evidence that much agriculture continued. This is only to be expected. Even in an island sliced up by closed *civitas* borders and tribal conflict, subsistence agriculture would continue and, increasingly, it is being suggested that land divisions and field systems can show evidence of continued usage in some areas from the Roman period into the post-Roman period and beyond.[64] Indeed, with people leaving the towns, agriculture might even have been expected to increase in safer areas. The pollen evidence for Britain suggests something rather like this. Not enough pollen evidence is available to give a clear picture of developments right across the island. However, in some instances, particularly in the west of Britain, there are clear indications that the level of agriculture remained the same at the end of the Roman period

71   The amphitheatre at Cirencester, which was probably transformed into some kind of stronghold in the post-Roman period

and, in some places, there are even signs of increased activity.[65]

However, in southern and northern England broadly, there are signs of a decrease in agricultural activity. A detailed study of the Upper Thames Valley, for instance, seems to show that in the post-Roman period, agriculture on the first terrace gravels and alluvium was abandoned, even though agriculture on the second terrace gravels continued.[66] The Upper Thames Valley, as already mentioned, was a site of potential conflict between the Catuvellauni, Dobunni and possibly Atrebates, and tribal conflict could generally have done severe damage to British agriculture in many parts of the island. It may even have caused famine which could have exacerbated conflicts, as tribes clashed over food-producing areas. There is an interesting passage in Gildas which may reflect some memory of such a situation:

> So the Britons turned their arms against each other, and, in an effort to grab just a little food, dipped their hands in the blood of their fellow countrymen. In this way, foreign disasters were worsened by domestic turmoil, and as a result, the whole country had no food, except what the hunters could find.
>
> Gildas, *On the Ruin in Britain* 19

Interestingly, there seems to be particular evidence of a collapse in the amount of land in use in the area around Hadrian's Wall.[67] It may be that this is the result of the disappearance of garrisons from the forts there (though it has been argued that there is evidence for significant continued occupation, or reoccupation, of sites along Hadrian's Wall well into the fifth century). Alternatively it might simply suggest that even where hoard and buckle evidence is thin, the period at the end of Roman rule was far from peaceful.

We have looked at possible refugee occupation in the towns, now it is time to consider the situation in that respect in the countryside. As mentioned earlier, one well-known aspect of late fourth-century rural archaeology is what used to be called 'squatter occupation', in which villas, previously occupied by wealthy inhabitants, suddenly see occupation of a much less affluent kind. Often occupation is restricted to a few rooms in a large building and little notice seems to have been taken of the expensive decor of previous years. In the villa at Lufton, for example, a large hearth is built straight on top of a mosaic in room 2, while an oven cuts through the mosaic in room 3. In room 4 a mortar floor is slapped over the mosaic and a partition wall is also built across it. At Barnsley Park the only hypocaust-heated room goes out of use, along with the hypocaust, while the flue of the old bath house is blocked and moulded pilasters are reused and laid as yard paving. At Witcombe old roof tiles are laid as a floor, and an oven and a temporary roof supported on timber posts appears in one of the old rooms. In two more rooms, fires were simply being lit on the existing floors.[68]

It has been argued that this simply implies a change of the owners' lifestyle or perhaps represents occupation by caretakers while the owners went elsewhere. However, it is hard to believe that anybody connected in any way with the owners, who had lavished so much time and money on embellishing their villas, would have been permitted to perpetrate the often extensive damage of the villas' decor that often occurs. On the strength of Bosnia, I would say that 'squatter occupation', in fact looks very much like refugee occupation (or possibly, even, occupation by people who had made the original owners of the villas into refugees) (*72*). Refugees frequently occupied buildings abandoned by their owners who had fled elsewhere. Often they would just make a few rooms in an abandoned building habitable, and often they would make 'adjustments' to the buildings. In one case, in a fine nineteenth-century building, the refugees had knocked holes straight through walls and mouldings so they could feed through the chimney pipes for the wood burning stoves that were their only means of keeping warm and cooking.

Though more work needs to be done on this, it is also interesting to note that there is at least some correlation between signs of destruction and 'squatter

72 At Rockbourne, in the West Wing, in the late fourth century, a mosaic was broken up and fires lit on the floor. Limestone roofing slates were laid as a rough corridor floor. It is possible this represents refugee occupation or occupation by those who made the original owners of the villa into refugees

occupation'. Thus a number of the villas affected by fire near Wansdyke show reoccupation but only of a much less affluent kind. At King's Weston, for instance, the destroyed west wing was not rebuilt, and occupation continued in probably just three rooms of the east wing and the corridor. A door into the corridor from one room was blocked and a cooking platform was built against it using rubble from a damaged portico. At Keynsham too, a cooking platform was built in the main corridor using rubble from the destruction. At Box, fires were regularly lit on the pavement square. At Atworth, roughly paved floors replaced the former more affluent style and a corn-drying oven was built into a bathroom.[69]

Almost all villas, however, show abandonment at the end of the Roman period. Even with significant numbers of displaced people around, this would be no surprise. For short-term use, refugees are likely to use existing available buildings, even ones far too large for them. However, practicalities of size, the disappearance of the economic structures that had supported the villas, the increasing dereliction of the villas over time and the gradual fading of a system of values in which villa-occupation equalled wealth and success, would logically have led any occupants eventually to move to smaller, more practical and more easily maintained constructions.

Discovering what these constructions were and where they were located is, of course, a rather harder question. While the Roman-style villas and towns seem to have collapsed entirely at the end of the Roman period, there is evidence that some of the British-style settlements survived at least a little longer.[70] There is also the possibility that some of the simple habitations previously attributed to early Anglo-Saxon settlers, could be linked to the surviving British population as well. It is hard to find close continental Germanic parallels for one of the main types of building in the fifth-century settlements. These are rectangular buildings that are usually larger than the sunken-featured buildings and, as Arnold points out, there is no sign of the bow-sided construction and animal stalls seen on the most similar continental buildings.[71] Dark suggests that there are good reasons for doubting the Anglo-Saxon, as opposed to British, nature of a number of fifth- and sixth-century settlements. Thus, for instance, he points out that the Frilford and Chalton settlements show the same grass-tempered pottery found on nearby Roman-period British sites and that the Bentley Green settlement has produced nothing explicitly Germanic and lies just half a kilometre from a Roman-period British settlement.[72] As we shall further consider in Chapter 8, there is also increasing evidence for Britons continuing to live in the areas of central and eastern England that see early Anglo-Saxon settlement, often sharing the same cemeteries and sharing some of the same cultural customs.

One possible objection to the tribal war scenario might be a lack of bodies showing signs of violent death. By analogy with Bosnia one might expect to find mass graves. For a start, though, it is hard to know how many bodies we would be looking for. In the Wessex law code of Ine from the Anglo-Saxon period, any group of more than 35 armed men could be termed an army. It is unlikely that whatever confrontations there were at the end of the Roman period were individually large-scale, and it does not take massacres of the size of Srebrenica to persuade people to leave an area.

Then there is the point that a percentage of whatever bodies there were, would simply have been left on the surface and, after the attentions of the elements and wild animals, would leave no trace. Gildas describes such a scene:

> Human body parts, covered with bright, clotted blood, looking like they had been mangled in a press, and with no hope of burial, except in ruined houses, or in the hungry bellies of wild animals and birds.
>
> Gildas, *On the Ruin of Britain* 24

73 Skeleton from the end of the Roman period, or later, found buried face down in a shallow grave at Rockbourne Villa

Add to this the fact that, of those bodies that were buried, only some would have had anything on them to identify them as late Roman and only a percentage of those who had died a violent death would show clear evidence of it on their surviving remains. A skull split in two by a sword or, as with the famous skeleton from Maiden Castle, a ballista bolt in the vertebrae are easy-to-spot signs of violent death, but, as discussed earlier, neither swords nor ballistae would probably have been in common use in any tribal wars at the end of the Roman period. Knife or spear scratches on a rib cage are going to be rather more difficult to spot. Finally, there is the fact that, compared to the likely millions living in Roman Britain, very few Roman-period burials of any century have actually survived. The same low percentage of survival will apply to burials of those killed in any conflicts at the end of the Roman period.

Broadly speaking, even where we do know of significant conflict from the historical sources, it is rare to find the skeleton evidence to back up a picture of large-scale killing. There are, for instance, only a very small number of corpses that have been specifically linked to the events of 60-61, and it is rare, even with later conflicts, to come across unequivocal evidence of more than a few violent deaths.

What can be said, though, is that some people do definitely seem to have died in violent ways at the end of the Roman period. There is the recently discovered famous instance of the corpse pushed inside a corn-drying oven at Sedgeford in Norfolk and we have already mentioned the assorted human remains found in some villas in the west of England. Equally, there are a number of late Roman burials which look as if they were conducted in emergency circumstances (*73*). Thus, for instance, bodies are found at the end of the Roman period inside towns, a location that would have been highly unusual in the preceding centuries. In Canterbury, there is the Stour Street burial in which an entire (possible) family (man, woman, two children and two dogs) were found buried in a pit dug into a probable temple area.[73] At Cirencester, bodies even seem to have lain unburied in a ditch dug beside a main street.[74]

In conclusion, therefore, one can say that while it is impossible to be 100 per cent sure that Britain was ripped apart by a series of ethnic conflicts at the end of the Roman period, this scenario does seem to fit the evidence (and as discussed in the Introduction, the simple fact of a sudden power vacuum after the disappearance of Roman control from a group of only very partially integrated tribes with a history of hostilities, does in itself indicate a high likelihood of conflict). Whatever the causes and whatever the results, however, there is certainly ample evidence that, at the beginning of the fifth century, the *civitates* and whoever was in political and military control of them, had some very serious problems to contend with. As in pre-Roman times, one option that was open to them was to introduce new players onto the British tribal political scene.

CHAPTER 7

The First of the Anglo-Saxons

The Saxons make an appearance relatively late in the list of fourth-century threats to Britain south of Hadrian's Wall. The Picts and Scots, with occasional walk-on parts for the Attacotti, feature most regularly and prominently. It is easy with hindsight, and with the thundering rhetoric of Gildas ringing in one's ears to see the Saxons as a dark force hanging over Britain in the fourth century and at the beginning of the fifth, but the evidence for this is slim. The Saxon Shore forts system with its imposing series of fortifications was once thought to demonstrate the magnitude of the Saxon threat in the fourth century. However, this traditional view has fallen apart. As discussed in Chapter 4, Caister, Reculver and Brancaster probably date from the first half of the third century when the Saxons were not even a conceivable threat to Britain. Other forts in the system were constructed under Carausius and Allectus when the central government in Rome was a more likely invader than the Anglo-Saxons. Portchester, for instance, was probably built in, or around, the 280s, while Pevensey was built in 293 or shortly afterwards.[1]

The role of the Saxons in 367-369 is unclear. A reading of the actual text of Ammianus indicates that they were mainly raiding Gaul at this time. With the narrowness of the Straits of Dover there must always have been some danger of overspill, but Britain does not seem to have been their main target. An entry in the *Gallic Chronicle* for 409-410 does record Britain being attacked by Saxons, but the evidence of the *Gallic Chronicle* is not something it would be wise to place too much unquestioning reliance upon. Its entry, for instance, for 441 states, 'Theodosius II, 18th and 19th year. The Britons, who up until this point had gone though assorted disasters and tragedies, submit to the control of the Saxons.'

Archaeology makes it clear that the Britons had not all submitted to the control of the Saxons by 441. Indeed the archaeology suggests that the first Anglo-Saxons were probably only just settling in Britain around 441, and were therefore still a long, long way from taking over the country.[2] So, if the Anglo-

Saxons were not taking control of Britain in 441, the crucial question is what were they doing there?

In the next chapter we will discuss the archaeology and history of how the centre and east of Britain became Anglo-Saxon England. First, though, it is time to consider some possible historical scenarios of why the very first Anglo-Saxons came to settle in Britain.

> Then the council, along with the proud tyrant, were so blind that, attempting to ensure their country's safety, they instead ensured its doom, by inviting in (like wolves into a sheep-fold) the savage and heathen Saxons, a race hated by both God and man … They first landed on the eastern coast of this island, invited in by the unfortunate king.
>
> Gildas, *On the Ruin of Britain* 23

Everyone interested in the Anglo-Saxon arrival, of course, knows of Gildas' '*superbus tyrannus*' and the Hengest and Horsa of the *Anglo-Saxon Chronicle* in Kent. However, the archaeological evidence suggests that the first arrival of Anglo-Saxons on a significant scale actually took place to the north of Kent, mainly in Catuvellaunian territory.

Böhme identified a category of early Germanic metalwork in Britain (including, for instance, supporting arm brooches and early cruciform brooches) which he originally dated to the first quarter of the fifth century (*74*). Revised dating now places this metalwork and the accompanying Germanic cremation burials in the period 425-450 (*76*).[3] The dates are, of course, significant. Apart from anything else, they confirm that the chaos in Britain at the end of the Roman period is not likely to have been mainly caused by an influx of Anglo-Saxons. As we saw in the previous chapter, Britain seems to have been in severe trouble long before 425.

In some manuscripts of Gildas his '*superbus tyrannus*' is identified as Vortigern, and Bede, in his version of the arrival of the Anglo-Saxons, explicitly links the account by Gildas of Saxons being invited in by a British king with the Kentish Vortigern, Hengest and Horsa story of the *Anglo-Saxon Chronicle*. In the process he also uses the *Chronicle* date of 449 for the arrival, a date consistent with the archaeology of Anglo-Saxon settlement in Kent.[5] While it cannot be proved beyond doubt that the '*superbus tyrannus*' should be identified as Vortigern, there are currently no other candidates. There are many reasons why Gildas might ignore the initial Anglo-Saxon settlement in Catuvellaunian territory. Obviously, he may simply not have been aware of it. He seems to have been writing probably in the west of Britain, in the early to mid sixth century, and events in, for instance, Mucking, a century earlier, may not have featured largely in his life.

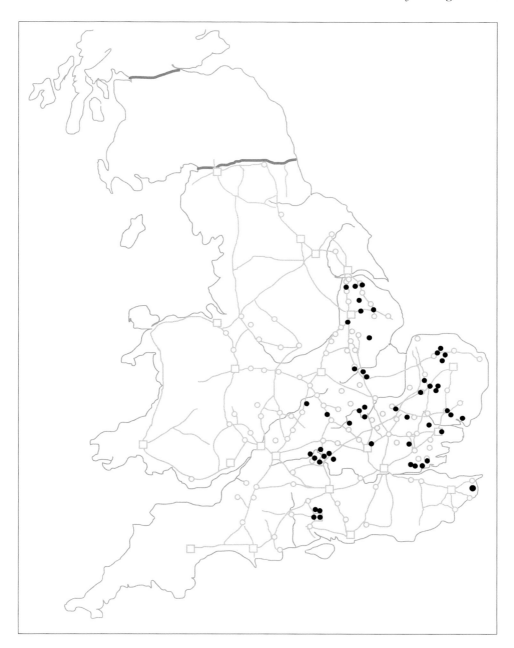

74   Distribution of the earliest Anglo-Saxon metalwork (shown by black dots). See Notes.[4] *After Böhme, Dark with additional material*

75   Anglo-Saxon supporting arm brooch and cruciform brooch

There is, however, a more intriguing alternative. Gildas is launching a diatribe about the Saxon invaders taking over Britain. Maybe he is discussing Kent because the Anglo-Saxons did take over there, but does not mention the earlier Anglo-Saxon settlements to the north because they did not take over there. The account by Gildas (which must be treated with some respect since it is, for all its

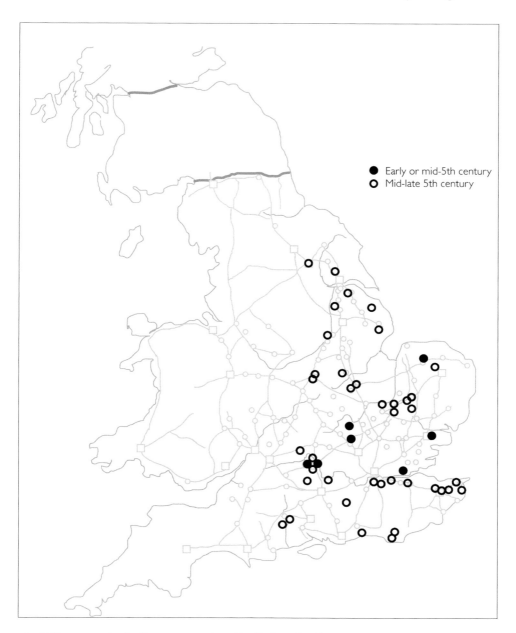

76   Fifth-century Anglo-Saxon cemeteries. *After Dark, with additions*

drawbacks as a historical record, the closest we have to a contemporary account of the arrival of the Anglo-Saxons) indicates that they originally came as *foederati* (under a *foedus* or treaty setting out their obligations and rewards) to help defend part of Britain and then subsequently rebelled. When he describes the rebellion itself, he uses the phrase '*rupto foedere*', meaning 'treaty broken.'[6]

> So the barbarians were brought into the island as soldiers, claiming falsely that they would face any danger defending their hosts. They were given generous rations which for a while, as the saying goes, kept the dogs' jaws busy. Nevertheless, they complain that their rations are not enough, and they aggravate each quarrel, threatening that, unless their rations are increased, they will break the treaty and ransack the whole island. Shortly, they back up their threats with action.
>
> Gildas, *On the Ruin of Britain* 23

There seem reasons to believe that the settlers in Catuvellaunian territory were also brought in to defend part of Britain but then did not subsequently rebel (or at least, not before the time of Gildas). Maybe their remuneration package was just that bit more generous!

It has long been a puzzle why some of the earliest Anglo-Saxon settlers suddenly appear so far inland in Britain and so far from the North Sea coast or the Channel coast. Some of the earliest Anglo-Saxons settle almost in the middle of the country, in the area around Dorchester on Thames. Obviously they could have sailed up the Thames, but it is a long way for a small force to travel through a hostile neighbourhood, and with only one conceivable narrow track for the journey, i.e. the Thames, it would have given locals ample time to react and resist. Our review of the possible collapse of Britain into tribal warfare (particularly around Catuvellaunian borders where, due to the empire-building of Tasciovanus and Cunobelin, land disputes were probably acute) suggests an alternative explanation for the Anglo-Saxon settlement in this area.

As previously discussed, the area to the west and north of Dorchester on Thames was probably disputed territory between the Dobunni and the Catuvellauni, with the Catuvellauni expanding into previously Dobunnic territory there in pre-Roman times and with a heavy concentration of pre-Roman defensive works. As we have also seen, this area was included in the Catuvellauni's fortification of their borders after 155, suggesting possible conflict with the Dobunni at that stage. It also features again in the list of potential flashpoints in the last decades of Roman rule. From the point of view of strategic communication routes, the Dorchester on Thames area also controls the Thames where it enters Catuvellaunian territory and the Thames crossing point for the Icknield Way before it heads up into the Chilterns. It, therefore, seems a perfect spot for the Catuvellauni to defend with some extra muscle hired from abroad.

77 Mosaic at North Leigh Villa. This villa has Dobunnic mosaics and Dobunnic belt fittings were found at the adjacent Shakenoak Villa. South Leigh Villa, a few miles away, has produced a Catuvellaunian buckle. This area was the border between Dobunni and Catuvellauni and is also near the edge of early Anglo-Saxon settlement

A comparison of the earliest Anglo-Saxon settlement in this area with the distribution there of the coins of Tasciovanus and Cunobelin is instructive. In the south, they all spill across the Thames at exactly the same point to create a limited 'bridgehead' near Abingdon. In the north, the border area lay somewhere in the region of Woodstock and Charlbury. In the pre-Roman era, this is the region which marks the furthest west penetration in quantities of Catuvellaunian coinage. It is also the site of the North Oxfordshire Grim's Ditch which has been suggested as the pre-Roman boundary between the two tribes.[7] In the late Roman period, the area remained a probable boundary between Dobunnic and Catuvellaunian influence. At North Leigh Villa a Cirencester school mosaic was unearthed,[8] and just over a mile away, at Shakenoak Villa, three Dobunnic-style belt fittings were found (77).[9] At South Leigh, by contrast, just about three miles from North Leigh, a Catuvellaunian-style belt fitting has been discovered.[10] In the post-Roman period, this area sees the furthest west examples of early Anglo-Saxon settlement.[11]

As already discussed, despite the views of Gildas, probably forged by his experience of Anglo-Saxon expansion in the sixth century, the Saxons may not have been viewed by the Britons as the prime threat in the late fourth century and early fifth centuries and employing them would continue a long tradition of Roman recruitment of Germanic volunteers. There is an interesting example of this, involving Britons, recorded from perhaps just 15 years prior to the first major appearance of Anglo-Saxons in Britain. When the British leader Gerontius rebelled against Constantine III in 409 and established Maximus as emperor in Spain, he used elements of the Suevi/Alans/Vandals in Gaul to attack Constantine. Constantine, who was certainly from Britain, and since he succeeded another usurper, Gratian, who was British and selected the British Gerontius as one of his major commanders, may even have been British, immediately reacted by trying to raise an army of Franks and Alemanni to counter the threat.

Perhaps more to the point, it would continue a long tradition of British tribes recruiting help overseas in their battles with their neighbours. The Parisi and Commius may well have arrived on this basis, and certainly it is likely that both Julius Caesar on his second expedition and Claudius were invited into Britain by tribal leadership anxious to gain a military edge against its rivals. For a more recent parallel, we can again turn to Bosnia and Croatia in the early 1990s. Here, as in late fourth-century Britain, societies where extensive military experience was comparatively rare were confronted with the need to fight wars. In that situation, foreign volunteers with the necessary recent military experience were often welcomed with open arms. One should probably see, though, the earliest Anglo-Saxons in Catuvellaunian territory as *foederati*, like Gildas' Saxons. Germanic female brooches are some of Böhme's earliest indicators of Anglo-Saxon settlement, implying the arrival of whole families rather than just young men on their own.

Supporting evidence for the idea that the initial Anglo-Saxon settlement in the Upper Thames area was undertaken under Catuvellaunian control comes from the *Anglo-Saxon Chronicle* for 571. The passage is admittedly a controversial one, though it is disputed not on textual grounds but because it contradicts preconceived notions of the spread of Anglo-Saxon control. It reads:

> This year Cuthwulf fought against the Britons at Bedcanford and captured four towns, Limbury, Aylesbury, Benson and Eynsham.

All the places mentioned in the 571 entry, plus the site of the battle (if Bedcanford is to be identified with Bedford, as is often assumed) lie in Catuvellaunian territory and if Britons controlled them in any sense in 571, presumably they did in 425-450 as well. Both Benson and Eynsham lie directly in the Upper Thames area of early Anglo-Saxon settlement. Archaeological evidence also gives some sense of a mingling of Britons and Anglo-Saxons in this area in the fifth century. For instance, a sunken-featured building of a type traditionally associated with early Anglo-Saxon activity has been found here, not far from a Roman-style masonry building, both probably being of fifth-century date.[12] In addition, several cemeteries in the area have burials which appear to be British, post-Roman and contemporary with early Anglo-Saxon settlement. The cemetery at Queenford Farm, Dorchester on Thames, for example, has 200 graves recorded dating from about the fifth to seventh centuries, with all but two west-east burials without grave goods. While at Frilford, it is suggested that only 13 cremations and about 28 inhumations out of about 212 burials can be categorised as Anglo-Saxon.[13] Across the Thames at Barton Court Farm near Abingdon, a small hut or cottage built on the site of a third-century villa seems to have been abandoned some time in the fifth century, but early fifth-century Germanic carinated pottery found on the site suggests some form of possible continuity of occupation from the Roman period into the Anglo-Saxon period.[14]

So what of the location of the other sites of earliest Anglo-Saxon activity as identified by early Germanic metalwork and by early to mid fifth-century cemeteries? When we look at the different places involved, they can all (with the exception of the Spong Hill, Winchester and north Lincolnshire groups which we will discuss later) be understood in terms of Catuvellaunian strategic imperatives. It is hard not to see this pattern as significant.

Moving clockwise from the upper Thames region, the next concentration of the earliest Anglo-Saxon metalwork and cemeteries lies in the Bedford/Luton region. Limbury, now a suburb of Luton, is mentioned in the 571 entry as under British control up to that point and Bedford is widely thought to have been the site for the battle mentioned in 571. From the point of view of Catuvellaunian strategy, note that the area sits between Watling Street and Ermine Street. Towcester, one of the towns burnt in 155, lies nearby. The early Anglo-Saxon cemetery at Kempston near Bedford, in addition to early Germanic metalwork, has also produced much Roman material, again suggesting a mingling of Britons and Anglo-Saxons.[15]

Moving round again, we come to the Water Newton/Peterborough area. This lies across Ermine Street where it enters Catuvellaunian territory, and is also at the heart of the Nene Valley area which may have been disputed territory between the Corieltauvi and Catuvellauni at the end of the Roman period. There is, in addition, some suggestion of continuity of occupation into the Anglo-Saxon period in this area. Most famously, at Orton Hall Farm, timber buildings, including both post-built and sunken forms, appear on a Roman-period villa site with the new buildings carefully arranged so as to respect the Roman-period buildings.[16]

Moving around again, we come to the area near Cambridge and the Cambridgeshire/Suffolk border. This is the border region between the Catuvellauni and the Iceni, defended with linear defences probably in pre-Roman and certainly in post-Roman times, and one of the major possible flashpoints in the period at the end of Roman rule. The main concentration of early Anglo-Saxon metalwork lies slightly to the east of the main area of early Anglo-Saxon cemeteries in this area. This may reflect movements of borders here in the post-Roman period. Linear defences which are possibly post-Roman in their final form cut the Icknield Way in five places from Bran Ditch, near Heydon, as far east as Black Ditches near Cavenham. This may indicate a frequently moving and, therefore, presumably contested border. It is an obvious place for the Catuvellauni to locate a garrison of *foederati* and there is also evidence of links between Anglo-Saxons and Britons in the region. It is, for instance, well known that one of the major Anglo-Saxon settlements in this area, at West Stow, sits right next to a major late Roman site at Icklingham and considerable quantities of Roman pottery and coinage have been found at West Stow.[17] At St John's College cricket field, Cambridge, it has been suggested, due to the presence of Roman brooches, pottery, artefacts and coins in the early Anglo-Saxon cemetery, that a mixed British and Anglo-Saxon community was burying and cremating its dead there.[18] In the large cemetery at Girton too, some burial practices suggest continuity.[19]

To the south and east of this area, a few pieces of the earliest Anglo-Saxon metalwork have been found around and to the north of Colchester. The late fourth-century buckle evidence, with belt fittings of a similar style appearing in both the territory of the Catuvellauni and the Trinovantes, suggests that the pre-Roman confederation of these tribes was maintained in post-Roman times. Again, Colchester, pre-Roman capital of the Trinovantes and burnt in 60-61, plus the territory around (possibly attacked again by the Iceni in the late second century) would be a reasonable position to place additional manpower. There is also evidence in this region for cooperation between Britons and early Anglo-Saxon settlers. At the villa at Rivenhall, for instance, carinated 'Germanic' pottery was found on the floor of a fourth-century aisled barn, which seems to have continued in use into the fifth century.[20] Not far away at Heybridge lies a significant early Anglo-Saxon settlement which has already been suggested as a location of Germanic mercenaries.[21]

Finally, we reach the Thames in the area of Mucking. While Dorchester on Thames controls access to the Catuvellaunian stretch of the river from the west, Mucking controls access to it from the east. It has long been recognised that there is evidence of contact at Mucking between the earliest Anglo-Saxons and Britons. Dixon's discovery of the apparent continued use of Roman measurements in the construction of many of the huts at Mucking is interesting in this context,[22] as is the appearance of Roman and British buckles in the cemetery there. Again, it has already been suggested by a number of people, including Dark, that the early Anglo-Saxon settlements in this region may have been established there to protect a British political entity inland.[23] In other words, at almost every major strategic point along the Catuvellauni's borders is the site of one of the small number of very early Anglo-Saxon settlements (*74, 76*). It is hard to imagine that this can be a coincidence. The only area that does not appear to be protected by this ring is the south, although this was probably not the case for long.

In the earliest years of the Anglo-Saxon *foederati*, it may have been thought that the Thames was a sufficient defensive barrier. However in the next decades of Anglo-Saxon settlement, an arc of burials appears south of the Thames at Croydon, Orpington and Beddington, each astride one of the Roman roads into London from the south. As with the settlements in the Mucking region, it has already been argued by others that this represents a post-Roman defence of London.[24] I would agree with that, but would add that it should almost certainly be seen specifically in the context of the Catuvellauni's defence of their borders. It is true, as discussed in the previous chapter, that a post-Roman linear defence appears to have been built north of London facing Catuvellaunian territory at some stage. However, London was well within the territory of Tasciovanus and Cunobelin, and there are no early Anglo-Saxon settlements north of the area to protect it. The Anglo-Saxon name for the area of settlement to the south of London also seems to suggest a connection with Catuvellaunian territory to the north. The name Surrey derives from the Anglo-Saxon name '*suthre ge*' meaning the southern region. The ending 'ge' is thought to be an early Anglo-Saxon term, indicating that this territory was called the southern region from early in its history, and it has been suggested that calling this the southern region must indicate that it was linked to a northern region, presumably on the other side of the Thames.[25] At the time of settlement, the area north of the Thames, probably including London and definitely beyond London, was Catuvellaunian.

As we saw in earlier chapters, British tribes were often quick to adopt successful military and political strategies from their neighbours. In the period before the Roman invasion, for instance, the Atrebates and Catuvellauni may both have competed to win Roman support and assistance, while in Roman times not just the Catuvellauni but also the Dobunni and the Corieltauvi seem to have fortified their borders in the period after 155. Then in the fourth century, not just the Catuvellauni/Trinovantes but also the Dobunni, the Corieltauvi and the Iceni developed their own style of military buckles, and probably their own

78 Buckle from near Mucking, showing stylistic links both to late Roman triangular plate buckles and later Anglo-Saxon triangular plate buckles

79   Scabbard chape of a type found in early Anglo–Saxon graves

militias. It would be no surprise, therefore, if, in the wake of the Catuvellauni, other tribes also introduced Anglo-Saxon troops along their borders.

Mention has already been made of the Spong Hill concentration of early Anglo-Saxon burials and metalwork. This is one of only three of the earliest concentrations of Anglo-Saxon material to lie away from Catuvellaunian borders. It is, however, still arguably placed in a strategic location, though this time from an Icenian, rather than a Catuvellaunian point of view. Spong Hill lies at a distance from the coast and from coastal access (making it less likely that Anglo-Saxons would settle here of their own volition) and is instead situated about three miles to the east of the Launditch, probably, in its final form, a post-Roman linear defence protecting Icenian territory as mentioned in Chapter 6. It is, therefore, conceivably connected with the disputed ownership of the fenlands also discussed in that chapter.

Equally, in the north of Lincolnshire, to the south of the Humber Estuary, is another group of early Anglo-Saxon metalwork (Elsham, Hibaldstow, Kirmington) and early Anglo-Saxon cemeteries (Cleatham, Elsham) (*colour plates 18 & 19*). This was a highly strategic area for the Corieltauvi, controlling, as it did, routes north into the territory of the Parisi and the Brigantes, a tribe the Corieltauvi had quite possibly clashed with before. It is also an area that shows a heavy concentration of buckles and belt fittings from the late Roman period, some of them even coming from the same sites as the early Germanic metalwork. Hibaldstow and Kirmington, for instance, have both produced late Roman buckles.[26]

The Winchester group of early Germanic brooches is curious. Unlike with the other concentrations, there is little cemetery evidence to clarify and explain their presence. However, Winchester, as the capital of the *civitas* of the Belgae which was probably torn apart by civil conflict in the fourth century, would be an obvious place to locate some Anglo-Saxon military assistance. It is also an interesting echo of the presence in Lankhills cemetery of probably foreign soldiers from the late fourth century. Certainly the presence of the Winchester group so far inland and so far from other groups, confirms that the arrival of the earliest Anglo-Saxons should not be seen in terms of seaborne raiders simply settling in the most convenient places.

Moving into the second half of the fifth century, when the Anglo-Saxon cemeteries start appearing to close the Catuvellaunian ring to the south of London, there is evidence of Anglo-Saxons appearing in more tribal border areas. To the south, the Anglo-Saxons appear in the territory of the Cantii, the Regni and the Atrebates, which is where we once again come to Gildas and the *Anglo-Saxon Chronicle*. In Victorian days, it was thought that the combination of details from Gildas, Bede and the *Anglo-Saxon Chronicle* gave us a clear, detailed account of the Anglo-Saxon arrival in this country. Now the situation is almost reversed, with all but possibly Gildas and his *superbus tyrannus* deemed to be virtually worthless. It may, however, as is the nature of these things, be time for a re-evaluation of the re-evaluation.

Let us start by saying what the section of the *Anglo-Saxon Chronicle* covering the fifth century and early sixth century is clearly not. It is clearly not the kind of contemporary account that the *Anglo-Saxon Chronicle* of the tenth century (despite being occasionally slanted by Wessex propaganda) is generally considered to be.

Yorke, Sims-Williams and Dumville among others have quite correctly highlighted a number of features of the early *Anglo-Saxon Chronicle* for the fifth and early sixth centuries which clearly contradict any idea that what we have here is any sort of eyewitness year-by-year record.[27] Some of these features, such as the apparent repetition of Cerdic's arrival in Wessex, probably represent some form of mistake. Others suggest a poetic filling-out of available information. In this category falls the introduction of characters who seem to owe their existence to clumsy attempts to explain place names. For instance, the *Anglo-Saxon Chronicle* entry for 501 states, 'This year Port and his two sons, Bieda and Mægla, came to Britain, with two ships, at a place called Portsmouth'. Sims-Williams has also drawn attention to the somewhat parallel chronological structures between the Kent and Wessex accounts where a landing occurs, the kingdom is established five or six years later, then there are a few battles and an heir succeeds about 40 years later.[28] This too might represent the arrangement in a poetic framework of available material. Many modern scholars have taken these anomalies (some with apparent relief) as indications that the *Anglo-Saxon Chronicle* account of fifth and early sixth-century Britain is of too late an origin to be relevant and can be safely ignored entirely. Attention in this respect has been drawn to the work of David Henige which suggests that oral tradition cannot accurately reflect events more than 200 years previously.[29]

However, such a wholesale rejection of the *Anglo-Saxon Chronicle* may in itself be as unwise as a wholesale acceptance. For a start, with some of the central accusations against the *Chronicle* there are mitigating circumstances. In the instance of fictitious characters derived from place names, it is noticeable that this does not apply to any of the major characters. Then there is the claim that the Wessex and Kent *Chronicle* accounts are unlikely both to be true, because they mirror each other in terms of the number of years between events happening. Certainly I would not suggest that we take the exact dates quoted in the *Chronicle* too seriously (for instance, as Dumville has pointed out, there are slight discrepancies between the length of reigns suggested in the *Anglo-Saxon Chronicle* and those in the king lists for Wessex[30]). The chroniclers must have been relying on an oral tradition and if one thinks of one's own life, it is often easy to remember major events many years ago quite clearly, but precise timing and sometimes even the sequence can get slightly confused. It may well be that poets, or the *Chronicle* compilers, slotted different stories into similar chronological frameworks. However, it does not seem warranted to use such similarities to reject the entire narratives, which have fundamental differences. Most obviously, unlike in the Kent story, Cerdic is not said to have been invited in by Britons.

Equally, there are reasons to question the relevance of the claim that the *Chronicle* cannot be relied upon because oral traditions cannot retain detail accurately over more than 200 years. For a start, Gildas, writing maybe less than 100 years after the event, does include the apparent core of the Hengest and Horsa story, with the *superbus tyrannus* (possibly a translation of the British name Vortigern) inviting Saxons to fight for him on the east side of the island, only to see them rebel. In addition, there are good reasons to believe that Gildas may even then have been relying on an Anglo-Saxon account of the events. Using an Anglo-Saxon word, he mentions that the Anglo-Saxons arrived in three *cyuls* (ships) and states that one of the Saxons had forecast they would hold the island for 300 years, both comments which look as if they would have come from an Anglo-Saxon version of the story. In other words, the core of the Kentish foundation story may well have been in existence and (considering Gildas was a British monk in the west of Britain) widely known, less than 100 years after the events, conceivably, if you think of a grandparent talking to grandchild, almost within living memory. This core, of course, may not have consisted of much more than something like one of the Welsh triads, thought by some to have originated as memory aids to assist oral poets in their composition. A typical Welsh example from the *Red Book of Hergest* is:

> Three handsome princes of the island of Britain: Owain son of Urien, Rhun son of Maelgwn, radiant Rhufawn, son of Dewrarth Wledig.

In this way, the Sussex story could have been as concise as 'Ælle's three battles, Andredslea, Mearcredesburnansted and Andredesceaster'. It is perfectly conceivable that such limited and condensed information could have survived intact and accurately remembered for later inclusion in the *Anglo-Saxon Chronicle*.

Archaeology also offers some reasons for thinking that the core of the *Chronicle*'s foundation stories are worth considering seriously. For instance, there is the way in which the *Anglo-Saxon Chronicle* version corresponds with the archaeological evidence. It lists Kent, Sussex and Wessex as three of the areas of early major Anglo-Saxon settlement, and this seems to be perfectly correct. Much more significantly, there are grounds for considering whether the *Anglo-Saxon Chronicle* may get the geography right on a much more detailed level as well.

If the *Chronicle's* account was simply fictitious, one might logically expect fairly linear accounts of the founding figures of Kent, Sussex and Wessex fighting their way into the areas of their future domains from the coast and then establishing their kingdoms. Instead, the narratives are rather more complex, with the battles that can be traced often located in peripheral zones and/or far inland. When linked to archaeological evidence which, as in Catuvellaunian territory, suggests early Anglo-Saxon settlement in Sussex and Wessex near the borders of *civitates*, this raises the possibility of early Anglo-Saxon combat in Wessex and Sussex not being focused inward towards the heart of the respective kingdoms, but outwards towards other *civitates*. We know from Gildas that some of the earliest Anglo-Saxon settlers had *foederatus* status and it seems likely that so did the earliest settlers in Catuvellaunian territory. The possible fit between *Chronicle* evidence and archaeological evidence may suggest a similar scenario applying to Kent, Sussex and Wessex.

On balance, therefore, it seems quite likely that the *Anglo-Saxon Chronicle* accounts of the foundation of the three kingdoms do contain a significant element of truth. It would be simple to reject the *Anglo-Saxon Chronicle* wholesale, but when so little historical information is available for this period, it seems unwise to do the easy thing, rather than attempt to use what is available with due and proper caution. After all, nobody suggests total rejection of Gildas just because he says Hadrian's Wall was built at the end of the Roman period. In light of all this, it is worth re-exploring the specific *Anglo-Saxon Chronicle* accounts in detail and seeing how they appear when compared to both the archaeological evidence and our reconstruction of tribal politics in pre-Roman, Roman-period and post-Roman Britain.

KENT

In the case of Kent (assuming the Gildas reference should be linked to the *Anglo-Saxon Chronicle* account) the Anglo-Saxons are said by Gildas to have been invited in to fight 'the northern nations', by which it is generally assumed he means the Picts whom he mentions somewhat earlier in his diatribe. This is interesting on two accounts. Firstly, because it continues the tradition that raiders from the north were the main threat to Britain south of Hadrian's Wall in the fourth and early fifth century, and secondly because it lacks a certain plausibility. If you are going to fight Picts, Kent is not the obvious place to do it from. An alternative suggestion would be that the Anglo-Saxons were invited into Kent to protect it from enemies rather closer to home, 'a northern nation' in a rather more localised sense, perhaps the Catuvellauni and their Anglo-Saxon allies sitting to the north and west of Kent. This would fit with the locations of two of Hengest's four battles that can reasonably be identified (Crayford and Aylesford).[31] After all, even if Anglo-Saxons were the new masters in Kent, they would still have the neighbours to deal with. West Kent may have been a battleground for the Catuvellauni and other competing tribal factions in the pre-Roman period and the probably post-Roman linear defence of Faesten Ditch, only about four miles from Crayford, suggests that there was post-Roman conflict in the area exactly where the *Anglo-Saxon Chronicle* places it. The archaeology of early Anglo-Saxon settlement in Kent also tends to support the idea of a frontier in this area. In the late fifth century there is a cluster of cemeteries around Canterbury. Moving further west however, there is then a gap until one comes to the Anglo-Saxon cemeteries, probably those of Catuvellaunian *foederati*, lying to the south of London. This gap is only filled in the sixth century.[32]

It has been claimed that Hengest and Horsa cannot be real, since their names are both a variant on horse and it is argued that instead they must represent archetypal mythical founding twins. This is possible. The Kent royal genealogy does go back to Woden, and another figure in the Kent *Anglo-Saxon Chronicle* story and genealogy, Oisc or Esc, has a name that could be derived from an Anglo-Saxon word for god (though it could also be an abbreviation of a name like Oswine, Osbert etc). Equally, however, it is possible that Horsa, who disappears from the story early on, was mythically added to a real Hengest (a figure called Hengest, for instance, makes a solo appearance in the Finnsburh episode in Beowulf). Alternatively, it is possible that both Hengest and Horsa were real or at least had real counterparts with other names. After all, power politics both in pre-Roman and post-Roman Britain was very much a family matter, with brothers often cooperating (as well as often opposing each other) and the Anglo-Saxon tendency for family members to have alliterative names is well attested. It might be that Hengest and Horsa were bynames or nicknames, animal terms being a common source of such names down the ages.

Certainly, the basic *Anglo-Saxon Chronicle* outline of Hengest and Horsa's claimed actions in Kent (a rebellion, followed by four battles) is hardly the stuff great mythology is made of. Moreover, they are very consistent with the kind of actions claimed for Ælle in Sussex and Cerdic in Wessex, where there is no suggestion of these being divine characters in human disguise. Elements that appear in the *Historia Brittonum*, such as the marriage of Vortigern and Hengest's daughter Rowena and the massacre of British leaders at a feast after a sudden drawing of daggers, by contrast, do have much more of a mythical feel about them. It is, however, perfectly feasible to see these as a later poetic gloss on a basically factual story that need not invalidate the core events. Just as Welsh poets wove mythical stories around the historical fact that Magnus Maximus took an army to Europe to try to seize power there,[33] so they and their Anglo-Saxon counterparts may well have done the same with Hengest and Horsa.

The idea of a force of Anglo-Saxons arriving (at least initially) in cooperation with the local Britons, rather than as a straightforward invading force, is also supported by evidence of significant continuity between the *civitas* of the Cantii and the Anglo-Saxon Kingdom of Kent. The name of the kingdom remained the same, and the capital of the *civitas* of the Cantii, Canterbury, seems to have remained a major centre throughout the period. There is evidence for a continued British presence in Canterbury in the fifth and sixth centuries, with a (probably) fifth-century British family burial being found at Stour Street, and some evidence for the survival of a church there in this period. In addition, unlike in many other Roman-period cities, there is evidence of early Anglo-Saxon settlement inside Canterbury itself, with sunken featured buildings dating to the fifth and sixth centuries found in a number of places.[34]

This sense of Cantii and Germanic newcomers living side by side and cooperating is reinforced by the evidence of the so-called Quoit Brooches.[35] These are intricately decorated brooches apparently dating from the fifth century and originating in Kent. As discussed in the last chapter, there are good reasons for also linking some of the buckles associated stylistically with these brooches to mainstream late Roman and British buckle design. However, there are design elements on some of the Quoit Brooches themselves which seem to incorporate Germanic elements. The repeated friezes of crouching animals that appear on a number of the pieces[36] (while they may ultimately derive from the pair of crouching lions found on

80   Repeated animal frieze on Quoit Brooch Style object from Kingsworthy, which seems to show Germanic as well as British stylistic influence

some late Roman belt fittings) seem closest to parallel animal friezes on Germanic metalwork, for instance on some equal-arm brooches (*80*).[37] The relief modelling on items such as the Howletts Quoit Brooch[38] is also much closer to Anglo-Saxon chip carving than to anything characteristically British like the incised designs on Dobunnic buckles. Again, the round human faces with round eyes that feature on a number of the pieces[39] have close links to Anglo-Saxon metalwork (for instance, the well-known button brooches, *colour plate 21*).

It is, of course, impossible to say that a series of stylistically mixed artefacts indicates an ethnically mixed population. Matters of taste are often dictated by more than mere ethnicity. Just as the ethnically non-Roman Britons across central, southern and eastern England widely adopted Roman culture, so it is likely that Britons under new Germanic leadership would adopt some elements of Germanic style. Nevertheless, the best guess one can make from the mixture of Quoit Brooch Styles in the case of Kent is that it represents social and ethnic mixing as well.

SUSSEX

In Sussex, apart from an initial fight upon landing (which seems implausible for reasons we will return to) all Ælle's actions as listed by the *Chronicle* can be located on the borders of the *civitas* of the Regni. This is in line with the archaeological evidence which suggests that the earliest Anglo-Saxon settlement took place almost entirely in the far east of the *civitas*, in a narrow strip between the Rivers Ouse and Cuckmere. In his first battle, Ælle is said to pursue Britons into the wood of Andredslea. Andredeslea is assumed to be the Andredesweald, or The Weald. Unfortunately this does not tie the action down much, since the term was used in Anglo-Saxon times for an area stretching from Hampshire, through Sussex to Kent. The borders of the *civitas* of the Regni, however, certainly touched the Andredesweald in a number of areas, for instance in the east, and may even have followed most of it. Andredesceaster, or Pevensey, is listed as the site of his second battle (*81*). The evidence for the tribal control of the area around and east of Pevensey in pre-Roman and Roman times is not entirely clear. A small number of Atrebatic coins have been found in the area. However, the distribution of pre-Roman pottery types used in Atrebatic areas does not extend as far east as Pevensey and Cunliffe suggests that generally the pre-Roman ceramic tradition of parts of East Sussex has more in common with Kent.[40] The Roman road network in the area to the east of Pevensey also links to towns in Kent rather than to West Sussex. In other words, probably at Andredesceaster (and quite possibly at Andredeslea too) Ælle is conducting

81 Pevensey Castle. Situated in the region of the border between the *civitates* of the Regni and the Cantii, and site of one of the battles attributed to Ælle by the *Anglo-Saxon Chronicle*

his operations near a border with a neighbouring tribal area, or neighbouring Anglo-Saxon kingdom. The evidence for the later border of the Anglo-Saxon Kingdoms of Kent and Sussex in this area suggests a rather fluid situation which would sit well with it being disputed territory. A charter of Offa, for instance, granting land at Icklesham, well within East Sussex today and only about 15 miles from Pevensey, refers to the '*cantwara mearc*'. Equally, details of a ninth-century estate at Burmarsh in Kent refer to '*suthsaxa land*'.[41]

Mearcredesburnansted, the site of another of Ælle's battles is unlocated, but the element '*mearc*' again suggests that this battle should be located on a border. If Ælle is concentrating on fighting Britons on the borders of the *civitas* rather than in its heart, it suggests either that (despite the *Chronicle*'s account of him 'fighting his way off the beachhead') Ælle was initially invited in by the British authorities in control of the *civitas* of the Regni, or that he rapidly pulled off a coup d'état, taking over the running of the Regni state from the top. The former is probably more likely, since Ælle's landing place, Cymenshore, is placed near Selsey by a tenth-century charter[42] (admittedly an Anglo-Saxon forgery of the time, but while this may invalidate the legal claim of the charter, it need not invalidate the basic geography). Archaeology shows no Anglo-Saxon settlement in this area until well after the alleged date of Ælle's arrival, so if the landing at Cymenshore did happen, the most likely scenario would be Anglo-Saxon mercenaries coming ashore near the pre-Roman and Roman-period capital of the area before being despatched eastwards to guard the *civitas* boundaries. In this scenario, the *Chronicle*'s account of Ælle fighting his way off the beachhead would be a later interpretation of events, designed to show Ælle as a conquering invader rather than a hired sword.

Certainly, there are interesting signs of cooperation between early Anglo-Saxon settlers in Sussex and the existing British community. The early Anglo-Saxon cemetery and settlement at Highdown Hill is in the immediate vicinity of a late Roman villa and a group of probably post-Roman barrow burials. One barrow contained three west–east burials with hands folded on pelvis, in a way found in British post-Roman cemeteries in the west of Britain.[43] Equally, at Beddingham Villa near the eastern borders of the Regni and the Kingdom of Sussex, the excavator believed that Roman and early Anglo-Saxon pottery were both in use at the same time.[44] At Thundersbarrow, Old Shoreham, early Anglo-Saxon cremations including late Roman pottery are found near a Roman-period British settlement, where occupation probably continued up until at least the fifth century. While at Rookery Hill, Bishopstone, some of the many inhumations of late fifth- to sixth-century date buried in a crouched position north–south, are thought perhaps to represent some form of British cultural continuity.[45]

WESSEX

Finally, we come to Wessex. The archaeology here makes it clear that if Cerdic did land in this area around the beginning of the sixth century, then he was certainly not the first Anglo-Saxon to do so. We have already noted the presence of early Anglo-Saxon metalwork at Winchester. Equally, there were Anglo-Saxons living around the Salisbury area decades before Cerdic and, again, the archaeological evidence suggests, already cooperating in some way with the local Britons.

As Draper has emphasised in his recent study, the fifth and sixth centuries in eastern Wiltshire seem to show a blending of British and Anglo-Saxon culture rather than a straightforward replacement of British culture by a Germanic one. At Ashton Keynes, Avebury, Highworth, Liddington and Swindon, early Anglo-Saxon settlements are found in close proximity to (and sometimes actually on

82   The hillfort at Old Sarum, Salisbury. According to the *Anglo-Saxon Chronicle*, the site of one of Cynric's battles, it is in an area of early Anglo-Saxon settlement and is also close to the border with the Durotriges

top of) Roman-period British settlements. (The phenomenon of early Anglo-Saxon settlements appearing in very close proximity to British settlements of the Roman period is one we will come back to time and time again. It is uncertain to what extent it represents new Anglo-Saxon arrivals settling into an already existing system of land division and to what extent it represents Britons with a new Anglo-Saxon culture moving accommodation out of a decaying old settlement onto a new greenfield site. It may very well, of course, be a mixture of the two. In any event, it represents some form of continuity.) It is also now becoming clear that organic-tempered pottery of the period which appears on Anglo-Saxon settlements and in Anglo-Saxon burials in this area, and used to be thought to signify an exclusively Anglo-Saxon presence, is also to be found in association with a significant number of British settlements of the Roman period. At Coomb Down, in Enford Parish, for instance, a sunken-featured building was found associated with organic-tempered pottery and Roman artefacts on the outskirts of a significant Roman-period British settlement.[46] Having said that, the *Chronicle* account is, apart from the replication of Cerdic's arrival, similar in strategic outline to events in Kent and Sussex. Cerdic's fighting and that of his successor Cynric, where it can be located, is done on the borders of Atrebatic territory rather than in its heart. Thus, there are battles at Netley/Charford, Old Sarum and (if the usual identification of Beranbyrig is correct) Barbury Castle (*82*). It is true that an element of suspicion may hang over the appearance of Cerdicesora, Cerdicesford and Cerdicesley in the *Chronicle* account, but there is a familiar geographical logic to those battles that can be located and there is certainly no particular reason to question the idea that Cynric might have been fighting near Old Sarum or Barbury Castle.

As explored in the previous chapter, both the Durotriges and Dobunni would be likely enemies for any Anglo-Saxon fighting on behalf of an Atrebatic state, or on behalf of an Anglo-Saxon successor to an Atrebatic state. Bokerley Dyke suggests some kind of hostility between the Durotriges and the Atrebates or their successors in the post-Roman period, and it is likely that the Dobunni and the Atrebates were involved in fighting over the dismantling of the *civitas* of the Belgae. Eagles has already raised the possible strategic significance of the early Anglo-Saxon settlements near Salisbury, suggesting that they might be a garrison, settled by Atrebatic authorities, to act as a buffer against the Durotriges and the Dobunni.[47]

The Battle of Guoloph is also probably worth a very quick mention at this point. There is a statement in the *Historia Brittonum* that:

> From the reign of Vortigern to the conflict between Vitalinus and Ambrosius are twelve years, that is Guoloppum, the Battle of Guoloph.
>
> *Historia Brittonum 66*

The *Historia Brittonum* is hardly the most reliable of sources and, as mentioned earlier, does incorporate what is clearly much poetic and fictitious material. However, the sheer baldness of the statement (there is no explanation, for instance, of who Vitalinus was or what the conflict was about) does imply that, at the very least, there was a much fuller account than that offered by the *Historia* in existence at some previous stage. Working from the chronology given, the date of the supposed battle would be something like 437, and one of the most likely locations is one of the villages still called Wallop (the English equivalent of Guoloph) which are near the great hillfort at Danebury in Hampshire. This would place a battle between Britons only about 11 miles from the fighting mentioned by the *Anglo-Saxon Chronicle* at Old Sarum and just a little further from the Battle of Cerdicesford/Charford. Interestingly, three of the four Dobunnic belt fittings found inside Atrebatic territory (see Chapter 6) are also grouped in this area, with one from Nether Wallop itself, another from Houghton Down, just a few miles away, and a third at Popham, about 12 miles away. In isolation, the evidence of the *Historia Brittonum* on Guoloph might be regarded as of very little value. However, in the light of the overall picture of possible conflict in this area in the late and post-Roman period, it is at least mildly interesting.

It has been argued that the story of Cerdic's battles is later Wessex propaganda designed to reinforce Wessex's claim to a Jutish area in Hampshire and the Isle of

Wight.[48] Certainly the entry for 534, where Cerdic and Cynric are said to have given the Isle of Wight to Stuff and Wihtgar, may fall into this category, but if the chronicler was trying the same for the mainland it is hard to see why he located Cerdic's battles right on the western edge of this area (or in the instance of Old Sarum, actually outside it) rather than in the centre, at Winchester maybe, or Southampton. Alternatively, why did he not make some bold simple statement, as with the Isle of Wight, like 'Cerdic gave territory on the mainland to the Jutes'?

Interestingly, of course, Cerdic is itself probably a British name (a fact which incidentally supports its historicity – an Anglo-Saxon scribe writing in ninth-century Wessex is hardly likely to have created a British name for the founder of the Wessex dynasty). Cerdic's name is not the only British name in the Wessex king list either. As late as the seventh century, a king of Wessex had the very British and very un-Anglo-Saxon name of Cædwalla. This suggests a strong element of cooperation between elements of the local British aristocracy and the incoming Anglo-Saxons. Perhaps Cerdic should be seen as a product of a probably mixed British and Anglo-Saxon society that had, by the early sixth century, developed along the western borders of Atrebatic territory. If he did land on the British coast with a group of Anglo-Saxons (rather than this being a later interpretation by one of the compilers of the *Chronicle*) he may have had to cross the Channel to fetch them in the first place.

Any attempt to rehabilitate the fifth- and sixth-century foundation accounts of the *Anglo-Saxon Chronicle* is bound to be highly controversial, but I hope that this exercise has shown that taking the core details of the stories and setting them in the context of both the archaeology and the previous tribal history of the relevant areas can produce abbreviated narratives that are both feasible and logical. That does not, of course, mean that they are true but it means that, at least, they might be true.

At this point, it is worth briefly mentioning another aspect of fifth-century metalwork in Britain. In Chapter 6 we explored the spread across the country of buckles derived from late Roman dolphin designs. In the later fourth century another type of zoomorphic buckle appeared widely across parts of the Roman Empire on the continent. These buckles feature animal heads which may be derived from late Roman *draco* standards and it seems reasonable, therefore, to refer to them as dragon buckles.[49] Such dragon buckles, however, do not seem to have become popular with Britons. It may be that by the time the dragon buckle style appeared in Britain, the dolphin buckle style had already taken such a grip that it could not be shifted. Maybe, with the direction of flow of Roman troops in the late fourth century being

83 Fixed-plate dragon buckle from Britain. As opposed to the situation with dolphin buckles, there is little difference between these buckles on either side of the Channel suggesting the British examples are more likely to be imports

more out of, than into, the country, Britons were never exposed to the style in sufficient depth to adopt it. Whatever the reasons, dragon buckles are only found in small quantities in Britain and, where they are found, they are usually almost identical to examples from the continent, suggesting that British dragon buckles may be almost all imports rather than of local manufacture. On the continent, the dragon buckle style continued into the first half of the fifth century. The main distinguishing feature of fifth-century dragon buckles was their fixed, often slightly trapezoid, buckle plate, rather than the rectangular, hinged version seen on fourth-century examples (*83*).[50] These fifth-century dragon buckles, where they are found in Britain, are again, stylistically, very close to continental examples, suggesting again that they are imports. However,

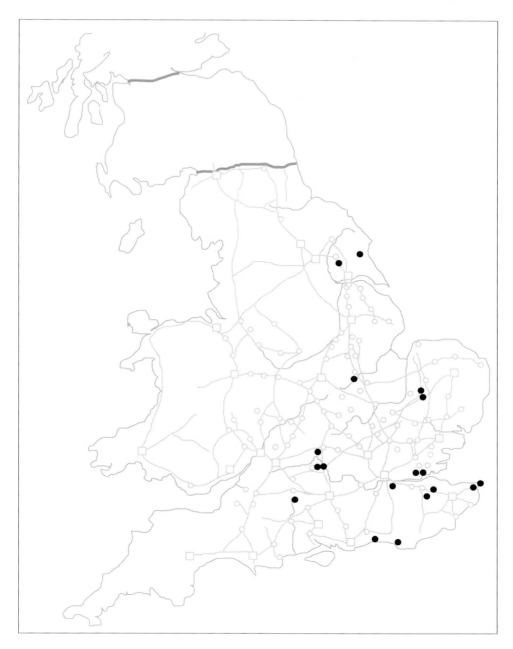

84 Distribution of fifth-century fixed-plate dragon buckles and associated strap ends in Britain. Their distribution has close parallels with that of the earliest Anglo-Saxon settlements and suggests links, direct or indirect, with the Roman military prior to the new immigrants' arrival in Britain. See Notes for more information[51]

fifth-century dragon buckles and their associated belt fittings are not found in large quantities in Britain either. Since many probably date from after the end of Roman rule here, this is hardly surprising. What is particularly interesting about fixed-plate dragon buckles in Britain, though, is their distribution (*84*). They appear in many of the areas of earliest Anglo-Saxon settlement and in very few other places. This distribution, with the addition of the date evidence and the indications that they are imports, suggests that the buckles and belt fittings may have accompanied the earliest Anglo-Saxon settlers when they arrived in Britain. In other words, it seems likely that a number of the earliest Anglo-Saxon settlers did not arrive here, direct from their homelands with absolutely no prior experience of Rome and the Roman military, because they were already wearing Roman military kit. This does not, of course, indicate that they had fought for the Romans, but it is another indication that their arrival should be seen in the context of Roman military tradition. They might not have been actual *feoderati* before they arrived in Britain, but there again, they may have been. They appear at any rate to have had some form of contact, direct or indirect, with the Roman military.

Certainly when all the evidence of archaeology, geography, Gildas and the *Anglo-Saxon Chronicle* is taken into account, it can be suggested that, as with the arrival of the Romans in Britain, maybe the arrival of the Anglo-Saxons should be seen as an event in many ways dictated by the dynamics of British tribal politics. That being so, it is now time to examine in detail how the British tribes of central and eastern Britain became the Anglo-Saxon kingdoms of England.

CHAPTER 8

The First of the English

Dark has done much valuable work on the west of England and Wales analysing how the tribes and *civitates* became the post-Roman kingdoms, often, in the process, showing a large degree of continuity. There is even a degree of name continuity. Thus the territory of the Dumnonii becomes the Kingdom of Dumnonia and there is epigraphic evidence in a sixth-century inscription from Devon showing the name Dobunni surviving into the sixth century.[1] The first element of the name of the Durotriges survives in the Anglo-Saxon name for their core area, Durosæte/Dorset, and in Wales, a Class I inscribed stone at Penbryn in Cardiganshire records a man named Corbalengus as an *Ordous*, an Ordovician.[2]

However, even where the name of the entity has changed, Dark has identified a strong degree of territorial continuity. We have already mentioned how Dark has located post-Roman Durotrigan and Dobunnic entities on either side of Wansdyke. To the south of Wansdyke is an area which saw the reuse of hillforts and the appearance of imported fifth- and sixth-century Mediterranean pottery. To the north is an area where neither of these factors applies, but instead grass-tempered pottery is found when it is largely absent to the south. In Wales, the Kingdom of Brycheiniog seems to have originated in post-Roman times, on land at the edges of the tribal territories of the Demetae, Ordovices and Silures, but apart from this, the Roman intervention in Britain appears to have left the tribal geography of Wales and the West relatively unchanged. Dark argues convincingly that the tribal area of the Demetae becomes Dyfed (with Ceredigion eventually splitting from it), that the Ordovician territory is renamed eventually as Gwynedd, that the Cornovii are reborn as Powys, and that the territory of the Silures is split in two, to become in the west, the territory known as Glywysing and, in the east, Gwent (named after Venta Silurum, the former capital of the *civitas* of the Silures).[3] This feature of *civitates* splitting in two is an interesting one and one that we shall return to on a number of occasions when considering the fate of the eastern *civitates*. British tribes were probably often composed of separate constituent parts, in a manner parallel to the Scottish septs system. This separate identity within a tribe could have been developed and harnessed by the development of separate market centres during the Roman period.

The Corieltauvi are a possible example of this, with major Roman period centres at both Leicester in the south and Lincoln to the north. There is evidence of pre-Roman settlement at both sites, and the appearance of more than one name on Corieltauvian coins at the same time may suggest joint rulers in separate parts of the tribal territory. Similarly, in Dobunnic territory, there may be evidence in pre-Roman times of a separate identity to the southern part, with different styles of pottery and some evidence, at some points, of different coinage circulating in the different areas. The coins of Bodvoc, for instance, do not seem to circulate in this lower region. It is probably no accident that the Romans chose to include this part of Dobunnic territory into the *civitas* of the Belgae, and it is this part of the Dobunnic territory that seems to have been lost to the Durotriges in post-Roman times with the construction of Wansdyke on its northern border.

Since Dark's analysis of the transition from Roman-period *civitas* to post-Roman British kingdom in the west is convincing, the key question now becomes, how did the end of Roman power affect the political and ethnic landscape of central and eastern Britain?

> So vengeance's fire, justly sparked by earlier crimes, burned from coast to coast, fanned by the hands of our enemies in the east. It did not stop, until, after ravaging neighbouring towns and territories, it came to the far side of this island and dipped its wild and crimson tongue in the western sea.
>
> Gildas, *On the Ruin of Britain* 24

> So some of those left in this misery were captured in the mountains and slaughtered en masse. Others, driven by starvation, surrendered themselves to the enemy and lifelong servitude, taking the risk of instant execution, which truly would have been their best bet. Others crossed the seas, weeping loudly…
>
> Gildas, *On the Ruin of Britain* 25

Gildas gives such vivid descriptions of destruction and murder by Anglo-Saxon invaders, accompanied by pitiable accounts of British refugees fleeing abroad, that in Victorian times it was taken for granted that the Anglo-Saxons had largely erased any British ethnic, and definitely political, legacy in central and eastern Britain.

It is true that the origins of the British/Breton identity in Brittany do appear to date from this time and there seems no reason to doubt that a significant number of Britons did become either internally or externally displaced, fleeing from the Anglo-Saxons (or, at least, culturally Anglo-Saxon forces). However, Gildas was probably writing in the west, possibly in Durotrigan territory, sometime in the early to mid sixth century, and it is hard to know how much his vivid descriptions represent conditions across Britain and across the period 425-550 as a whole, and how much it reflects his or his sources' local experience of warfare. It was commonplace, for instance, during the 1990s for writers to describe Bosnia as totally ravaged by war, yet in reality there were, throughout the war, large parts that were physically untouched by shell or bullet (though still, of course, affected by the more general results of the war, such as the collapse of the economy). Equally, one could enter a village that had been described as 'shelled to pieces' only to find that, yes, it had been shelled, but most of the buildings were, while scarred, still substantially intact and many were not even touched. It has been the same situation in Iraq recently. Despite the widespread chaos, there have been large areas, for instance in the Kurdish north, relatively unaffected by the fighting (apart from, again, in terms of the more general issues).

Recently, those who believe that Anglo-Saxon immigration must have been large-scale have concentrated on the dominance of the English language in England. They point to the very small number of British words surviving in English and the lack of evidence of British influence on English speech patterns.[4] This is indeed striking, but it still need not necessarily imply large-scale Anglo-Saxon immigration. Supporters of the idea that the dominance of English must indicate large-scale Anglo-Saxon replacement of Britons in England point across the Channel to France where, by contrast, incoming Germanic dynasties eventually adopted the language of their local Gallic subjects rather than vice versa. This is a fair comment, except that the local language in question was derived from the Latin of the Roman conquerors of Gaul, not from the original Celtic languages of Gaul. Nobody is suggesting large-scale Roman ethnic replacement of Gauls, so this is a stark illustration that language replacement need not mean ethnic replacement. The example of Gaul may also shed light on why Celtic languages have left so little trace in England and English. As we have seen, Britain during the Roman period was sharply divided into a culturally Romanised centre, east and south, and a culturally un-Romanised west and north. We do not know what language was being spoken in the Romanised parts of Britain at the end of the fourth century, but, on the evidence of Gaul, it may well have been some form of Latin. If Anglo-Saxon replaced Latin, rather than a Celtic language, it would explain the lack of Celtic influences on speech patterns in English. In this scenario, why Anglo-Saxon replaced Latin, but took much longer to replace the Celtic languages spoken in the west of Britain, is a different point. It is presumably linked to earlier Anglo-Saxon control in the east and perhaps a loss of cultural self-confidence when Romanised Britons were separated from Rome in the early fifth century. With Roman authority increasingly weak and increasingly distant, Latin was no longer the language of power and aspiration.

In recent times, there has begun to be a widespread acceptance that whatever did happen in the centre and east of Britain in the fifth and sixth centuries, it did not result in the complete annihilation of the British there. The new source of evidence, as far as British and English identity goes, is genetic-based research. This has already produced some fascinating insights into the history of these islands and, undoubtedly, as techniques are refined and developed, it will reveal many more. Unfortunately, finding a definitive answer to the question, 'How much of the British population in central and southern Britain was replaced by Anglo-Saxon immigration?', may be beyond current genetic research and may always remain so. For a start, current estimates, depending on the approach taken, seem to vary widely between the belief that the Anglo-Saxon immigration was very limited,[5] to the view of other researchers who claim that more than half the British population was replaced.[6] Even some of the high-end estimates of Anglo-Saxon immigration, though, still suggest that a substantial number of Britons remained in the centre and east of Britain.[7]

In addition, while genetic research can demonstrate links between modern day people living in England and modern-day people living in Holland, northern Germany and southern Scandinavia, what it cannot do so easily or accurately is reveal when these links were established. The period of the Anglo-Saxon immigration is, of course, one point at which these links may have developed. However, there is also the later Viking immigration to contend with. In areas of heavy Viking settlement, such as the North and East Anglia, it becomes very hard to tell when the genetic material from across the North Sea arrived. At least with the Vikings, though, it is feasible to localise the areas that saw Viking settlement. More problematic still in isolating information about Anglo-Saxon genes is the high likelihood of genetic sharing across the Channel and North Sea in pre-Roman and prehistoric times. The possibility of Belgic immigration as claimed by Caesar, presumably to southern England (in other words those areas where the genetic picture is not already blurred by Viking immigration), has already been discussed in Chapter 1. The Belgae seem to have been, at least in some sense, a Germanic tribe who lived near the North Sea coast.[8] Therefore they presumably shared at least some genetic characteristics with the Anglo-Saxons and Danish Vikings.

More problematic still, in terms of attempting genetically to define the extent of Anglo-Saxon immigration, is the possibility of genetic links in prehistoric times. Initially, there is the possibility that both central and eastern Britain were colonised in post-glacial times by people genetically similar to those colonising the North Sea coast region in mainland Europe at a similar time. Then there is the possibility of immigration from the continental North Sea coast region into Britain in the thousands of years before historical evidence for Britain. Some researchers looking at this question have estimated that the close genetic links between England and the Anglo-Saxon homelands are more likely to have been formed at least 5000 years ago, rather than 1500 years ago.[9] For all these reasons, it may, at the very least, be a long time until genetic science can give precise and uncontroversial answers about the origins of the Anglo-Saxon political landscape in central and eastern Britain and its ethnic construction. However, using the more traditional methods of analysing cultural identities as expressed in artefacts and burial rites, and by drawing on our analysis of the tribes in pre-Roman and Roman times, we may still be able to develop a reasonably revealing portrait of the period. The great unknown with this method, is, of course, the extent to which British people may have started using Anglo-Saxon artefacts and rites in the post-Roman period. After all, Britons had extensively adopted Roman culture during the Roman period and even, often, adopted Roman names. In archaeological terms they appear Roman. Obviously, this was in the context of massive political influence, of a sort which would not have been a factor in the early years of Anglo-Saxon settlement. However, equally, there were issues involved in the fifth century, that were not present earlier and that increase the probability of adoption by Britons of a foreign culture.

As we saw in Chapter 6, much commerce in late Roman Britain may have become concentrated in large industries, exporting long distances. Such industries would have replaced much local small-scale craft production. The potteries are the classic example, where a large number of local industries were widely replaced by a much smaller number of big industries. The sudden demise of these large-scale industries, however, in the chaos at the end of the fourth century and beginning of the fifth would have left Britons lacking access to certain basic craft skills. An influx of newcomers with these skills from territory that had never seen large-scale commercial production could have received a ready welcome from the Britons.

On a broader scale too, one should perhaps think of cultural demoralisation in Britain at the beginning of the fifth century, as touched upon in our earlier discussion of the adoption of the Anglo-Saxon language. Rome, which had played such a massive part in dictating British cultural trends during the occupation and which for centuries had been the epitome of power and wealth, had suddenly left Britain. In this context, Roman culture in Britain could quickly have lost much of its attraction and direction, and there is comparatively little evidence of Britons in the east and south of the island managing to create their own independent post-Roman cultural identity. In this situation, a new, self-confident culture imported by Anglo-Saxon warriors, coming to assist, might have been welcomed to fill the cultural gap. There is, again, an interesting potential parallel from Bosnia. During the war, small numbers of Islamic fighters from Middle-Eastern countries travelled to Bosnia to fight for the Sarajevo government. The Mujahideen were generally welcomed because they came enthusiastic to fight, many with fresh experience of war from places like Afghanistan. However, they also brought with them an Islamic culture very different from the mainly secular attitudes of Bosnian Muslims. Sometimes this caused tension, but it also led to a certain Islamicisation of some areas where the Mujahideen were based. The process stopped abruptly when many of the Mujahideen were pushed out of Bosnia after the Dayton Peace Agreement, but the potential parallel of a demoralised local culture absorbing cultural elements from foreign fighters come to help, is an interesting one.

A further factor worth bearing in mind when considering the possible adoption by Britons of Anglo-Saxon culture, is some of the similarities between Anglo-Saxon and British culture. Early Anglo-Saxon pottery, while very different from the wares in use in Roman-period Britain, is similar on a basic level to some pre-Roman British pottery. Equally, many Anglo-Saxon brooches probably ultimately derive from Roman originals (with cruciform brooches, for instance, being descended from crossbow brooches[10]). Again, while there may seem to be a huge difference between the standard of accommodation available in some of the large villas of the Roman period and that available in early Anglo-Saxon dwellings, it needs to be remembered that most Britons throughout the Roman period lived in much more modest accommodation than the big villas. Plus, as discussed in Chapter 6, by the time of the arrival of the Anglo-Saxons, many of the villas and towns were probably little more than shelters for refugees, featuring widespread use of simple, small structures.

In addition (though it is not clear to what extent Christianity may have survived in early, pagan Anglo-Saxon kingdoms) there were strong similarities between the British pagan pantheon of the Roman period and that of the Anglo-Saxons. Clearly much of Britain was, on some level, Christianised by the end of the fourth century, but continuation of some pagan temples up to at least the 390s[11] indicates significant possible pagan survival too. It would not be hard to imagine British pagans adapting their religion to that of the Anglo-Saxons, just as they had adapted pre-Roman British religion to integrate with Roman religion. Take, for instance, our days of the week. In Britain, the days mostly incorporate the names of Germanic pagan gods, while across the Channel in France for instance, the names of days, inherited from the Romans, still mainly feature the names of Roman gods. However, it is notable that the Germanic gods

85 Fragment of early Anglo-Saxon pottery showing sun face. In English, the old Roman '*dies solis*' becomes Sunday, suggesting how easy it might have been for any British pagans to adapt their beliefs to Anglo-Saxon paganism

of the relevant days often have very similar attributes to those of the Roman gods. Thus Monday, the day of the Moon, is in France *Lundi*, the day of Luna. Tuesday, the day of Tiu, Anglo-Saxon god of war, is in France *Mardi*, the day of Mars. Thursday, the day of the thunder god Thor, is in France, *Jeudi*, the Day of Jupiter the Thunderer. Friday, the day of either Frig or Freya (depending on your point of view), the Anglo-Saxon goddess of married women or of love and beauty, is in France *Vendredi*, the day of Venus. With Saturday, the original Roman god was not even replaced. The old Roman '*dies solis*', the day of the sun (renamed in France, *dies Domini*, *Dimanche*, in the Christian period) becomes simply Sunday in English (*85*).

As mentioned in the last chapter, and as we will explore further in this one, there is increasing evidence of Britons continuing to live in the centre and east of Britain after the arrival of the Anglo-Saxons.[12] In that context, there seems no particular reason to doubt that a significant number of those using 'Anglo-Saxon' artefacts in the fifth and sixth centuries and employing 'Anglo-Saxon' customs must have been British just as most of the people using Roman artefacts and Roman customs during the Roman period had been. The increasing number of burials which seem to mix Anglo-Saxon artefacts with Roman-period customs suggest as much. Thus, for example, at Great Chesterford a young girl, wearing a single penannular brooch at the shoulder in British fashion was also buried with an Anglian girdle-hanger.[13] At Apple Down, Compton, a number of burials featuring Anglo-Saxon grave goods, also feature Roman coins, unpierced and apparently left as obols in Roman fashion. Similarly, at Barton Court Farm, among a group of apparently Anglo-Saxon inhumations, one man was buried with a Roman coin in his mouth.[14] Nevertheless the spread of Anglo-Saxon customs and artefacts can still be effectively used to chart the spread of Anglo-Saxon cultural influence and, at least help clarify the corresponding development of Anglo-Saxon political involvement in Britain. Interestingly enough, when this is done, the picture ultimately created may well have much more in common with Dark's portrait of contemporary western Britain than previously thought.

One of the major existing theories of Anglo-Saxon kingdom development is based on a document known as the Tribal Hidage. This is, in origin, probably a seventh- or eighth-century document, giving rough values for the size and economic importance of the various regions of England. The Tribal Hidage features all of the major Anglo-Saxon kingdoms of England of the period (*86*). Among the names of these kingdoms, though, a significant number of much smaller units are also mentioned. While the larger kingdoms have values measured in tens of thousands of hides, these smaller units are usually measured in just hundreds. It has been argued that these much smaller entities represent the first stage of Anglo-Saxon kingdom development. In other words, at some stage after the Anglo-Saxon immigration, central and eastern Britain found itself divided into a large number of small districts in the region of 300–600 hides each. Some of the units mentioned in the Tribal Hidage seem to have names linked to individuals, for instance the Færpinga ('Færpa's people') or the Spalda (assumed to be identifiable with present-day Spalding, 'the people of Spalda'). The argument runs, therefore, that these original fragments, possibly based on small family units, later coalesced into medium-sized units and finally into the largest units, the Anglo-Saxon kingdoms themselves.[15] In many ways, it is a process analogous to that by which the original British tribes must have formed in pre-Roman times.

There are, however, a number of problems with applying this scenario to the creation of the Anglo-Saxon kingdoms. A comparatively minor one, first, is that where the smaller units in the Tribal Hidage can be located, many of them seem to be just in one area, around the Chilterns and slightly further north, suggesting that these small political/economic entities may be more a specific feature of this

86   Early Anglo-Saxon political geography

region than a general one. This is an interesting factor that we will return to later.

Probably much more of a problem is the timescales involved. The Anglo-Saxon kingdoms are widely accepted to have existed much in the form represented in the Tribal Hidage by around the end of the sixth century at the very latest, and some, like Kent, almost certainly existed much earlier. This only gives around 150 years at most, to move from tiny, perhaps family-based groups to kingdoms, which, considering the amount of warfare almost certainly involved in forming so many disparate groups into large, hierarchical structures, seems far too short. It is, for instance, worth bearing in mind at this point, the at least 200-300 years of hard fighting that it took for the different Anglo-Saxon kingdoms of the Tribal Hidage to coalesce into a united kingdom of England. However, the most damaging fact for the 'small units coalescing into big units' theory of Anglo-Saxon kingdom formation is the geography.

By following the development of the tribes from pre-Roman times, through the Roman period and into the post-Roman years, we can now understand tribal geography much more clearly. When we look at the early Anglo-Saxon kingdoms in the light of all that evidence, it becomes clear that there is, in most cases, a marked similarity between the boundaries of the Anglo-Saxon kingdoms of central and eastern Britain and the pre-existing tribal and *civitas* boundaries in those areas. It is hard to see how such a widespread similarity could have come about through a process where the *civitates* of central and eastern Britain were fragmented into small family units and then the Anglo-Saxon kingdoms formed from them. It would be almost like taking a completed jigsaw, breaking it up into pieces, throwing the pieces up in the air and watching the jigsaw land again, miraculously, in its completed form.

It seems much more likely that the similar geography of the *civitates* and the early Anglo-Saxon kingdoms derives from a widespread taking over by new Anglo-Saxon authorities of existing British political entities, either by coups d'état, as probably in Kent, or by a process based on cooperation with elements of the existing British aristocracy, as perhaps in Wessex, rather than straightforward invasion and conquest. Such territorial and political continuity has already been suggested in a number of cases.[16] However, in light of what we have seen about how the tribes developed in pre-Roman and Roman times, it now seems possible to take a step further. Let's see if the main Anglo-Saxon kingdoms represent simply a new version of the existing tribal territories, just as in the west the British post-Roman kingdoms represented the new face of the tribes there.

There are interesting signs of a similar survival of tribal entities within a new Germanic culture across the Channel in former Gaul. Here, while many of the Roman names for *civitas* capitals were lost, their ethnic identities were often clearly retained, with the cities simply being referred to by the name of the tribe. Thus, for example, we have Paris from the Parisi, Soissons from the Suessiones, Trier from the Treveri, and Vannes from the Veneti. It is interesting to note, as an illustration of how long-lasting some tribal identities were, that even some of the earliest known tribal names from Gaul (which as discussed in Chapter 1 may have been in existence by the fifth century BC[17]) survive in this way. Thus, Bourges comes from the Bituriges, Sens comes from the Senones and Le Mans probably from the Cenomani. In Gaul, the tribes did not reassert their political independence because of the rapid transfer from Roman political control to control by new, large, Germanic kingdoms created by large, cohesive, Germanic immigrant ethnic groups. Instead, tribal identity seems often to have survived in some sense through the method of ecclesiastical administration. A study, for example, has indicated that the boundaries of the *civitas Atrebatum* in northern Gaul were probably almost identical with those of the medieval diocese of Arras.[18] In central and eastern Britain, by contrast, the tribes may have survived just as completely but were able to reassert themselves politically as well, though with new Anglo-Saxon identities.

This is not to suggest that significant numbers of Anglo-Saxons did not cross the North Sea and Channel in the post-Roman period. Significant numbers probably did arrive in Britain at this time, though we may never know exactly how many is meant by significant in this context or, for that matter, when they arrived in the 100 years between around 420 and 520 (the settlers in the earlier decades may well have only represented a small proportion of the final number). What seems equally likely, however, is that significant numbers of Britons may have remained in the centre and east of Britain and helped create the Anglo-Saxon kingdoms in the place of the British *civitates*, adopting Anglo-Saxon culture and becoming, in terms of the archaeological record, Anglo-Saxon (just as they had previously adopted Roman culture and become, archaeologically, Roman). In the same way as the tribes survived the arrival of the Romans as Roman-style *civitates*, so they may have survived the arrival of the Anglo-Saxons as Anglo-Saxon-style kingdoms, and the tribal battles for supremacy, partly suspended under Roman rule, may have resumed with full vigour.

THE KINGDOM OF KENT

As discussed in the previous chapter, the most logical scenario for the emergence of the Anglo-Saxon Kingdom of Kent is a coup d'état some time in the mid fifth century, either by Hengest and Horsa, or by similar but now nameless figures. This would conform to the evidence of Gildas and his *foederati* rebelling on the 'east side of the island' and the later appearance of the story in the *Anglo-Saxon Chronicle*. In whatever way Anglo-Saxon control originated though, there has long been a measure of acceptance that the Anglo-Saxon Kingdom of Kent should in many ways be seen as a successor to the *civitas* of the Cantii, rather than as a new creation.[19] As mentioned in the previous chapter, the name Kent itself is a survival of the name of the Cantii, and the capital of the *civitas* of the Cantii, Durovernum, survives as the capital of the Kingdom of Kent (in the form of Canterbury, the *burg* of the men of Kent). It is even arguable that there is continuous occupation at Canterbury from the Roman period into the Anglo-Saxon period. Clearly, this was not occupation comparable to that at the height of the Roman period (with timber-framed buildings almost blocking streets at the Marlowe site some time after 388 in a manner reminiscent of slums, and a possible family burial being dug into a probable temple precinct in Stour Street[20]). Nonetheless, it does suggest a strong degree of continuity from the Cantii to Kent.

Mention has also already been made of Quoit Brooches, a number of which seem to show an amalgam of Germanic style with British style, and it is probably best to see the Cantii as being early adopters of new Germanic styles imported from the continent by the *foederati*, just as they had been early adopters of continental styles in the pre-Roman period. Kent is, of course, one of the areas that Bede asserts was settled by Jutes. Archaeology has indeed demonstrated a connection between Kent and Jutland in the form of bracteates found in both areas,[21] though this evidence does not seem to stretch back as far as the middle of the fifth century. It is possible, therefore, that a takeover by rebelling *foederati* was followed by another takeover by incoming Jutes.[22]

There is also, however, extensive evidence of Frankish influence on Kent, including, for instance, the naming of one of its early kings Irmenric (Irmen being a common Frankish name element), the marriage of King Æthelbert to a Frankish princess, and the appearance in the area of rich garnet and glass inserts on jewellery. There are even suggestions that at one stage political power extended across the Channel,[23] and it may be that kings of the Franks exercised some kind of authority over Kent. Such cross-Channel authority would echo that suggested by Caesar in pre-Roman times. It is quite interesting to note that it was the Suessiones who were suggested by Caesar to have exerted cross-Channel authority and that that the post-Roman city continuing their name, Soissons, was one of the two major royal Frankish centres at the time of their possible overlordship of Kent. In other senses too, politically, the history of the Anglo-Saxon Kingdom of Kent looks very much like a continuation of the pre-Roman history of the Cantii. A major concern was probable disputes over the territory of West Kent with neighbouring rivals. We have already mentioned a possible Catuvellaunian-sponsored presence south of London in post-Roman times (which would reflect Catuvellaunian expansion in this area in pre-Roman times) and the possibility of the battles listed in the Hengest and Horsa story in some way relating to conflict with Catuvellaunian power.

In pre-Roman times, the Atrebates were also political players in this area, with, for instance, the Atrebatic ruler Eppillus at one stage issuing coins in Kent. It seems likely that, in post-Roman times too, Anglo-Saxons from the area of the Atrebatic *civitates* again clashed with the political entity based on East Kent. We have already mentioned possible conflict between Ælle and Kent in the south around Pevensey and Kentish interest in the area is demonstrated by the finding of a number of pieces of Quoit Brooch-Style metalwork within the territory of the Kingdom of Sussex. The earliest reference to Kent in the *Anglo-Saxon Chronicle*, after the fifth century, is an entry for 568 which records Ceawlin and Cutha of Wessex defeating Æthelbert of Kent at Wibbandun. Unless this is Wimbledon (as once thought, though it now seems unlikely) the clash is unlocatable. However, the geographical logic is that it is likely to have taken place somewhere in the Surrey region. It is a story we will return to later from the Wessex point of view.

West Kent's separate status (probably already evident in the pre-Roman and Roman periods as discussed in Chapter 1) seems to have continued to be recognised well after the initial Anglo-Saxon arrival. In the first half of the seventh century when other Anglo-Saxon kingdoms had only one diocese each, Kent already had a second diocese (in addition to that of Canterbury) based at Rochester. It has also been demonstrated that in the seventh and eighth centuries, Kent often had two joint rulers, with some of these rulers having authority only in West Kent. Even more significantly, a number of the rulers of West Kent seem to have come from the Kingdom of Essex across the Thames to the north,[24] thus, perhaps, replicating control of this area by the Catuvellaunian/Trinovantian confederation in pre-Roman times.

For a time, in the late fifth and early sixth century under Æthelbert, Kent became a major player on the Anglo-Saxon political scene, even at one stage expanding its authority north of the Thames to include London (perhaps echoing Ptolemy's claim that London was originally a city of the Cantii). However, ultimately, just as the tribal territory of the Cantii seems, in the late first century BC and the first century AD, to have become a battleground between the Atrebates from south of the Thames and the Catuvellauni from north of the Thames, with both entities intermittently controlling Kent (possibly occasionally interrupted by brief periods of independence), so the Anglo-Saxon Kingdom of Kent ultimately became a battleground between

Wessex from south of the Thames and Mercia from north of the Thames, with control by Wessex alternating with control by Mercia, and occasional brief periods of Kentish independence.

THE KINGDOM OF THE SOUTH SAXONS

The Anglo-Saxon Kingdom of Sussex occupied most of the territory of the *civitas* of the Regni. Certainly its extent along the southern coast is likely to have been the same in its early years. In the west, by the sixth century, it probably terminated near the Solent (the granting of the Meonware by Mercia to Sussex in the seventh century implies it did not control it before) and in the east it may have terminated near Pevensey. As we have seen, this is also likely to have been the eastern border of the Regni. The Kingdom of Sussex may not have extended much north of the historic county of Sussex,[25] but then, as discussed in the previous chapter, the same may well also have been true of the *civitas* of the Regni. In his book on the Regni, for instance, Cunliffe takes the approach that the northern border of the territory of the Regni was roughly similar to that of the county of Sussex.[26]

As mentioned in the previous chapter, early Anglo-Saxon settlement takes place almost exclusively in the east of the *civitas* of the Regni/Kingdom of Sussex, with the area around the capital of the Regni, Chichester, initially without any Anglo-Saxon presence. It has been suggested that this may represent a British enclave briefly holding out against Anglo-Saxon expansion from the areas of earliest settlement to the east. However, as mentioned in the previous chapter, there is archaeological evidence of cooperation between the earliest Anglo-Saxon settlers in Sussex and the Regni, and Ælle's locatable battles, apart from the probably fictitious 'fighting his way off the beach' scenario, are all compatible with the earliest Anglo-Saxon settlers arriving in Sussex to work within the framework of the *civitas* of the Regni rather than to break it up.

The *civitas* of the Regni was probably Atrebatic and to the immediate west of Chichester lay other Atrebatic areas. By contrast, to the east of the *civitas* of the Regni lay the Cantii, with whom the Atrebates may have had occasional disputes. In this context, it would make strategic sense for any Anglo-Saxon mercenaries to be located in the east of the *civitas*, not in the area around Chichester. As with Canterbury, there is evidence that occupation in and around Chichester survived well into the fifth century. A supposedly 'late Roman' cemetery outside Chichester's Eastgate contains pottery associated with post-Roman occupation at Chilgrove Villa and it is likely that the cemetery too dates to the second quarter of the fifth century or later.[27] As in Canterbury, again, the type of developments possibly to be associated with refugee occupation appear, with hearths and wattle partitions being built over the floors of Roman-period town houses.

In addition, even though the earliest Anglo-Saxon settlement may well have been to the east, Chichester seems, in some sense, to have retained its position as the political centre of the area. By the sixth century there is evidence of Anglo-Saxon influence on the region, with archaeological evidence of a mingling of British and Anglo-Saxon traditions. In the Anglo-Saxon cemetery at Apple Down, Compton, are also found a series of inhumation burials which may well be of Britons.[28] By the second half of the seventh century at the latest, the South Saxon kings were ruling from sites in the region of Selsey, the location of the pre-Roman capital of the area, and nearby Chichester, the Roman-period capital.[29] One thing that did, of course, change with this political entity, unlike with Kent, is the name of the area. By the end of the fifth century and beginning of the sixth, this was no longer the territory of the Atrebates or of the Regni, it was the Kingdom of the South Saxons. This, however, of course, does not mean that all the people living in the territory were genetically Saxon, any more than does the adoption of Saxon brooches and other elements of Saxon culture across the area. Just as the arrival of Commius and other Atrebates in the area probably prompted a change of name without any sign of mass displacement of the original population, so quite probably did the arrival of the Saxons.

At an early period Sussex may have been a significant power, with Bede describing Ælle as the first *Bretwalda*, a title linked to an Anglo-Saxon king pre-eminent in his era. However, it seems to have rapidly lost importance. The *Anglo-Saxon Chronicle*'s next mention of Sussex is in 607 when Ceolwulf of Wessex is found fighting against the South Saxons. Sussex had its own kings at least as late as the eighth or ninth century, but one of their main tasks seems to have been struggling to retain their independence against Wessex, their neighbour to the west. In terms of the pre-Roman and Roman-period political geography of Britain, this would hardly be surprising. Wessex was based on the core of the pre-Roman Atrebatic tribal territory and the *civitas* of the Regni was also, in some sense, Atrebatic tribal territory. Perhaps the eventual absorption of Sussex by Wessex should be seen as re-establishing a pre-Roman unity.

THE KINGDOM OF THE WEST SAXONS

Myres suggested years ago that Wessex should be seen, in some sense, as a successor to the tribal territory of the Atrebates.[30] However, this is an aspect of Wessex that has received little attention in recent years, with instead much closer scrutiny being focused on the possibility of an early Jutish kingdom in the area.[31] There seems little reason to doubt that there were Jutes in the region of Hampshire. Archaeologically there is comparatively little specific evidence for them but there are a number of place names linking the area to Jutes (Ytene Forest, Yting Stoc, Ytedene) plus there is Bede's specific statement about a Jutish population in the region.

Significantly, however, while there is evidence of a Jutish kingdom on the Isle of Wight (and additional proof in the form of Kentish brooches, of contact with the, at least in some sense, Jutish Kingdom of Kent) there is no explicit evidence that the Jutes on the mainland opposite ever constituted a kingdom in their own right (as opposed to just inhabiting a territory). No historical source lists Jutish kings of the area and as we have seen with the Catuvellauni, early Anglo-Saxon settlement need not imply early Anglo-Saxon political control.

In addition, there is the Wessex foundation story in the *Anglo-Saxon Chronicle*. As mentioned in the previous chapter, it has been suggested that the *Anglo-Saxon Chronicle* account of the founding of Wessex represents ninth-century propaganda to help establish an early claim by a Wessex royal house springing (as some assert) from the early Anglo-Saxon settlements in the Upper Thames region, to the territory of the Jutes in Hampshire. However, it is hard to see why, if the locations of Cerdic's battles were chosen to establish a claim over Jutish territory, they should all be located on the edges of the Jutish area (and in the instance of Old Sarum, outside it) rather than right in the middle of it.

Equally, there are a number of reasons to doubt the claim that the Upper Thames was the cradle of Wessex. The only potential evidence linking the origins of the royal line of Wessex to the Upper Thames is the location at Dorchester on Thames of the first base of the diocese of the Gewissae, an early name for the inhabitants of Wessex. It is true that the Anglo-Saxon settlements in the Upper Thames would have been in place in time for the founding of Wessex, but so would the Anglo-Saxon settlements around Salisbury which is an area much more consistent with the *Anglo-Saxon Chronicle* account. In addition the diocese at Dorchester on Thames is not established until 635, and its location there need not necessarily say anything about political geography over 100 years earlier. What is more, the base of the diocese only stayed at Dorchester for about 25 years, before being moved south to Winchester, former Atrebatic capital of the *civitas* of the Belgae in about 660.[32] As discussed in the previous chapter, it seems to make more sense to see the area around Salisbury as the probable cradle of the Kingdom of Wessex (*87, 88*). This is consistent with both the archaeology and with the *Anglo-Saxon Chronicle*'s reference to Cerdic and Cynric's early battles being close to this area.

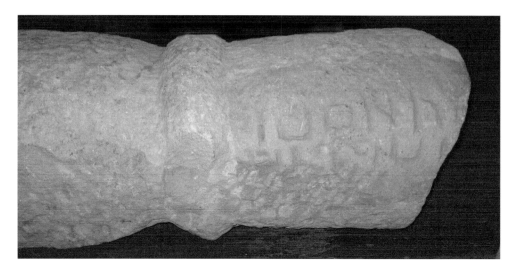

87   British inscription at Wareham of post-Roman date illustrating British culture prior to the expansion westwards of Anglo-Saxon culture and identity

If the core of the *Anglo-Saxon Chronicle* foundation story of Wessex is true, the creation of Wessex should probably be seen very much in terms of a continuity of British politics. As mentioned, Cerdic is a British name, his locatable battles are all on the western border of Atrebatic tribal territory, and archaeology in the area suggests cooperation between the Atrebates and the earliest Anglo-Saxon settlers, with Eagles already suggesting that the settlement around Salisbury might be seen as a settlement specifically created to defend Atrebatic areas from the Durotriges and the Dobunni to the west.[33] It is perfectly feasible that the Jutes in Hampshire were also there at the invitation of local Atrebatic authorities.

As discussed in Chapter 6, the discovery of no less than three early fifth-century supporting arm brooches (a type hardly found in other areas of Jutish settlement such as Kent and the Isle of Wight) in the Winchester area suggests that prior to the Jutes, there may have already been other Germanic *foederati* and settlers based in the ethnically Atrebatic capital of the *civitas* of the Belgae.[34] There is some archaeological evidence in the region to suggest cooperation between the local Britons and subsequent Germanic newcomers too. At both the post-Roman settlements at Chalton in Hampshire and at Cowdery's Down near Basingstoke, rectangular structures have been found which may represent a combination of British and Anglo-Saxon traditions.[35] At Horndean, Hampshire, it is claimed that there is definite continuity of burial from the pre-Roman period, through the Roman period and into the Anglo-Saxon period. While in the late fifth-/sixth-century cemetery at Mount Pleasant, Alton, an elderly

88   The Anglo-Saxon St Martin's Church at Wareham, of eleventh-century date, illustrating the expansion westwards of Anglo-Saxon culture and identity

woman aged 60-80 years was found buried with a necklace of Roman-period British beads, two perforated Roman coins and a Roman-period British brooch on each shoulder.[36] Bearing in mind the date of the cemetery and the age of the woman, it is even possible that she owned these items before the arrival of the Jutes in the area and was buried with the items long after their arrival.

In fact, if one looks at the area probably covered by fifth-century Jutish settlement[37] and adds the area probably covered by other fifth-century Anglo-Saxon settlement in the region, then what we arguably have is the Atrebatic half of the *civitas* of the Belgae, with Jutes occupying the centre of the area and an additional Anglo-Saxon presence on its western borders. As discussed in Chapter 6, there are reasonable grounds for supposing the *civitas* of the Belgae to have been the site of extensive tribal conflict in the fourth and early fifth centuries, and it would not, therefore, be a surprise to find the area heavily populated with *foederati*.

This sense of continuity between the *civitas* of the Belgae and the Kingdom of Wessex is strengthened by the re-emergence of two Atrebatic centres in the *civitas* of the Belgae, Salisbury (in the form of nearby Wilton) and Winchester, as major royal centres in the Kingdom of Wessex. Unlike Kent and Sussex, of course, Wessex does not slip from prominence in the historical sources after an initial phase – quite the contrary, in fact, as the various sources chart the rise and eventual victory of Wessex in the competition between the kingdoms for power in England. However, as with Cerdic and Cynric's actions before the battle at Old Sarum, events after Old Sarum are perhaps just as easily understood in terms of the strategic priorities of the British tribes, as they are in terms of the Anglo-Saxon kingdoms. There is the added bonus, of course, in this case that with events in the later sixth century, as opposed to the earlier part, we are getting increasingly close to the date when Anglo-Saxon monks are likely to have started recording contemporary historical events and, therefore, we can have more confidence in the pattern of events described.

In 556 Cynric and Ceawlin fought the British at Beranbyrg. If, as is widely supposed, this is to be identified with the hillfort of Barbury Castle, then it suggests the prototype Kingdom of Wessex, possible successor to an Atrebatic entity, turning against the Dobunni, who as we have seen, may have clashed with the Atrebates in the late fourth century. Certainly by 577 Ceawlin and Cuthwin are confronting elements from the Dobunnic heartland, fighting forces from Gloucester, Cirencester and Bath, at the Battle of Deorham, probably to be identified with the modern village of Dyrham near Bath. However, this is not the only direction of expansion by Wessex. We discussed in Chapter 2 the probable battle for supremacy in pre-Roman times between the Atrebates and the Catuvellauni. It is unclear where all the flashpoints at that stage may have been, though the area of the Upper Thames is a likely one. In pre-Roman times the conflict ended in defeat for the southern kingdom, the Atrebates. This time around, in the post-Roman era, the confrontation went rather differently. As mentioned previously, in the *Anglo-Saxon Chronicle* entry for 571, one Cuthwulf (assumed from the similarity of his name to that of Cutha and Cuthwin, to be a member of the Wessex dynasty) is said to have taken Benson, Eynsham, Aylesbury and Limbury from the Britons at the Battle of Bedcanford. Since all four places are taken after one battle, it is a reasonable assumption to make that these all represented part of the same British political entity at the time and, if so, that entity must have been Catuvellaunian in nature, since they all lie well within what was Catuvellaunian territory at the time of Tasciovanus. Ceawlin and Cutha then proceeded to fight Britons at the Battle of Fethanleag in 587. It is hard to know who the Britons involved were precisely. However, if the location has been correctly identified from a twelfth-century document, as at Stoke Lyne, near Bicester,[38] it could easily be seen as another stage in winding up Catuvellaunian power west of the Chilterns and solidifying Wessex's control of the Upper Thames region.

There is, however, one notable omission from this list of battles and fighting. No mention is made of the forces of Wessex fighting in the area around Silchester, the core of the *civitas* of the Atrebates and a major chunk of pre-Roman Atrebatic territory. There is also no sign of early Anglo-Saxon settlement in the area and it has been widely assumed that a British enclave survived here for some time.[39] However, as early as 568 Ceawlin and Cutha are said to clash with Æthelbert of Kent at the Battle of Wibbandun. There is no specific reason to assume that this should be equated with Wimbledon. However, it is difficult to see where such a clash could have taken place apart from somewhere in the historic county of Surrey and, this being the case, it is hard to think how Ceawlin and Cutha could have reached the battle except through the supposed British enclave around Silchester. The lack of any indication of Ceawlin and Cutha having to fight for access to this territory seems to suggest a political link between it and Wessex by the middle of the sixth century at the latest.

As mentioned earlier, there are what are probably post-Roman linear ditches defending Silchester. However, they face north (where the Roman road beyond them to Dorchester on Thames and Catuvellaunian territory went out of use) and west, towards Dobunnic territory.[40] Though admittedly at some stage the south-western gate was reduced to half its width, as was the western gate, there is noticeably no similar linear defence system to the south where the Jutes were settled. The implication seems to be that, in post-Roman times, the inhabitants of Silchester perceived their major threat as coming from areas other than those occupied by the Jutes to the south and the Anglo-Saxons to the south-west.

In light of all this it seems feasible at least to suggest that the area around Silchester was either from the start part of the same political entity as the developing Anglo-Saxon Kingdom of Wessex, or certainly became part of it shortly afterwards, in a largely peaceful fashion. It remains unclear why Silchester was eventually abandoned (there is no sign of violence) but perhaps the lure of alternative political centres within Wessex became too strong. Whatever the reason, probably by the middle of the sixth century at the latest, the Atrebatic half of the *civitas* of the Belgae had been reunited with the *civitas* of the Atrebates, and with the ultimate absorption of Sussex into Wessex, the entire pre-Roman Atrebatic tribal territory was reunited. In many ways, therefore, the view of Myres that the Anglo-Saxon Kingdom of Wessex should be seen as a continuation of an Atrebatic political entity seems justified.

As touched on in the instance of Kent, the rise of Wessex and its competition for power against the Kingdom of Mercia to the north in the seventh century and beyond also has strong echoes of the probable competition for power between the Atrebates and the Catuvellauni in the first centuries BC and AD. Though the southern player remains almost the same, the northern player is centred slightly further west (though, by that stage, incorporating a significant chunk of previously Catuvellaunian territory). Nevertheless the sense of continuity in the face-off between the southern kingdom and a kingdom to the north is strong. In pre-Roman times, the northern element seems to have won out. In post-Roman times, the southern contestant was ultimately to be victorious.

There is an interesting footnote where Wessex is concerned on the question of adoption of Saxon identity by Britons. The laws of Ine, king of Wessex, set different amounts of compensation for killing a Saxon or a Briton. Generally, the amount for a Briton is set at about half that of a Saxon. Some have suggested that this should be seen as a sign of an apartheid regime which, literally, thought a Saxon worth twice a Briton. If this was the case, however, it is hard to see how a seventh-century king of Wessex could have as distinctively a British name as Cædwalla. It is perhaps more likely that the Britons concerned were those in the newly conquered British territories to the west, like Dorset, who had yet to adopt Saxon customs and a Saxon identity. Certainly, by the time of the laws of Alfred, all such ethnic/cultural distinctions had disappeared.

MIDDLE SAXONS, MIDDLE ANGLES, SURREY AND EAST SAXONS

The defining event of British history in the century before the Roman intervention must, as explored in Chapter 2, be the rise of Catuvellaunian power. By contrast, the defining event of British history in the 100 years after the Anglo-Saxon arrival seems to have been the collapse of Catuvellaunian power. Why this should be, is hard to decide. The scarcity of hoards from the Catuvellaunian and Trinovantian heartlands at the end of the Roman period suggest that, whatever border conflicts took place at that time, most Catuvellaunian territory was not in significant danger. In addition, if the opening movement of the Anglo-Saxon settlement was to ring the territory of the Catuvellaunian and Trinovantian federation with garrisons, then at that stage the Catuvellauni still appear to have been in a very strong position. Certainly, there is extensive evidence for post-Roman survival at Verulamium, the capital of the Catuvellauni, perhaps more extensive here than at any other Roman-period city in Britain. Frere identified a sequence of construction in *insula* XXVII which seems to end well into the fifth century, with a carefully dug trench holding a timber water pipe suggesting complex utilities still in use at a very late date. Nibblet has identified post-Roman occupation in timber buildings at a number of places in Verulamium. The shrine of St Alban at Verulamium seems to have survived the departure of Rome as well (*89*), with the *Life* of St Germanus recording a visit by the saint there in around 420. There is also even the possibility of continuation of villas in the region with, for instance, some indications of continued fifth-century occupation at Park Street.[41] In addition, as discussed in the previous chapter, there is significant evidence in some Catuvellaunian towns, such as Dorchester on Thames, of a flourishing British presence surviving alongside an Anglo-Saxon one well into the sixth century.

So what went wrong for the Catuvellauni? Why did their tribe not go from being one of the largest, most successful British tribes to being one of the largest, most successful Anglo-Saxon kingdoms? The answer may lie in pre-Roman history and the Tribal Hidage. The core of Catuvellaunian territory seems to have been in and to the south of the Chilterns. This is where Verulamium, the capital of the Catuvellauni, lay and where, in the pre-Roman period, continental styles such as cremation were adopted most vigorously. However, under Tasciovanus and Cunobelin, the Catuvellauni also seem to have had control of territory beyond the Chilterns, as far north as the Nene Valley. This part of Catuvellaunian territory incorporated what was to become the wealthy location of the Nene Valley pottery industries. As we have seen, it was one potential flashpoint at the end of the Roman period and probably saw the arrival under Catuvellaunian sponsorship of an Anglo-Saxon settlement/garrison in the early fifth century.

However, at some time between then and the date of the probably seventh- or eighth-century Tribal Hidage, the political geography of the region was transformed. As mentioned above, in the Tribal Hidage, alongside the large Anglo-Saxon kingdoms are also a significant number of small political units, of about 300-600 hides each. Some of these cannot be located but, of those that

89 From Roman Britain to Anglo-Saxon England. Looking through the Roman walls of Verulamium to the Abbey of St Albans on a hill outside the old Roman city

can be, almost all seem to be in roughly the region that would have constituted Catuvellaunian territory in the Chilterns and to the north of the Chilterns. Thus, for example, the Cilternsætna were obviously located in the Chilterns. The Hicca are probably to be associated with the area around Hitchin. The Gifla may be associated with the region around Sandy and the River Ivel. The North and South Gyrwe were located in the fenland area. The Spalda are probably to be associated with Spalding in the far south of Lincolnshire. The Witherigga are probably linked to Wittering etc.[42] One unit, the Færpinga, cannot be located but an annotation on the earliest manuscript of the Tribal Hidage indicates that the Færpinga were located in Middle Anglia which is roughly the same region. Dumville suggests that the Færpinga may have been based in the region of Charlbury in Oxfordshire.[43] As we will see, as we progress across the country, there is little evidence elsewhere of the *civitates* fragmenting into units as small as some of these. The Tribal Hidage, therefore, suggests a unique and catastrophic fragmentation of the northern half of Catuvellaunian territory at some stage in the centuries after 410.

To the south of the Chilterns it seems to have been a different story. A significant part of the core of Catuvellaunian territory there survived intact as the region of the Middle Saxons. It is unclear whether the Catuvellaunian capital of Verulamium/St Albans ever formed part of this territory. By the late seventh century it seems to have been part of Mercia. However, both Hemel, just to the west of St Albans, and Hatfield, just to the east, seem to have been part of the territory of the Middle Saxons,[44] so it may be that St Albans was originally part of the same territory and was annexed, with its famous shrine, by Mercia at a later date.

Whether the Middle Saxons ever represented a kingdom in their own right remains controversial. However, what seems highly significant, in light of the Catuvellaunian/Trinovantian confederation in pre-Roman and probably post-Roman times, is that Middlesex, at least until the eighth century, seems to have remained firmly linked to Essex. This was the Anglo-Saxon kingdom which was to take over almost all of the tribal territory of the Trinovantes and has indeed been suggested as a successor state to that of the Trinovantes by Bassett and others.[45] A number of charters of Offa, king of the East Saxons, confer land in the territory of the Middle Saxons, including in the area of Hemel in present-day Hertfordshire, as well as at Harrow and at Sunbury.[46] The fact that the Middle Saxons do not appear in the Tribal Hidage and the apparent discrepancy between the Tribal Hidage figure of 7000 hides for the East Saxons, compared with the Domesday Book figure of 2700 hides for Essex, also suggests that the Tribal Hidage classified the Middle Saxons as part of Essex.[47]

South of the Thames lay the Anglo-Saxon Kingdom or sub-kingdom of Surrey. As discussed in the previous chapter, this may represent Catuvellaunian territory south of the Thames, the southern *ge* or region of Catuvellaunian territory. Such a suggestion receives additional support from the fact that, like the region of the Middle Saxons, Surrey was, at least for a time, subject to the kings of Essex.[48] In addition, there is the occurrence here of an unusually high number of place names with British origins, for instance Chertsey, Caterham and Penge. Attention has been drawn to this unusual concentration before. It is unparalleled in eastern England and suggests particularly strong continuity with the area's British past.[49]

The probable unity of at least much of the territory of the Catuvellauni as late as 571 is suggested by the *Anglo-Saxon Chronicle* indicating that Benson, Eynsham, Aylesbury and Limbury (four settlements stretching across Catuvellaunian territory) were still under British control at this time but were all taken after a single battle. Support for this idea also comes from the appearance of British-style penannular brooches across much of the region in the fifth and sixth centuries, including those areas where there was extensive Anglo-Saxon settlement (*colour plate 23*).[50]

The Kingdom of the East Saxons seems, by the standards of Anglo-Saxon kingdoms, to have been a late creation. As discussed in the previous chapter, there is good evidence of a mingling of British and Anglo-Saxon culture around Colchester, suggesting a strong sense of continuity here between the Roman and Anglo-Saxon periods. Further inland, the same seems to have applied. In the inhumation/cremation cemetery at Great Chesterford, for instance, it has been suggested that the unaccompanied burials, particularly those with coffin nails, possible hob nails and the occasional Roman coin, represent British burials within an Anglo-Saxon cemetery. Equally, the Anglo-Saxon cemetery at Saffron Walden has produced many inhumations and Roman artefacts including Samian Ware and bracelets.[51] Dark, among others, has raised the possibility of a continuation, for a period, of British political control in Essex, and certainly the historical evidence and the list of Anglo-Saxon kings is consistent with a creation date for the Kingdom of the East Saxons some time in the second half of the sixth century. This is also a date that cannot be too far distant in time from 571.

As Iraq has shown most recently, the military defeat of a strong central power can often lead to the fragmentation of a political entity. Perhaps we should associate the fragmentation of Catuvellaunian territory in and north of the Chilterns as well as the disappearance of British power to the south of the Chilterns and in Essex, with the events of 571. It is notable that after his victory in 571, Cuthwulf is said to have died. It may, therefore, be that the victory by Wessex was sufficient to smash Catuvellaunian power, but the death of the victor may indicate why Wessex was not able to hold onto the area around and east of Ayelsbury. In the ensuing power vacuum, the core territories of the Catuvellunian/Trinovantian confederation south of the Chilterns changed identity to become the Anglo-Saxon Kingdom of Essex and its linked region of Middlesex. The areas in the Chilterns and beyond, though, having been less directly connected to the heart of Catuvellaunian power and more immediately affected by the incursion of 571, collapsed into small-scale political fragments. It may, thus, be that 571 should be seen as the death blow for the Catuvellaunian empire, a death blow administered by Wessex, the successor to the Atrebatic state that had been the loser against the spread of Catuvellaunian power in the pre-Roman period. There is, however, a further factor which may have helped guarantee the breakup of Catuvellaunian tribal territory, or at least helped ensure that, once it had broken up, the area never again became a political powerhouse.

The question of the extent to which ethnic makeup can be determined by the cultural affinity of artefacts and customs in a period of history as remote as the fifth century is, as already mentioned, a vexed one. However, just as

Bede indicated that there was a Jutish element in the settlement of Kent, so he defined two other differing cultural zones of immigration – one connected with the Angles from southern Denmark and another connected with the Saxons from northern Germany.

It is clear that, as with their genetic makeup, there was an element of cultural overlap between these two groups. However, Bede's comments do, in some sense, seem to reflect a genuine difference visible in English archaeology, with brooch types defined as Anglian appearing generally above a line along the Chilterns to Ipswich and brooch types defined as Saxon generally appearing below that line. There is again overlap, with some Saxon brooches appearing in the Anglian cultural zone and vice versa, and again it is not possible to say with definite certainty that a person buried with an Anglian brooch was Anglian rather than Saxon, or indeed, of course, British. Nevertheless, there is a broad sense of cultural difference between the areas indicated by Bede, one that may even have survived as late as the Viking period. It is noticeable, for instance, that the Scandinavian Vikings largely seem to have settled in areas where the culture was originally defined by the Angles, also from Scandinavia, and seem to have avoided (or been more strenuously prevented from) settling in areas where the culture was originally defined by the Saxons from northern Germany. The reason for this demarcation in the initial settlement is far from clear. It may reflect some chronological difference in settlement or perhaps an administrative one, with different British entities looking for assistance from different groups of Anglo-Saxons. It is interesting to note that in the instance mentioned in the previous chapter, where the Briton Gerontius used Germanic immigrants to attack Constantine III, who then responded by finding Germanic allies of his own, the two opposing leaders chose forces from different Germanic ethnic groups. Gerontius used warriors from the Suevi/Alans/Vandals group. Constantine III responded by approaching Franks and Alemanni. Obviously, it would make sense to avoid recruiting warriors from the same ethnic group as your enemy, and it is possible that something like that may have been happening in Britain.

However, one thing is certain – the Catuvellauni were the only one of the main eastern British tribes with a territory that straddled the eventual dividing line between Anglian and Saxon regions. This probably was not the case at the time in the early and mid fifth century when the Catuvellauni ringed their *civitas* with Germanic garrisons. The evidence at that stage suggests that even the garrisons in territory later to become culturally Anglian, may have been initially culturally Saxon (or at least mixed).[52] Nevertheless, with the development of a stronger Anglian cultural identity in East Anglia and Mercia to the north, Anglian culture seems to have become dominant in formerly Catuvellaunian territory to the north of the Chilterns. At some stage (whether as a cause or as a result) this cultural split was also displayed as a political one, with the territory to the south of the Chilterns looking to the Kingdom of the East Saxons and the territory to the north of the Chilterns looking either to Anglian Mercia or, along the eastern borders, to East Anglia. In pre-Roman terms, both developments make perfect sense, with Mercia reclaiming territory possibly taken by the Catuvellauni from the Corieltauvi and in the east, the East Angles probably reclaiming territory taken from the Iceni by the Catuvellauni.

Essex continued to have kings until the ninth century although it was under the control at times of either Mercia or Wessex. In the early years its capital may have been at Prittlewell, perhaps reflecting the origins of Anglo-Saxon settlement in Essex as a border guard along the Trinovantian coast. However, London and Colchester, the two main cities of the area in the Roman period, once again became major centres later in the Anglo-Saxon period. Any hope that St Albans may have had of reviving as a major political centre, though, was probably blighted by its position along the divide between culturally Anglian and culturally Saxon territory. In the late seventh and early eighth century there is what may in some sense be regarded as the last glimmer of the great empire of Tasciovanus and Cunobelin. For a time, Essex seems to have exerted some kind of authority in Kent, with kings ruling in Essex also ruling in West Kent, just as they had in the years before the Roman invasion.[53]

THE KINGDOM OF THE EAST ANGLES

The Anglo-Saxon Kingdom of East Anglia covered the territory that had once been the *civitas* of the Iceni. If there was, as suggested in Chapter 6, a confrontation line in north-west Norfolk, to the east of the Fens, it may not have stayed there very long. Anglo-Saxon influence appears in the area to the west of Spong Hill in the early sixth century and the region seems to have become fully incorporated into the Kingdom of the East Angles. On the Icknield Way, the border of the East Angles with the Catuvellauni seems to have stayed in roughly the same position as the border of the Iceni with the Catuvellauni. As mentioned previously, the linear earthworks cutting the Icknield Way near Cambridge include probably pre-Roman, late or post-Roman, and definitely Anglo-Saxon period examples (*90*).

As discussed above, though, the increasingly Anglian nature of the area, certainly to the east of Cambridge in the sixth and seventh centuries, does suggest that the Kingdom of the East Angles may have been nibbling away at Catuvellaunian and post-Catuvellaunian territory in this area, perhaps recovering ground lost by the Iceni to Tasciovanus and Cunobelin. Further south, the East Anglian border, probably reflected by later diocesan boundaries in the area, follows a line

90 Devil's Dyke near Cambridge, probably marking a new shift in the border between the Catuvellauni or their successors and the East Anglian successors to the Iceni

roughly similar to that of the Icenian *civitas*, meeting the sea probably just south of Ipswich.[54] Geographically, there are obvious reasons to see the Kingdom of the East Angles as a successor state to the Iceni and archaeology lends additional support to this view.

The point has already been made by other writers that in the area covered by the Kingdom of the East Angles, there is evidence of a strong correlation between the earliest Anglo-Saxon cemeteries and British sites of the Roman period. Spong Hill and Caistor by Norwich, the capital of the *civitas* of the Iceni, are the two most well-known examples where very early Anglo-Saxon cemeteries are located right next to major British sites of the Roman period, but in addition such a correlation is also evident at Burgh Castle, Stanton Chair, Great Thurlow, Brettenham, Bridgham, Thornham, and Caistor on Sea.[55]

Generally, there is a higher proportion of early Anglo-Saxon cremation graves in East Anglia than further south. On one level this could be seen as indicative of a strongly Anglian flavour to the culture. However, O'Brien suggests that to some extent the popularity of cremation in the area continues a late Roman tradition of cremation there. In addition, there is also evidence of continuing British practices within early 'Anglo-Saxon' cemeteries in the region. In the cremation cemetery at Spong Hill, for instance, there are a number of inhumation graves that may belong to Britons, while in the cemetery at Morning Thorpe, no fewer than nine penannular brooches have been found, at least three of which were being worn singly, in the traditional British way.[56]

In political terms, the course of possible continuity is slightly harder to track, though that does not mean it is not there. Though the area around Caistor by Norwich, or at least Norwich itself, would later regain its pre-eminence as a regional centre, the archaeological evidence suggests that the Roman-period capital of the Iceni itself was abandoned, at the latest, shortly after the initial Anglo-Saxon settlement there. The region around Spong Hill, however, seems to have retained its importance in the Kingdom of the East Angles, with nearby North Elmham being, for instance, the probable base of a diocese. Another area that retained its importance from pre-Roman and Roman times was the Thetford region. This had been the location of a significant Icenian site and in the Anglo-Saxon period Thetford was a major centre, becoming one of the largest towns in East Anglia. The main power base of the kingdom for the East Angles, however, was in the area around Ipswich, at Rendlesham. On some level this seems to show a lack of continuity with the Icenian past. However, two points can be made. Firstly, the dynasty ruling from here, the Wuffingas, may well not have been the first generation of Germanic rulers in the territory. The dynasty seems to have had much closer links with Sweden than any earlier rulers, suggesting, that as with Commius, a foreign dynasty may have taken power here in an existing territory in Britain. The great ship burials at Snape and Sutton Hoo, for instance, have parallels in central Sweden and on the west coast of Norway but are unparalleled in other regions of Britain (*91*). Similarly, O'Brien draws attention to the appearance at both Snape and Sutton Hoo of cremations deposited in bronze bowls, something which she also sees as a distinctively Scandinavian custom with parallels in western Norway.[57] Bede also indicates that the founder of the dynasty was Rædwald's grandfather Wuffa (from whom the dynasty was called the Wuffingas). Rædwald is known to have been active in the early seventh century, which cannot place Wuffa much before 550, at the earliest. Secondly the lack of continuity in this area is probably more apparent than real. Icenian material is found as far south as this, including an Icenian buckle of the late Roman period found at nearby Ufford, and a comparison of early Anglo-Saxon burials in the area with Icenian coins found there throws an interesting light on the question (*92*). There appears to be a distinct correlation in the two groupings suggesting a strong continuity of habitation in the region. In addition, the hillfort at nearby Burgh by Woodbridge may have been an important Icenian

91   The burial ground at Sutton Hoo

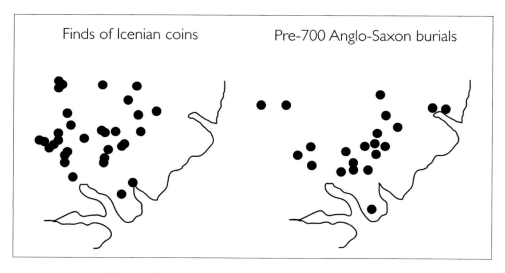

92   Comparison of the distribution of Icenian coin finds and Anglo-Saxon cemeteries and single burials pre-700 in the area around Rendlesham. *After Cunliffe and Campbell*

centre, before possibly being taken over by the Catuvellaunian/Trinovantian confederation (see Chapter 1).

The division of East Anglia into North Folk (Norfolk) and South Folk (Suffolk) probably does represent some sort of administrative division in the early Anglo-Saxon period, but the border area between the two counties may also have been comparatively lightly settled in pre-Roman and Roman times. The area remained largely lacking in settlement until towards the Late Iron Age[58] and, even then, the distribution of Icenian coins found in East Anglia shows something of a corridor running just north of the border in which few coins have been found.[59] This suggests that the division between North Folk and South Folk is either just a matter of geography or reflects existing divisions in pre-Roman and Roman times. Either way, it need not stand in the way of any argument for political continuity.

Historically, nothing is known of East Anglia's relations with neighbouring kingdoms before 600. It may be, though, that East Anglia expanded south at the expense of the Trinovantes/East Saxons. The southern border of the East Angles seems, away from the coast, generally to have been a little further south than that of the Iceni, particularly the line it took in the period of Cunobelin. Such expansion would not be surprising. We saw in Chapters 1 and 2 how Cunobelin probably pushed into Icenian territory in this area, and both the events of 60-61 and the period after 155 may have included Icenian pushes south against the Trinovantes. In addition, as discussed in Chapter 6, concentrations of fourth-century buckles, belt fittings and hoards along this border suggest tension in the area.

In the early part of the seventh century, the Kingdom of the East Angles rose to brief prominence under Rædwald, a king Bede marks out as notable by attributing the title of *Bretwalda* to him. In 616, Rædwald confronted Æthelfrith of Northumbria at the Battle of the River Idle and killed him. In 655, however, Bede records the death of King Æthelhere of the East Angles at the Battle of Winwæd against the Northumbrians. On this occasion, the East Angles were fighting alongside the Mercians. However, the alliance was not to last, with Mercia increasingly pushing down into East Anglian territory. In 794, for instance, Offa had the king of the East Angles killed and took direct control of the kingdom. It is possible that a confrontation between the East Angles and, first the Northumbrians and then, subsequently, the Mercians in disputed territory in the eastern Midlands and fenlands, should be seen as a continuation of tensions between the Iceni and the Corieltauvi over control of fenland salt-extraction areas. Like Mercia and Middle Anglia, East Anglia formed part of the Anglian cultural zone discussed above. Cultural contacts between the different political entities within this group seem to have remained fairly strong. However, as one might expect, there is also some sign of political separation reflected in slightly divergent cultural tendencies. There is, for instance, a marked difference between burial practices in Middle Anglia and East Anglia.[60]

THE KINGDOMS OF MERCIA AND LINDSEY

While, in many ways, Mercia is one of the most important Anglo-Saxon kingdoms, for instance coming close to winning the competition for ultimate supremacy among Anglo-Saxon kingdoms, its origins are also among the most obscure. The element Merc in Mercia refers to a border, so essentially the name Mercia means 'borderland'. The name first appears in the seventh century and there has been much academic dispute over which border is being referred to. Brooks and Stenton both suppose that the border in question is simply one between Anglo-Saxons and Britons. Hunter Blair, by contrast, believes that the border is that between the Northumbrians and Anglo-Saxons south of the Humber Estuary.[61] Both these suggestions, however, rely on the border in question being one primarily of importance to Anglo-Saxons, and, as we have already seen, there is plenty of reason to believe that the geography of the earliest Anglo-Saxon settlements was dictated by British priorities not Anglo-Saxon ones. In order to understand the origins of Mercia, therefore, we need to go back to the earliest Anglo-Saxon settlement in the East Midlands. In light of discussion about the possible use of *foederati* in strategic areas of tribal territories, the context of early Anglo-Saxon settlement in the area of Lindsey and Mercia is very interesting. For a start, there are strong indications of continuity from the Roman into the post-Roman period in the region. At Lincoln, for instance, a Roman-period church at St Paul in the Bail seems to have remained in continuous use until replaced by an Anglo-Saxon building in the early seventh century. In addition, Type G and Class 1 penannular brooches, both widely reckoned to be a sign of British cultural influence, are found here in some numbers.[62] A figure featuring in the list of 'Anglo-Saxon' kings of Lindsey has a British name, Cædbæd, suggesting a situation similar perhaps to that in Wessex, where the ruling dynasty probably originated in a fusion of British and Anglo-Saxon elements. Equally, Penda of Mercia, an 'Anglo-Saxon' king, had no problem allying himself with Britons against other Anglo-Saxons. Penda fought alongside Cadwallon, king of Gwynedd, against the Northumbrians at the Battle of Hatfield Chase in 633 and seems to have fought alongside other Welsh princes in other battles, including the Battle of the Winwæd in 655. It is even arguable that Offa's Dyke, the one feature of Mercia's landscape most widely known today, is essentially a piece of British military engineering ordered by a king with an Anglo-Saxon name. There is, after all, a much stronger tradition in Britain than in the continental homelands of the Anglo-Saxons of building linear defences.

In the cemeteries too, there are signs of British continuity. It has been suggested for instance that the mixed inhumation and cremation cemetery at Quarrington might represent continuity from the Roman to the Anglo-Saxon period, while in the fifth- to sixth-century cemetery at Sleaford, a group of west–east burials without grave goods, and with those buried lying on their sides with their knees bent and hands by the face, may be British. Loveden Hill is also thought to show a mix of British and Anglo-Saxon customs.[63] As one might expect, evidence for survival of British customs in cemeteries only gets stronger as we move further west in the area. At Stretton-on-Fosse, radiocarbon dates suggest continuity of use of the cemetery from the third century to the seventh century. Equally, at Wasperton, out of 200 inhumations, only 117 have been identified as showing Anglo-Saxon cultural identity. Evidence of varying combinations of metalwork, hobnails, mutilation and orientation, however, suggest 36 are probably culturally British burials.[64]

Perhaps even more significant, though, is the geography of early Anglo-Saxon cemeteries in the area. In the north of Lincolnshire, as discussed in the previous chapter, there is a cluster of early Anglo-Saxon cemeteries south of the Humber. This is also an area where a substantial number of late Roman military belt fittings have been found and it is arguably a strategic area, both because of its access to the Humber Estuary, but also because of its control of routes leading south from the territory of the Parisi and the Brigantes. To the south, the area around Lincoln sees little early Anglo-Saxon settlement. Further south still, though, there is a concentration of early Anglo-Saxon evidence. In this region, a large proportion of early Anglo-Saxon cemeteries are located next to Roman-period British settlements, strongly suggesting the Anglo-Saxons arrived here with some kind of British involvement. Such cemeteries appear at Leicester, Medbourne, Barrow/Quorn, Kirby Bellars, Wymeswold/Willoughby, Mancetter and Ancaster. Caves Inn and Thistleton do not have cemeteries directly associated with them, but there are cemeteries within a mile of both.[65]

From a strategic point of view it is easy to see why the Corieltauvi might want to concentrate imported military muscle in this area. Not only does it face south to the Nene Valley, a possible flashpoint at the end of the Roman period, it also faces south-west towards Dobunnic territory, and north-west towards Brigantian territory. In fact, this is not far from the border region that seems to have been fortified in the period after 155 and is in the same area where the Watling Street Burgi fortifications appear around the end of the third century or the beginning of the fourth. If we are looking, in our search for the origin of the Merc element of Mercia, for an area of early Anglo-Saxon activity that has a strong association with borders, it would be hard to find a better candidate than this.

This area of early Anglo-Saxon activity to the south of Lincoln basically comprises the southern half of Corieltauvian territory. The area around Lincoln and to the north comprises the northern half and was to become the Anglo-Saxon Kingdom of Lindsey, independent for a time, before being overrun by Northumberland and subsequently incorporated into Mercia.

We have seen tribal areas splitting in the post-Roman period before. In South Wales, Dark argues that the *civitas* of the Silures splits into Glywysing and Gwent, while just to the south of the area we are discussing, Catuvellaunian territory splits into the Middle Angles and the Middle Saxons. The southern part of Dobunnic territory, which formed part of the *civitas* of the Belgae, appears to have become united with Durotrigan territory in the post-Roman period. It seems perfectly plausible, therefore, to suggest that the Anglo-Saxon Kingdoms of Lindsey and Mercia originated as the result of a split in the *civitas* of the Corieltauvi. It is worth remembering here that, as discussed in Chapter 1, Corieltauvian territory may have consisted of two semi-independent halves in pre-Roman times.

Both king lists of Mercia and Lindsey trace back to what may be a single king in the late sixth century. In the Mercian king list this character is recorded as Creoda, while in the Lindsey king list he is referred to as Cretta. It seems quite possible that this is the same figure and, if so, presumably he ruled a kingdom composed of the territory of both early Mercia and Lindsey. Equally, there is some interesting ceramic evidence that suggests a cultural and economic unity between the two areas in Anglo-Saxon times. Vince's work on early and middle Saxon granitic tempered pottery in eastern England produces a distribution[66] that not only incorporates both the areas under discussion, but also bears very close comparison with the distribution of pre-Roman Corieltauvian coins (*93*).

One objection to the idea of early Mercia as the southern half of the Corieltauvian *civitas* is that Leicester, the major southern Corieltauvian centre, would be expected to be in Mercia. However, by 737 it seems to have been regarded as part of Middle Anglia. This is not necessarily, though, a major problem. Leicester was located close to the border with Catuvellaunian territory. Towards the end of the fourth century, the forum, basilica and market hall were burnt and not rebuilt,[67] and Leicester seems to have been largely abandoned at the end of the Roman period, though reoccupied later. Its importance to the early Kingdom of Mercia, therefore, may have been marginal. Certainly, the distribution of granitic tempered pottery in the area suggests stronger cultural affinities with Mercia and Lindsey than with Middle Anglia to the south. Why the Corieltauvian *civitas* would have split in two at the end of the sixth century is not clear. However, as we have seen, Rædwald was able to march through the area in 616, and it may be that a previous East Anglian defeat of a united political entity based on Corieltauvian territory had caused the area to fragment.

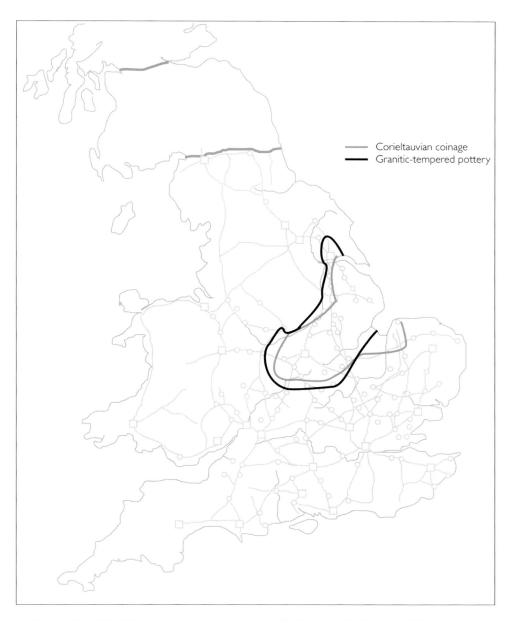

93 Distribution of Corieltauvian coins compared with distribution of early and middle Saxon granitic tempered pottery. *After Cunliffe and Vince*

Certainly this is not long after the time of the last king to hold both territories (if Creoda and Cretta are the same person).

If it is correct to view Mercia as the borderland of the Corieltauvian *civitas*, then the direction of some of its earliest expansion to the west is interesting. There is extensive evidence of Anglo-Saxon influence in the Peak District in the seventh century. As we have seen, this was a likely route to the south for raiding parties from the Brigantes, and possibly even from peoples further north in the Roman period. It raises the question of whether Anglo-Saxon control of the Peak District should be seen as garrisoning it against post-Roman raiders from the north. It is also possible that other early features of Mercian expansion should be seen in the light of Corieltauvian priorities.

We have already discussed how Mercian expansion into East Anglia may reflect a previous Corieltauvian and Icenian dispute over the Fens, and how Mercia took territory from the Catuvellauni around the Nene Valley possibly coveted by the Corieltauvi and incorporated it into Middle Anglia. Further to the west, Mercia expanded into formerly Dobunnic territory in north Gloucestershire. This is just to the east of an area where Dobunnic, Corieltauvian and Catuvellaunian coinage all seem to overlap in pre-Roman times, so it is possible that this should also be regarded as an area with a history of disputed territory. In addition, while Northumbria occupied Lindsey for a period, it eventually became part of Mercia, joining all the former Corieltauvian states together once more. Mercia, of course, under rulers such as Penda and Offa became the regional superpower in central England, before finally succumbing to a combination of attacks from Vikings and the rise to English dominance of the Kingdom of Wessex. As discussed previously, in some ways the struggle for power between Mercia from its heartland north of the Thames against Wessex, with its heartland south of the Thames, is also reminiscent of the pre-Roman rivalry between Catuvellauni and Atrebates.

THE KINGDOM OF DEIRA

Deira and Bernicia are the two component parts of the Kingdom of Northumbria and they go through a long complex process of unification which stretches throughout the seventh century. However, there are significant differences between the two kingdoms and it seems best to treat their origins separately.

Deira's southern border lay on the Humber Estuary. In the west and the north by the early seventh century, Bede indicates that Deira included both Catterick and York.[68] However, Dark has made a strong case for some kind of British post-Roman political entity, perhaps Brigantian, linking both these sites to areas around Hadrian's Wall,[69] and in its earliest form Deira may have stopped to the east of York. Its northern border might have extended as far as the Tees but there is comparatively little sign of Anglo-Saxon settlement in north Yorkshire in the period in question and the core of Deira seems to have occupied much the same territory as the core of the *civitas* of the Parisi. It is probably no coincidence that the name Deira seems to share its origin with the name of the most significant Roman-period town in the *civitas* (Derventio/ Malton) and it may even be derived from the name of the town itself. Certainly there is evidence of fifth- and sixth-century activity at Malton with a ditch from the period cutting the main street.[70] Brough on Humber seems to have been (at least at some stage) officially the capital of the *civitas* of the Parisi but never appears to have developed very successfully. In this situation, Malton may have effectively been the capital of the Parisi in the late Roman period and may well have continued to be the capital of a political entity based on the *civitas* of the Parisi in the post-Roman period.

The distribution of early Anglo-Saxon cemeteries in the area suggests that the first Anglo-Saxon settlement there should indeed be seen in a British context. There is a cluster of early Anglo-Saxon cemeteries in the region of Malton and O'Brien also draws attention to connections between the distribution of early Anglo-Saxon cemeteries and both Roman roads in the area and burial sites from the pre-Roman Arras Culture.[71] By the early sixth century, the pattern of Anglo-Saxon cemeteries in the area can be seen to roughly delineate the territory of the *civitas* of the Parisi as defined by the distribution of Arras Culture burials.[72] There may, of course, even be parallels between the arrival of the Anglo-Saxons and the arrival of the Arras Culture in this area. Maybe the bearers of the Arras Culture were invited in on a similar basis to help defend it against the same much larger neighbour.

The ruling dynasty of Deira may not have been established until well into the sixth century (Ælle ruling in 597 is the first Deiran ruler clearly identified in the historical sources) and it could well be that, as in Catuvellaunian territory, an explicitly British political entity survived for a period here after the end of Roman rule. It is even possible that the arrival of Anglo-Saxons in the area may have had less of an impact on political continuity there than the arrival of the Arras Culture. That, after all, seems to have led to the adoption of a completely new foreign name, the Parisi, whereas the 'Anglo-Saxon' kingdom seems to have inherited a pre-existing local name.

As mentioned earlier, at some stage prior to the early seventh century, Deira expanded westwards to incorporate both Catterick and York. If there was a successor state to the Brigantes in the area, at some point it must have fragmented, with the western part becoming the Kingdom of Rheged plus some other kingdoms in the Pennines. The small British Kingdom of Elmet seems to have been based in the Leeds area, and the small Kingdom of Craven may have been based around Bradford slightly further west. There is no evidence for when this fragmentation occurred. However, it is conceivable that the fall of York may have had a similar effect in fragmenting the surrounding areas that defeat at Bedcanford in 571 seems to have had on the northern part of Catuvellaunian territory.

The eastern part of Brigantian territory was, by contrast, incorporated into Deira and, possibly in the north, into Bernicia. In this scenario, the *civitas* would have broken along the Pennines. We have already noted elsewhere the phenomenon of *civitates* breaking up, and there would probably have been additional cultural factors involved in this case. As already mentioned, Roman culture was widely adopted in the eastern half of the *civitas* of the Brigantes, while the western half remained resolutely un-Romanised throughout the occupation. When this cultural divide is added to the natural barrier of the Pennines and any existing cultural and ethnic differences from pre-Roman times, it seems entirely conceivable that the *civitas* of the Brigantes would fracture at this point. As mentioned, Deira ceased to exist as a separate kingdom when it was united with Bernicia to form the Kingdom of Northumbria.

THE KINGDOM OF BERNICIA

The *Anglo-Saxon Chronicle* claims that in 547, Ida, founder of the Bernician dynasty, started his rule and established a defended base at Bamburgh. By the time Bernicia is mentioned again in the historical sources, it is at the beginning of the seventh century and Bernicia is already (if temporarily at this stage) united with Deira under King Æthelfrith and subsequently King Edwin. Bede mentions a royal site at Yeavering. Despite the thinness of the historical evidence, it seems clear, however, that the origins of Bernicia should be sought in a British context. In fact, in many ways, Bernicia should probably be considered more of a British kingdom than an Anglo-Saxon one. Having kings with Anglo-Saxon names does not make a kingdom Anglo-Saxon, any more than Roman names found in inscriptions in Britain in the Roman period and post-Roman period indicate that the people with those names were Roman. The name Bernicia itself is anyway probably British. It appears in the form Bryneich in early Wesh poetry and that may well be its original form.

In addition, while Bernician rulers may have had Anglo-Saxon names, there is evidence of extensive links between the Bernician dynasty and other Celtic kingdoms. For instance, when Æthelfrith was killed at the Battle of the River Idle, his sons fled for refuge to Ireland and the Celtic kingdoms of Scotland. Equally, between 653 and 657, Talorcan, son of a Pictish mother but the nephew of Oswiu of Bernicia, was king of the Picts, and Oswiu himself may have married Rhiainfellt, a princess of the British Kingdom of Rheged. Oswiu's brother Oswald is said by Bede to have been overlord of not just all the English kingdoms in Britain but also of all the British, Irish and Pictish ones as well. Oswald, in addition, having been converted in Dalriada, introduced Celtic Christianity into Bernicia with the help of missionaries from the Dalriadic centre of Iona.[73]

In archaeological terms there is a scarcity of cemeteries in the area that are culturally recognisable as Anglo-Saxon. Even where cemeteries have previously been identified as Anglo-Saxon, O'Brien questions whether some of them actually are, and even where a cemetery clearly is Anglo-Saxon, such as that at Norton on Tees, there is evidence within it of British customs as well, such as the wearing in burial number 65 of a single penannular brooch at the neck.[74] Equally, at the Bernician royal centre at Yeavering, firm links to British tradition are shown by, for instance, its location next to the largest hillfort in Northumberland and its inclusion of the so-called Great Enclosure dating from the fourth or fifth century. In addition, there is the unique 'amphitheatre', probably built for royal audiences but most closely resembling a Roman auditorium.

It is hard, realistically, to see any other scenario for the creation of Bernicia than a small Anglo-Saxon (by claimed identity, though not necessarily genetically or even culturally) group taking over control of a British political entity. This much seems to be widely agreed. More controversial has been the issue of what that British political entity was. For many years it was thought that the name Bryneich was in some way derived from the name of the Brigantes. This, however, is now regarded as unlikely. Bearing in mind the location of Bamburgh and Yeavering, both well north of Hadrian's Wall, in territory attributed by Ptolemy to the Votadini, it is probably best to see Bernicia as originating from the division into two of the tribal territories of the Votadini. We have seen such a scenario with other tribes (the Silures, the Corieltauvi, the Dobunni) and it is perfectly feasible here, particularly since there seems to have already been cultural differences between those Votadini in the area that was to become Bernicia, and the Votadini to the north of the area.

As O'Brien has pointed out, extended inhumations in cists and in dug graves are common in Votadinian territory north of the Tweed. However, in the Votadinian territory between the Tweed and the Tyne that was to form the core of Bernicia, the lack of evidence of burials or cremations indicates that the local population must have continued with the archaeologically invisible practices widespread in Britain to the south in pre-Roman times.[75] The split between the two areas of Votadinian territory may or may not have been violent but we need not necessarily think of the two areas as permanently locked in long-term bitter civil conflict. If the Catraeth of the *Y Gododdin* is Catterick, as it seems reasonable to suppose (and assuming the event recorded took place after the creation of Bernicia), then it is interesting to note, in this poem, that the Votadini ignore the 'Anglo-Saxon' presence in Bernicia, much closer to their heartland, and instead attack Deiran territory far to the south. It suggests that relations between Bernicia and the rest of the Votadini to the north were by no means always hostile. In fact, a look at a map suggests that any Votadinian raiding party heading south to Catterick would probably have had to pass through Bernician territory. Bernicia had an often fractious relationship with Deira and an alliance between Bernicia and the rest of the Votadini against Deira is by no means unimaginable. It is notable that, as with the Corieltauvi, the split in the territory of the Votadini was only temporary, with re-unification being achieved in the seventh century when Oswald of Northumbria took Edinburgh and, presumably, the rest of Votadinian territory.[76] Bernicia's main area of expansion, though, seems to have been to the south and west. Ptolemy arguably makes Corbridge a town of the Votadini and O'Brien's evidence of burial practices also suggests that the Bernicians may have had pre-existing ethnic links south of Hadrian's Wall. By the beginning of the seventh century, Bernicia and Deira were united under one ruler, and though there were intermittent breaks in this arrangement, the two did eventually form the united Kingdom of Northumbria.

Northumbrian power extended westwards in 616 with the expulsion of the king of Elmet and a victory at the Battle of Chester. Later in the seventh century, Northumbria seems to have taken over the Kingdom of Rheged and gained brief dominance over Mercia after Penda's death at the Battle of the Winwæd in 655. Mercia was, however, lost again shortly afterwards and defeat by the Picts at Nechtansmere in 685 and chronic instability in the eighth century helped prevent any further period of Northumbrian political eminence.

Conclusion

It is possible that, if Rome had never occupied Britain, the Catuvellauni might eventually have succeeded in uniting at least a large portion of present-day England. Cunobelin was already referred to by Suetonius as '*Britannorum rex*', King of the Britons,[1] and by the time of the Roman arrival in 43, the Catuvellauni/Trinovantes confederation was arguably closer to the proto-states encountered by Caesar in central Gaul than to the conventional British tribe. In addition to its own territory it seems to have already exerted authority over the territory of the Cantii and over at least a proportion of the Dobunni and the Atrebates. The confederation may have expanded its influence northwards into formerly Corieltauvian territory and probably significantly into Icenian territory as well. The Roman intervention reversed some of those gains and froze others. When the battle to take control in Britain recommenced with full vigour in the period after the Roman withdrawal, the possibility of the Catuvellauni or an Anglo-Saxon kingdom based in their territory ever being the one to succeed rapidly faded. Various other successor kingdoms competed to take advantage of the disappearance of Catuvellaunian power, fighting again over many of the same disputed territories that were already disputed in pre-Roman times.

The pre-Roman period saw the rise to prominence of various tribes and their subsequent decline. The fortunes of the Durotriges blossomed with their control of the cross-Channel link to the Atlantic trade routes then nosedived as cross-Channel trade went elsewhere. The Atrebates extended their influence into Kent, only to be overrun by Catuvellaunian expansion. So too the post-Roman period saw the rise and decline of Kent, of East Anglia, of Northumbria and, most dramatically, of Mercia. Finally, and ironically in the light of the Atrebates' probable defeat by the Catuvellauni in the pre-Roman power game, it was to be Wessex which united England. Not, however, before one last invasion.

The Vikings represent, in some ways, a continuation of the theme probably established by the Parisi and Commius in pre-Roman times, of foreigners taking political power within a British tribal structure. The Roman intervention was, in some ways, an extension of this tradition and so, even more clearly, was the arrival of the Anglo-Saxons. Concerning one of the earlier Viking raids, the *Anglo-Saxon Chronicle* for 838 records that:

> In this year a great armada came to West Wales [Cornwall], where the people joined them and started a war against Egbert, King of the West Saxons. When he learned of this, he set out with his army against them and fought them at Hengestdune, where he routed both the Welsh and the Danes.

This looks suspiciously like the people of Cornwall, the successors to the Dumnonii, reviving the old tradition of looking overseas for help against tribal enemies. Equally, it seems highly likely that elements within the power structures of the Anglo-Saxon kingdoms again looked to the new player on the British political scene for help against their enemies.

In 873-4 the Vikings assisted Ceolwulf, probably a member of the Mercian royal family and, judging by his name, possibly a descendant of the Mercian kings Cenwulf and Ceolwulf, to become King of Mercia. Equally, it seems likely that Æthelread and Oswald, the two kings who ruled East Anglia after the Viking conquest of the area and martyrdom of the previous king Edmund, did so with the cooperation and support of Viking forces.[2] There is a tendency to call such figures 'puppet rulers', just as figures like Togidubnus and Prasutagus tend to be dismissively called client kings. However just as those British rulers would undoubtedly have seen themselves as allies of the Romans, rather than servants, so Anglo-Saxon kings supported by the Vikings should not necessarily be dismissed as powerless figureheads. Another case of Anglo-Viking cooperation, for instance, is that of Alfred's nephew Æthelwold who, on failing to secure the kingship of Wessex, fled to the Danes of Northumbria, who are then said to have made him their king and followed him into battle against Wessex.[3]

In reality the balance of power between locals and Vikings in these territories is little understood and there is a certain amount of evidence to suggest administrative continuity into the Viking period from the pre-Viking period. Both Æthelread and Oswald, for instance, made use of the moneyer Beornheah for their coinage, who had also minted coins for Edmund, while an early issue of the Viking king Guthrum in the area shows similarities to coins of Æthelread and Oswald.[4] It is also notable that a peace treaty between Alfred and Guthrum, drawn up in Anglo-Saxon by someone within Alfred's court circle, is concluded on the 'Viking' side in the name of 'all the people in East Anglia',[5] suggesting the Wessex scribe perceived Guthrum's power base as decidedly Anglo-Danish rather than just Danish.

In other ways, however, the Viking invasion reflects a change from the past, and as much as anything it is a change of scale of political ambition on both sides. The Viking invasions destroyed Wessex's competitors for the position of pre-eminent Anglo-Saxon kingdom and ultimately helped Alfred and Wessex to move towards the goal of an English nation, led by Wessex. The treaty with Guthrum, mentioned above, is, on Alfred's side, confirmed by 'the councillors of all the English race'. Equally, among the Vikings, while many smaller entities existed, comparatively large-scale military and political units formed which were very different from the early groups of Anglo-Saxon mercenaries. The so-called 'great armies' of the Vikings could, and did, roam across Britain in a way not seen since the days of the Roman Army. At the end of the period, a king of Denmark, Swein Forkbeard, used his army to seize power in England as well. It would be wrong to define this as the Second World War model of state warfare mentioned in the introduction, but there are signs that point clearly towards medieval warfare, at least, rather than back towards the tribal raiding of old.

Some of the old tribal political borders, so faithfully reflected in the origins of the early Anglo-Saxon kingdoms, also begin to change at this time. Centuries of warfare between the Anglo-Saxon kingdoms had already started to blur the earlier political geography. Then the shire system of England took things a step further, creating a map of England with most of the shires present as they were to stay until 1974. In an era when regional, cultural and ethnic divisions in the country were beginning to be overtaken by a broader English identity, it became feasible to mark out a range of new boundaries based on contemporary realities. The shires created were based around large regional Anglo-Saxon urban centres, usually the defended *burhs* that were a major part of Wessex's military strategy against the Vikings (*94*). The process had probably started in Wessex some time previously, with the area around Hamptun (Southampton) becoming Hamptunshire or Hampshire, and the area round Wilton becoming Wiltshire. In the tenth century, the concept was extended north and west with new territories being created around the towns there. This was the case, for instance, in the old Catuvellaunian lands in the Chilterns and beyond. This area which never formed one of the independent early Anglo-Saxon kingdoms and appears as fragmented units in the Tribal Hidage, acquired a shire geography that was also fragmented. This is the origin of Hertfordshire, Cambridgeshire, Bedfordshire, Huntingdonshire, Oxfordshire and Northamptonshire.

However, at least some of the borders remained the same. The *civitas* of the Cantii, the Anglo-Saxon Kingdom of Kent, survives, with some border alterations, as the county of Kent, and Canterbury remains its capital. The *civitas* of the Trinovantes, the Anglo-Saxon Kingdom of Essex, survives as the county

94 Earthwork defences of the Saxon *burh* at Wareham

of Essex, with its main city still at Colchester. The *civitas* of the Regni, the Anglo-Saxon Kingdom of Sussex, survives, with minor border alterations, as the counties of East and West Sussex, with Chichester still prominent. The *civitas* of the Iceni, the Anglo-Saxon Kingdom of East Anglia, survives, with minor border alterations, as the counties of Suffolk and Norfolk, with Norwich still the major city, at least in Norfolk. In the north, the core of the *civitas* of the Parisi and the Anglo-Saxon Kingdom of Deira may survive as the East Riding of Yorkshire. In the west, the territory of the Dumnonii became Devon and Cornwall.

In an era of mass population mobility, of course, regional and county loyalties are not what they were, but many people do still retain a pride in, and affection for, their own tribal territory. One of the origins of sport is as a preparation for war. If so, maybe on some level there is a line that runs forward from the Cantii facing the Trinovantes, across the Thames Estuary, to Kent facing Essex on the cricket pitch. However, there is another, potentially less cosy, side to competing regional allegiances in Britain today. We live at a time when political fragmentation is again a genuine possibility. There is a real chance of both Welsh and Scottish independence at some stage in the next few decades. If so, we will have to hope that separation is dealt with intelligently and carefully, with politicians of goodwill on both sides keeping things calm and well-ordered. If ambitious politicians on either side of the borders set out to exploit the ethnic tensions that still exist in this island, then violence is not inconceivable.

Just as in late fourth-century Britain and in 1990s Bosnia, the most problematic situation is where political borders no longer fully represent the ethnic/cultural reality on the ground, as independence approaches. In this context, perhaps think of the English population that has moved into north-eastern parts of Wales, many of them commuting to English cities like Chester and Liverpool. Imagine a situation where an extreme Welsh nationalist government set out to make the English there feel like second-class citizens and where extreme English nationalist politicians set out, in turn, to exploit the situation. Fortunately, current politics in Wales, Scotland and England is mostly of a moderate kind and the idea of bloodshed currently seems extremely far-fetched. Yet who in the peaceful and affluent Yugoslavia of the 1970s and early 1980s would have predicted the chaos and bloodletting of the 1990s, and who in the peaceful and affluent Britain of the early fourth century would have predicted the chaos that would engulf the island within decades?

Notes

The following abbreviations have been used:
AE, *Année Epigraphique*
CIL, *Corpus Inscriptionum Latinarum*
RIB, *The Roman Inscriptions of Britain*, Vol. 1, eds. Collingwood & Wright, Oxford, 1965

INTRODUCTION
1 Millett 1990, 181-6.

CHAPTER 1
1 Oppenheimer 2006, 99.
2 Oppenheimer 2006.
3 See, for instance, Kilbride-Jones 1980, 12, 117-23.
4 See, for instance, a series of stone figures from North Humberside showing warriors carrying swords on their backs, Cunliffe 2004, 97.
5 Creighton 2000, 16-21.
6 Cunliffe 2004, 94.
7 Caesar, *Gallic Wars* 2, 6.
8 Cunliffe 2005, 541.
9 Cunliffe 2005, 592.
10 Collis 525-6, 2007.
11 Ptolemy, *Geography* 2.
12 Coins are identified as Dobunnic because of their apparent relation to the Roman-period capital of the Dobunni at Cirencester and then anywhere where the same coinage is later found also becomes Dobunnic.
13 Caesar, *Gallic Wars* 5, 11.
14 Cunliffe 2005, 166.
15 Caesar, *Gallic Wars* 5, 22.
16 Caesar, *Gallic Wars* 2, 4.
17 Cunliffe 2005, fig. 7.14.
18 Jones & Mattingly 1990, maps 6.24 pottery, 6.43 salt, 7.6 villas.
19 Niblett 2001, 49.
20 Caesar, *Gallic Wars* 5, 12.
21 Cunliffe 2005, 127.
22 Cunliffe 2004, 41-2.
23 Cunliffe 2005, 160.
24 Niblett 2001, 52.
25 Branigan 1985, 101.
26 Mattingly 2006, 384.
27 Branigan 1985, 158-62.
28 Cunliffe 2005, 169.
29 Cunliffe 2005, 170.
30 Frontinus, *Stratagems*, 2.13.11.
31 Creighton 2000, 192.
32 Henig 2002, 62.
33 Cunliffe 2005, 171.
34 Chadburn & Corney 2001, 23.
35 Mattingly 2006, 390.
36 Cunliffe 1973, 124.
37 RIB 1673.
38 Cunliffe 2005, 481.
39 Cunliffe 2005, 182-3.
40 Dark, 2000, 33.
41 Cunliffe 2005, 182.
42 RIB 1672-3.
43 Cunliffe 2005, 429.
44 Jones & Mattingly 1990, 181.
45 Puttnam 2000, 67-8.
46 Cunliffe 2005, 189.
47 Cunliffe 2005, 189-90.
48 Moore & Reece 2001.
49 Mattingly 2006, 409.
50 Mattingly 2006, 403.
51 Cunliffe 2005, 201.
52 Wacher 1995, 341.
53 Having said that, the cliffs and promontories of the area are also very similar to those in territory further south, so there may be an element of similar geography creating similar developments independently.
54 Cunliffe 2005, 207.
55 Jones & Mattingly 1990, 180.
56 Malim et al 1996, 101, 117.
57 Warner 1996, 34.
58 Cunliffe 2005, 198.
59 Mattingly 2006, 384.
60 Jones & Mattingly, 1990, map 6.24.
61 Davies & Williamson 1999, 21.
62 Todd 1991, 5.
63 Todd 1991, 80-1.
64 Todd 1991, 125.
65 Todd 1991, 119.

66 Jones & Mattingly 1990, map 6.24.
67 Cunliffe 2005, 195.
68 Cunliffe 2005, 215.
69 Jones & Mattingly 1990, 50-1 and map 3.12.
70 Cunliffe 2005, 85.
71 Stead 1979, 7-39.
72 Appels & Laycock 2007, fig. SL7.13.
73 Wacher 1995, 399.
74 Tacitus, *Agricola* 17, 2.
75 Salway 1993, 147.
76 Ptolemy, *Geography* 2, 2.
77 Hartley & Fitts 1988, 1.
78 See Cunliffe 2005, 214.
79 Hartley & Fitts 1988, 8.
80 Hartley & Fitts 1988, 10.
81 Cunliffe 2005, 211-12
82 Hartley & Fitts 1988, 87-9.
83 Hartley & Fitts 1988, 96-7.
84 Cunliffe 2005, 218.
85 Jones & Mattingly 1990, map 3.19. Cunliffe 2005, 217.
86 Cunliffe 2005, 217.
87 Dark 2000, 205.
88 Kilbride-Jones 1980, 171, 175.

CHAPTER 2

1 Caesar, *Gallic Wars* 4, 20.
2 Cunliffe 2005, 134.
3 Caesar, *Gallic Wars* 4, 20-36.
4 Caesar, *Gallic Wars* 5, 8-23.
5 Caesar, *Gallic Wars* 5, 11.
6 Rodwell 1976, 198-203.
7 Frontinus, *Stratagems* 2.13.11.
8 Creighton 2000, 19.
9 Cunliffe 2005, 145.
10 Crummy 1997, 20. Creighton 2000, 75.
11 Creighton 2000, 78.
12 Creighton 2000, 77.
13 Cassius Dio, *Roman History* 60, 20.
14 Suetonius, *Life of Caligula* 44.
15 Creighton 2000
16 Cunliffe 2005, 147.
17 Cunliffe 2005, 147. Creighton 2000, 78.
18 Suetonius *Life of Caligula*, 44-6. Cassius Dio, *Roman History* 59, 25.
19 Cunliffe 2005, 147.
20 Cassius Dio, *Roman History* 60, 19.
21 Suetonius, Life of Claudius 17.
22 Cunliffe 1971, I, xxv.
23 Manley 2002, 128.
24 Cunliffe 1973, 19. Cunliffe 2005, 171-2.

25 Some have suggested that Togidubnus also controlled the territory of the Catuvellauni and Trinovantes, but if so, it is hard to see how Tacitus, who mentions him as still ruling down to his time, makes no mention of him in relation to Boudica. There also seems little reason to associate Togidubnus with the Catuvellaunian leader Togodumnus who is said by Cassius Dio to have died in 43.
26 Crummy 1997, 44-5.
27 Salway 1993, 66.
28 Niblett 2001, 39-40.
29 Tacitus, *Histories* 14, 33.
30 See Crummy 1997, 66, for mention of the possibility.

CHAPTER 3

1 Tacitus, *Agricola* 14-16. *Annals* 14, 31-8.
2 Cassius Dio, *Roman History* 62, 1-12
3 Tacitus, *Annals* 14, 34.
4 Cassius Dio, *Roman History* 62, 7.
5 Cassius Dio, *Roman History* 62, 2.
6 Tacitus, *Agricola* 16.
7 Tacitus, *Agricola* 14.
8 Suetonius, *Life of Vespasian* 4.
9 Tacitus does contradict himself in the *Agricola*, by claiming the rebels attacked forts, but there is no archaeological evidence for this, and generally, it seems preferable to accept the evidence of the much fuller account in the *Annals*.
10 Crummy 1997, 55.
11 Ptolemy does make London a town of the Cantii, but under Cunobelin, at least, that part of the north shore of the Thames seems to have been firmly under Catuvellaunian control.
12 Malim et al 1996, 117.
13 Warner 1996, 34.
14 Potter 2002, 34.
15 Van Arsdell 1989, 24. Creighton 1994, 329.
16 Tacitus, *Annals* 12, 31-2.
17 Tacitus, *Annals* 14, 33.
18 Niblett 2001, 67-8.
19 Sealey 1997, 37.
20 Millett 1987. Niblett 2001, 67.
21 Niblett 2001, 59.
22 Niblett 2001, 58.
23 Niblett 2001, 55.
24 Crummy 1997, 55.
25 Crummy 1997, 90.
26 Crummy 1997, 86.
27 Hingley & Unwin 2005, 105.

28 Kemble 2001, 87.

29 Crummy 1997, 90.

30 Hingley & Unwin 2005, 80.

31 Fincham 2002, 72-3.

32 RIB 192.

33 RIB 1065.

34 AE 1956.249.

35 CIL xvi.49.

36 CIL xvi.163.

37 Allen 1989, 6. Niblett 2001, 39-40.

38 Mattingly 2006, 420.

39 Salway 1993, 479.

40 Watts 1998, 44.

41 Creighton 2000, 192.

42 Henig 2002, 62.

43 Niblett 2001, 46, 111.

CHAPTER 4

1 Breeze & Dobson 2000, 12.

2 Breeze & Dobson 2000, 11.

3 Breeze & Dobson 2000, 25-6.

4 Except possibly in the west, where if Ptolemy's Corio is Corbridge, Votadinian territory reached as far south as the wall zone.

5 Salway 1993, 146.

6 Shotter 1996, 127.

7 Kilbride-Jones 1980, 171, 175.

8 Breeze & Dobson 2000, 40.

9 Breeze & Dobson 2000, 57.

10 Shotter 1996, 127.

11 Breeze & Dobson 2000, 58.

12 Breeze & Dobson 2000, 90.

13 Breeze & Dobson 2000, 132.

14 Cassius Dio, *Roman History* 76, 5.

15 Cassius Dio, *Roman History* 77, 13.

16 Pausanias, Description of Greece 8, 43.

17 Hind 1977, 229-34.

18 Woodfield 1995, 135, 137.

19 Woodfield 1995, 129.

20 Woodfield 1995 129-45.

21 Rodwell 1975, 85-101.

22 Drury 1984, 29-30.

23 Robertson 2000, xxvi.

24 Faulkner 2000, 93.

25 Faulkner 2000, 207.

26 Woodfield 1995, 143.

27 Stevens 1937, 198.

28 Woodfield 1995, 145.

29 Millett 1990, 139.

30 Griffiths 2001, 50.

31 Bishop 1991.

32 (*Map data from: Bayley & Butcher 2004, figs. 175 and 178. Portable Antiquities Scheme, Knee Brooches: WILT-018473, LEIC-41BCF3, SUR-FBE846, NARC-F08813, NCL-D5E541, LEIC-CB1040, WMID-274835, NARC-27F046, DENO-6CB3E7, KENT-B694F1, NMS-F25D85, WMID-9DD187, NMS-38B382, NCL-3EDF87, NMS-F54095, BH-D92564, SUSS-B77D82, SUR-BFD652, NMS-C732D1, WMID-62C0D5, NMS-F3F636, NARC-91C143, NARC-15F652, LEIC-013041, SWYOR-6AE364, ESS-02DB54, NARC-344FE4, NLM-32F6E8, NLM-32F166, LIN-C355C3, YORYM-84B065, HESH-F47012, NLM-1ED374, SF-D14002, LEIC-EDC747, ESS-5D5EE7, NCL-B1FD43, LIN-78A600, LIN-909D01, WILT-B34E76, NCL-C94FE7, NCL-B9F3C1, LIN-1B0692, YORYMB1343, NMS1078, NMS1739, NMS1742, HAMP3516, HAMP3515, HAMP3004, HAMP1919, SF5366, NLM6118, NLM6045, NLM4488, HAMP1392. Portable Antiquities Scheme, Crossbow Brooches: LIN-E9ACB0, SF-C418A5, HAMP-F38377, HAMP-39A5D2, SF-3B5E74, LIN-6B48B6, NARC-B8DB28, NARC-57E995, LEIC-EEE688, SF-F76047, NMS-1D08B1, LEIC-9C94D1, LIN-D08A63, LIN-0B54E5, LEIC-8471B8, SUSS8-AB1D3, NMS-BC1567, LIN-95A403, NMS-2952C1, SUSS-B80335, NMS-9DEFA4, LIN-6249D0, LIN-4EFF36, NMS-F730D4, NLM-E41A21, SUR-BFFD73, NMS-7E9657, LIN-FEEF95, LIN-FEA194, BERK-CAC402, LEIC-055447, NARC-9DA9E1, LEIC-4E2E53, SUR-703E85, NMS-556012, KENT-3361E5, ESS-FA6464, SF-01BCE8, WAW-E6F6B3, SWYOR-AB7D42, WILT-E20915, WMID-FC5D73, SF-E58C02, SWYOR-19EED2, NMS-DE99E3, NMS-6AC912, LEIC-B84927, KENT-1475C7, LIN-D792B6, KENT-180214, KENT-178D71, LIN-D5C686, NMS-178, NLM5738, NLM4367, NLM4213, KENT538.

33 Collins 2004, 127-30.

34 Johnson 1989, 75.

35 Breeze & Dobson 2000, 136.

36 Breeze & Dobson 2000, 145

37 Ammianus Marcellinus, *Roman History* 28, 3, 8.

38 Gould 1999, 185-98.

CHAPTER 5

1 Salway 1993, 225.

2 Ammianus Marcellinus, *Roman History* 14, 6-9.

3 Breeze & Dobson 2000, 241.

4   For recall of *maijorinae* and *centenionales* from circulation in 354 and 365 see Hendy 1985, 470.

5   Breeze & Dobson 1985, 15-16.

6   Ammianus Marcellinus, *Roman History* 28, 3, 6.

7   Millett 1990, 153.

8   Shotter 1996, 121.

9   Clarke 1979, 276.

10 Clarke 1979, 275.

11 Appels & Laycock 2007, 169-75.

12 Map data from: Hawkes & Dunning 1961 figs. 4, 9. Leahy 2007 fig. 1. Corney 2001 fig. 3.2. Clarke 1979. Allason-Jones & Miket 1984. Map of Triangular Plate Buckles fig. 54.

13 See scarcity of buckles from areas distant from the *limes* in Sommer 1984. See Swift 2000, maps 17, 28, 29. See Böhme 1986 figs. 3, 11, 12. Buckles and belt fittings are scarce in southern Spain and southern France, *pers. comm.* Aurrecoechea Fernandez.

14 Macdowall 1995, 6. In 476, a law made it illegal for individuals to keep 'gangs of armed slaves, *bucellarii* or Isaurians', but the practice continued and in the sixth century Belisarius maintained up to 7000 *bucellarii*.

15 Aurrecoechea Fernandez 2001, 187-200 and *pers. comm.*

16 Aurrecoechea Fernandez, *pers. comm.*

17 Clarke 1979, figs. 68, 71, 72, 83, 100.

18 Wilmott 2002.

19 Swanton 1973, 48-50.

20 Cunliffe 2005, fig. 18.3.

21 Appels & Laycock 2007, Section 2, Chapters 5, 6, 7. Laycock forthcoming.

22 Icenian map data: Portable Antiquities Scheme SF-9EFED0, NMS-6B32A1, CAM-5DD0032. Norfolk Museums & Archaeology Service NHER16121, NHER28494. UKDFD.co.uk 3940. Appels & Laycock 2007 figs. SL5.10, SL5.4, SL5.6. West 1998, fig. 131.5. Ipswich buckle unpublished. Corieltauvian map data: Hawkes & Dunning 1961, figs. 17i, 18k. Portable Antiquities Scheme LEIC-0DAFA7, NLM5690, SF306, SF-800B97, LIN-BBF865, E4134, E4135. UKDFD.co.uk 176, 1037. Appels & Laycock 2007, figs SL7.3, SL7.4, SL7.7, SL7.13, SL7.2. Treasure Hunting Magazine June 2001, 34. Leahy 1996, fig. 11.16.3. Leahy 1984, figs 2.3, 2.13. Leahy ref. Navenby buckle. Cambridgeshire County Council FCB13954. Norfolk Museums and Archaeology Service NHER3182. Odell buckle unpublished.

   Catuvellaunian/Trinovantian map data: Hawkes & Dunning 1961, figs. 17e, 18j, 23h, 17k, 18d. Portable Antiquities Scheme NLM2741, SF-1EB4D0, SUR-00DEF4, NLM5692, BH-7FCB64, NARC-67B0F4, BERK-EB3477, BUC-B32F67, NLM-1278F5. Norfolk Museums Service NHER10657, NHER19544. Treasure Hunting Magazine, February 2000, 7 July 2001, 45. Appels & Laycock 2007, figs. SL6.7, SL6.5, SL6.10, SL6.11, SL6.17, SL6.14, SL6.8, SL6.9. Böhme 1986, fig. 27.7. West 1998 fig. 135.3. Museum at Square & Compass Pub in Worth Maltravers. Brill strap end unpublished. Dobunnic map data: Hawkes & Dunning 1961, figs. 1.16, 8, 13l, 15c, 15g, 15n, 15o, 15p, 15q. Eckhardt & Crummy, 2006 figs 1.127, 1.531, 7.1242. Portable Antiquities Scheme HAMP-722FA3, KENT-C4E293, KENT-AB6B72, WAW-6AD751, BUC-DB7A84, picture ID 001451BAE2901C4C. Böhme 1986, figs 28.2, 28.8, 28.9. Appels & Laycock 2007, figs. SL8.21, SL8.22, SL8.25. Brown & Henig 2002 363-5. Kemble 2001, fig. 35. Macgregor & Bolick 1993, fig 34.28. Hawkes 1974, fig 3.1. Robinson 1994, 14-15, UKDFD. co.uk no. 650. Henig 2002, fig. 56. Kingston-Deverill strap end ref. Brian Read. Strap end and buckle from near Buckingham ref. David Shelley. Honnington buckle ref. Nigel Sewell.

23 Appels & Laycock 2007, 191-4. Laycock forthcoming.

24 Cunliffe 2005, fig. 8.13.

25 Appels & Laycock 2007, 201-5. Laycock forthcoming.

26 Appels & Laycock 2007, 195-200. Laycock forthcoming. A row of dots sometimes appears marking the bridle on horsehead buckles even outside Catuvellaunian/Trinovantian territory, but constitutes a relatively minor element of the designs.

27 Appels & Laycock 2007, 212. Laycock forthcoming.

28 Appels & Laycock 2007, fig. SL 8.22. The Dorchester on Thames buckle plate, Hawkes & Dunning 1961, fig. 1.16, has a buckle, but the use of rivets to attach it to the buckle plate, rather than the usual hinge arrangement suggests it may not be the original buckle.

29 Appels & Laycock 2007, fig. SL 8.24. Hawkes & Dunning 1961, fig. 8.

30 Blair 1994, 13.

[31] Suzuki 2000.

[32] Suzuki 2000, nos. 6-10.

[33] Appels & Laycock 2007, fig. SL 10.30-32.

[34] Bayley & Butcher 2004, 194.

[35] Bayley & Butcher 2004, 196.

[36] Kilbride-Jones 1980, 170-83.

[37] See, for instance, Millett 1990, 175-6.

[38] See buckles and belt fittings in Laycock forthcoming and Appels & Laycock 2007, Section 2, Chapters 5, 6, 7.

[39] Marzinzik 2003, 60-1, 312.

[40] Gildas, *On the Ruin of Britain* 18.

[41] See Böhme 1986, fig. 14.

[42] Map data: Böhme 1986, fig. 14. UKDFD 18. Appels & Laycock 2007 SL1022, SL1023. Portable Antiquities Scheme, GLO-FA9938, LANCUM-0390F6, NARC-C6E5B8, LIN-6312A0, ESS-E52552, LIN-30F3D6, SF10430, NLM4207, NLM5502, NLM4281, SF8281.

[43] Frere 1967, 359.

[44] Pearson 2002, 163, fig. 77.

[45] Gildas, *On the Ruin of Britain* 18.

[46] RIB 1843, RIB 1844, RIB 1672-3, RIB 1962.

[47] Gildas, *On the Ruin of Britain* 18.

[48] Hawkes & Dunning 1961, fig. 15f, fig. 15g.

[49] Appels & Laycock 2007, 273-5.

[50] Gil, Filloy, Iriarte 2000, 26.

[51] Aurrecoechea Fernandez 1999, 64, figs. 4, 5.

[52] Myres 1986, 120-1.

CHAPTER 6

[1] Claudian, *de consulatu Stilichonis* 2, 250-5

[2] Faulkner 2000, 93.

[3] Faulkner 2000, 207.

[4] Brooks 1986. Millett 1990, 221.

[5] Crummy 1997, 130-1.

[6] Moorhead 2001. Abdy 2002, 64.

[7] Esmonde Cleary 1989, 93.

[8] Esmonde Cleary 1989, 139.

[9] Abdy 2002, 62.

[10] Moorhead 2001, 95.

[11] Abdy 2002, 64.

[12] There are a few mosaics in the west that probably date from later than 370, but they are either further north or further south than the area under discussion.

[13] Branigan 1977, 100-4.

[14] Esmonde Cleary 1989, 135. Tyers, P., Potsherd Atlas of Roman Pottery www.potsherd. uklinux.net/atlas/Ware/NFCC.

[15] Branigan 1977, 94-6.

[16] Dark 2000, 169.

[17] Vermaat.

[18] Dark 2000, 145-9.

[19] Daubney forthcoming.

[20] Davey 2004, 52-3.

[21] Cunliffe 2005, 189-90.

[22] Jones & Mattingly 1990, map 3.12.

[23] Van Arsdell 1994, 8.

[24] Bowen & Eagles 1990, 38-41.

[25] Chadburn & Corney 2001, 23.

[26] Corney 2001, 16-18.

[27] Griffiths 2001, 51, 68.

[28] Hawkes & Dunning 1961, fig. 18b.

[29] Hostetter, Howe, Allison 1997, 364-6.

[30] Wacher 1995, 420 fig. 186.

[31] Fulford 2000, 356-8.

[32] Portable Antiquities Scheme, HAMP-722FA3. Henig 2002, fig. 56. Hawkes & Dunning 1961, fig. 15p, fig. 15q.

[33] Limbrick 1998.

[34] Malim et al 1996, 65.

[35] Myres 1986, 107.

[36] Ordnance Survey 1966.

[37] Castle 1975, 267-77.

[38] For Foss Ditch see Clarke 1955, 192-5. For Launditch and Panworth Ditch see Wade-Martins 1974, 31.

[39] Fincham 2002, 72-3.

[40] Moorhead 2001, fig. 5.3.

[41] Portable Antiquities Scheme NMS-5A2005.

[42] Portable Antiquities Scheme CAM-5DD032. UKDFD.co.uk 3940. Appels & Laycock 2007, fig. SL5.10. Norfolk Museums & Archaeology Service, NHER 16121, NHER 28494.

[43] Cunliffe 2005, 144.

[44] Wacher 1995, 362.

[45] For the Colsterworth buckle, see Appels & Laycock 2007, 203. For the Little Downham buckle, see Laycock forthcoming.

[46] For Penycorddyn buckle see National Museums & Galleries of Wales 93.31H. For Blewburton Hill and Stanwick buckles, see Hawkes & Dunning 1961 fig. 14, fig. 15m.

[47] Foard, 6.

[48] Anderson 2000, 361 and Portable Antiquities Scheme website.

[49] Anderson 2000, 403-4 and Portable Antiquities Scheme website.

[50] Roger Bland, *pers. comm.*

[51] Millett 1990, 166, 172-3.

[52] Arnold 1984, 97-8.

[53] Dark 2000, 108. Gerrard 2004, 65-75.

[54] Lynn & Jefferies 1979, fig. 52.

[55] Tyers 2003, 80.

[56] Puttnam 2000, 67-8.

[57] Hartley & Fitts 1988, 97-98.

[58] Niblett 2001, 132.

[59] Dark & Dark 1998, 120-2. Esmonde-Cleary 1989, 147-8.

[60] Dark 2000, 102.

[61] Dark 2000, 100-1.

[62] Esmonde-Cleary 1989, 148.

[63] Dark 2000, 106.

[64] See, for instance, East Anglia, Esmonde Cleary 1989, 159.

[65] Dark & Dark 1998, 143.

[66] Esmonde Cleary 1989, 158.

[67] Dark & Dark 1998, 143-4.

[68] Branigan 1977, 101-3.

[69] Branigan 1977, 100.

[70] Esmonde Cleary 1989, 159.

[71] Arnold 1984, 70.

[72] Dark 2000, 66-7.

[73] Esmonde Cleary 1989, 150-1.

[74] Wacher 1995, 417.

CHAPTER 7

[1] Pearson 2002, 34, 36, 53-5.

[2] Dark 2000, 48.

[3] Dark 2000, 48-9.

[4] Additional map data: Elsham, Newball, Hibaldstow, Edlington, Heckington and Kirmington brooches ref. Kevin Leahy. For other additional brooches see Portable Antiquities Scheme, BUC-5FCFC5, HAMP-7E37B1, NARC-E36950, NMS-E4B006, HAMP-AB82B3, FASW-3D2EE0, SF-4805, SF1734, ESS-031E91, ESS-CA3565, LIN-A5C801, HAMP-118BD1, WAW-D009D7, SF-660192, NMGW-D5B047, KENT5139.

[5] Dark 2000, 11.

[6] Gildas, *On the Ruin of Britain* 23.

[7] Cunliffe 2005, 192.

[8] Ellis 1999, 202.

[9] Eckardt & Crummy 2006, fig. 1.1139. Böhme 1986, figs. 28.2, 28.9.

[10] Portable Antiquities Scheme BERK-EB3477.

[11] Shakenoak Villa, formerly in Dobunnic territory sees Anglo-Saxon settlement in the fifth century (see Blair 1994, 11) suggesting the border moved a mile or two west in the post-Roman period, the sort of border change that was probably common at the time, minor in some sense but still probably enough to cause conflict and interrupt any cross-border trade.

[12] Dark 2000, 59.

[13] O'Brien 1999, 161.

[14] Arnold 1984, 64-5.

[15] O'Brien 1999, 101.

[16] Arnold 1984, 63-64.

[17] Arnold 194, 66-7.

[18] O'Brien 1999, 101.

[19] O'Brien 1999, 101.

[20] Arnold 1984, 62-63 and Dark 2000, 100.

[21] Dark 2000, 100.

[22] Dixon 1993, 141-2.

[23] Dark 2000, 100.

[24] For instance, Dark 2000, 100.

[25] Yorke 1990, 46-7.

[26] Leahy 1985, 26-8.

[27] See Yorke 1993 for a discussion.

[28] Sims-Williams 1983, 35.

[29] Dark 2000, 43.

[30] Dumville 1985, 1986.

[31] It is widely assumed that Aylesford is the location of Agelsethrep, an improbable place name that seems to be a mangled version of Aylesford's Anglo-Saxon name.

[32] Dark 2000, 11.

[33] The Dream of Macsen Wledig.

[34] Dark 2000, 82, 101-2.

[35] Suzuki 2000.

[36] See, for example, Suzuki 2000, figs. 23, 24, 26, 31, 35.

[37] See Suzuki 2000, figs. 55-6.

[38] Suzuki 2000, plate 28.

[39] See, for example, Suzuki 2000, fig. 29, fig. 30.

[40] Cunliffe 2005, 166, 170-1.

[41] Welch 1989, 78-9.

[42] Welch 1989, 81.

[43] Dark 2000, 101.

[44] Dark 2000, 102.

[45] O'Brien 1999, 145.

[46] Draper 2006, 38-9, 46-8.

[47] Eagles 2001, 215-17.

[48] See Yorke 1989, 94-6 for a discussion of these issues.

[49] See Appels & Laycock 2007, Section 2, Chapter 11.

[50] Appels and Laycock 2007, 242. Hawkes and Dunning 1961 figs. 19 bis b, 20g, 20h.

[51] Data on map: Hawkes & Dunning 1961, figs. 1.11, 20g, 20h. Marzinzik 2003, plate 72, plate

72.2., plate 72.3. White 1986. Appels & Laycock 2007, figs. SL11.17, SL11.18. wiltshireheritage. org.uk, Roman Jewellery, Upavon buckle. Portable Antiquities Scheme KENTBFDB96. Böhme 1986, figs 19.5, 19.14 21.3, 21.5, 21.7, 21.10, 21.11.

CHAPTER 8

1   Dark 2000, 148.
2   Dark 2000, 178.
3   Dark 2000, 150-92.
4   Henson 2006, 111-14.
5   Oppenheimer 2006, 376. Sykes 2006, 286.
6   See Oppenheimer 2006, 356-61 on the debate.
7   See Oppenheimer 2006, 364 on the debate.
8   Julius Caesar, *Gallic Wars*, 2.4. Tacitus, Germania, 28.
9   Oppenheimer 2006, 372.
10 Leahy, *pers. comm.*
11 Watts 1998, 41.
12 See Dark 2000, 60-78 and Esmonde Cleary 1989, 201, 202, for instance, for the debate.
13 O'Brien 1999, 121
14 O'Brien 1999, 145. 161.
15 Bassett 1989, 23-4.
16 Henson, in his newly published book, has very briefly raised the possibility of a more general transferral, Henson 2006, 80-2.
17 Collis 2007, 525-6.
18 Delmaire & Delmaire 1990, 697-735.
19 See, for instance, Brooks 1989, 57.
20 Dark 2000, 101-102.
21 Dark 2000, 83-84.
22 Suzuki 2000, 120.
23 See, for instance, Henson 2006, 89, 90.
24 Yorke 1983, 1-20.
25 Welch 1989.
26 Cunliffe 1973, 2.
27 Dark 2000, 100-1.
28 O'Brien 1999, 145.
29 Welch 1989, 83.
30 Myres 1986 150-1.
31 Yorke 1989.
32 Yorke 1989, 93
33 Eagles 2001, 215-17.
34 Portable Antiquities Scheme, HAMP-7E37B1, HAMP-AB82B3, FASW-3D2EE0.
35 Arnold 1984, 69-70.
36 O'Brien 1999, 152.
37 See Yorke, 1989, 85 fig. 6.1.
38 Stenton 1971, 29.

39 Dark 2000, 101.
40 Wacher 1995, 420, fig. 186.
41 Niblett 2001, 131, 132, 145.
42 Yorke 1990, 12 and see Henson 2006, 208 for a fuller list.
43 Dumville 1989, 133-4.
44 Bailey 1989, 109-10, 116
45 Bassett 1989, 24.
46 Bailey 1989, 111.
47 Bailey 1989, 112.
48 Yorke 1990, 46-7.
49 Dark 2000, 99.
50 See Dark 2000, fig. 36, and fuller map in Laycock forthcoming.
51 O'Brien 1999, 121.
52 See, for instance, Leeds 1945, 81, on the area around Cambridge and see Dickinson 1979 on the early use of Saxon disc brooches in the area.
53 Yorke 1990, 49.
54 Campbell 1991, fig. 72.
55 O'Brien 1999, 114.
56 O'Brien 1999, 112, 117.
57 O'Brien 1999, 110.
58 Davies, John & Wlliamson 1999, 18.
59 Cunliffe 2005, fig. 8.15.
60 Henson 2006, 137.
61 See Brooks 1989, 162, for a discussion.
62 Dark 2000, 52, 130.
63 O'Brien 1999, 82.
64 O'Brien 1999, 93-4.
65 Liddle 2000, 1.
66 Williams & Vince 1997 and see Dark 2000, 86-8.
67 Wacher 1995, 362.
68 Bede, *Ecclesiastical History of England* 2, 14.
69 Dark 2000, 193-200.
70 Dark 2000, 195.
71 O'Brien 1999, 71.
72 Dark 2000, 11.
73 Yorke 1990, 8-86.
74 O'Brien 1999, 69.
75 O'Brien 1999, 62.
76 Yorke 1990, 84.

CONCLUSION

1   Suetonius, *Life of Caligula* 44.
2   Hadley 2006, 11-12.
3   Hadley 2006, 54-5.
4   Hadley 2006, 33.
5   Hadley 2006, 31.

Bibliography

Abdy, R. A. (2002) *Roman-British Coin Hoards*, Shire

Allason-Jones, L. & Miket, R. (1984) *The Catalogue of Small Finds from South Shields Roman Fort*, Society of Antiquaries, Newcastle upon Tyne

Allen, D. (1989) *Rockbourne Roman Villa*, Hampshire County Council

Appels, A. & Laycock, S. (2007) *Roman Buckles & Military Fittings*, Greenlight

Aurrecoechea Fernandez, J. (1999) 'Late Roman Belts in Hispania' in *Journal of Roman Military Equipment Studies 10*, 55–62

Aurrecoechea Fernandez, J. (2001) *Los Cinturones Romanos en la Hispania del Bajo Imperio*, Monographies Instrumentum 19

Arnold, C.J. (1984) *Roman Britain to Saxon England*, Routledge

Bailey, K. (1989) 'The Middle Saxons' in *The Origins of Anglo-Saxon Kingdoms*, Ed. Bassett, S., Leicester University Press

Bassett, S. (1989) *The Origins of Anglo-Saxon Kingdoms*, Leicester University Press

Bayley, J. & Butcher, S. (2004) *Roman Brooches in Britain*, Society of Antiquaries

Bean, S.C. (2000) *The Coinage of the Atrebates and Regni*, Oxford University School of Archaeology

Bishop, M.C. (1991) 'Soldiers and military equipment in the towns of Roman Britain' in *Roman Frontier Studies*, V. Maxfield and M. Dobson, Exeter, 21–7

Bishop, M.C & Coulston, J.C.N. (2006) *Roman Military Equipment*, Oxbow

Blair, J. (1994) *Anglo-Saxon Oxfordshire*, Sutton

Böhme, H.W. (1986) 'Das Ende der Römerherrschaft in Britannien und die Angelsachsische Besiedlung Englands im 5. Jahrhundert' in *Jahrbuch des Römisch-Germanischen Zentralmuseum Mainz 33* 469–574

Böhme, H.W. (1987) 'Gallien in der Spätantike' in *Jahrbuch des Römischen Germanischen Zentralmuseum zu Mainz 34*, 770–3

Bowen, H.C & Eagles, B.N. (1990) *The Archaeology of Bokerley Dyke*, Stationery Office Books

Branigan, K. (1977) *The Roman Villa in South-West England*, Moonraker Press

Branigan, K. (1985) *The Catuvellauni*, Sutton

Breeze, D. J. & Dobson, B. (1985) 'Roman Military Deployment in North England' in *Britannia 16*, 1–19

Breeze, D. J. & Dobson, B. (2000) *Hadrian's Wall*, Penguin

Brooks, D.A. (1986) 'A Review of the Evidence for Continuity in British Towns in Fifth and Sixth Centuries' in *Oxford Journal of Archaeology 5 (1)*, 77–102

Brooks, N. (1989) 'The formation of the Mercian kingdom' in *The Origins of Anglo-Saxon Kingdoms*, Ed. Bassett, S. Leicester University Press, 159–170

Brooks, N. (1989) 'The creation and early structure of the kingdom of Kent' in *The Origins of Anglo-Saxon Kingdoms*, Ed. Bassett, S., Leicester University Press, 55–74

Brown, C. & Henig, M. (2002) 'A Romano-British Buckle Plate from East Challow, near Wantage' in *Oxoniensia 67*, 363-5

Campbell, J. (1991) *The Anglo-Saxons*, Penguin

Campbell, J. (2000) 'Portrait of Britain AD500' in *History Today 50*, 29-35

Casey, P.J. (1979) 'Magnus Maximus: a reappraisal' in *The End of Roman Britain*, Ed. Casey, P.J, Oxford, 66-79

Castle, S.A. (1975) 'Excavations in Pear Wood, Brockley Hill, Middlesex 1948-73' in *Transactions of London Middlesex Archaeological Society 26*, 267-77

Chadburn, A. & Corney, M. (2001), 'Iron Age Resource Assessment' in *Archaeological Research Agenda for the Avebury World Heritage Site*, Trust for Wessex Archaeology 19-23

Clarke, G. (1979) *The Roman Cemetery at Lankhills*, Winchester Studies 3, Oxford

Clarke, R. (1955) 'The Fossditch — a Linear Earthwork in South West Norfolk' in *Norfolk Archaeology 31*, 178-96

Collins, R. (2004) 'Before 'the End': Hadrian's Wall in the fourth century and after' in *Debating Late Antiquity in Britain AD300-700*, Eds. Collins & Gerrard, British Archaeological Reports, British Series 365, 123-32

Collis, J. (2007) 'The Polities of Gaul, Britain and Ireland in the Late Iron Age' in *The Later Iron Age in Britain and Beyond*, Eds. Haselgrove & Moore, Oxbow

Corney, M. (2001) 'The Romano-British nucleated settlements of Wiltshire' in *Roman Wiltshire and After, Papers in Honour of Ken Annable*, Ed. Ellis, P., Wiltshire Archaeological and Natural History Society, 5-38

Creighton, J. (1994) 'A time of change: the Iron Age to Roman monetary transition in East Anglia' in *Oxford Journal of Archaeology 13*, 325-34

Creighton, J. (2000) *Coins and Power in Late Iron Age Britain*, Cambridge University Press

Crummy, P. (1997) *City of Victory*, Colchester Archaeological Trust

Cunliffe, B. (1971) *Excavations at Fishbourne 1961-69*, Society of Antiquaries

Cunliffe, B. (1973) *The Regni*, Duckworth

Cunliffe, B. (2004) *Iron Age Britain*, English Heritage

Cunliffe, B. (2005) *Iron Age Communities in Britain*, Routledge

Curteis, M. (1996) 'An analysis of the circulation patterns of Iron Age currency from Northamptonshire' in *Britannia 27*, 17-42

Dark, K. (1994) *Civitas to Kingdom, British Political Continuity 300-800*, Studies in the Early History of Britain, Leicester

Dark, K. & Dark, P. (1998) *The Landscape of Roman Britain*, Sutton

Dark, K. (2000) *Britain and the End of the Roman Empire*, Tempus

Daubney, A, (forthcoming) 'Deus Totatis; a cult of the Corieltauvi'

Davey, J. (2004) 'The Environs of South Cadbury in the Late Antique and Early Medieval Periods' in *Debating Late Antiquity in Britain AD300-700*, Eds. Collins & Gerrard, British Archaeological Reports, British Series 365, 43-54

Davies, J. & Williamson, T. (1999) *Land of the Iceni*, University of East Anglia

Delmaire, B. & Delmaire, R. (1990) 'Les limites de la cité des Atrébates (nouvelle approche d'un vieux problème)', *Revue du Nord 72*, 697-735

Dickinson, T.M. (1979) 'On the Origin and Chronology of the early Anglo-Saxon disc brooch' in *Anglo-Saxon Studies in Archaeology & History 1*, Ed. Hawkes, S.C, British Archaeological Reports, British Series 72, 39-80

Dickinson, T.M. (1982) 'Fowler's Type G penannular brooches reconsidered' in *Medieval Archaeology 26*, 41-68

Dixon, P.H. (1993) 'The Anglo-Saxon Settlement at Mucking' in *Anglo-Saxon Studies in Archaeology and History 6*, Oxford University Committee for Archaeology 125-47

Draper, S. (2006) *Landscape, Settlement and Society in Roman and Early Medieval Wiltshire*, British Archaeological Reports, British Series 419

Drury, P.J. (1984) 'The Temple of Claudius at Colchester Reconsidered' in *Britannia, 15,* 7-50

Dumville, D.N. (1985) 'The West Saxon Genealogical Regnal List and the chronology of Wessex' in *Peritia 4,* 21-66

Dumville, D.N. (1986) 'The West Saxon Genealogical Regnal List: manuscripts and texts', in *Anglia 104,* 1-32

Dumville, D. (1989) 'Essex, Middle Anglia and the expansion of Mercia in the South-East Midlands' in *The Origins of Anglo-Saxon Kingdoms,* Ed. Bassett, S., Leicester University Press

Eagles, B. (2001) 'Anglo-Saxon Presence and Culture in Wiltshire c. AD 450 – c.675' in *Roman Wiltshire and After, Papers in Honour of Ken Annable,* Ed. Ellis P., Wiltshire Archaeological and Natural History Society, 199-233

Eagles, B. (2004) 'Britons and Saxons on the Eastern Boundary of the Civitas Durotrigum' in *Britannia 34,* 234-40

Eckhardt, H. & Crummy, N. (2006) 'Roman' or 'native' bodies in Britain: the evidence of late Roman nail-cleaner strap-ends' in *Oxford Journal of Archaeology 25, 1,* 83-103

Ellis, P. (1999) 'North Leigh Villa, Oxfordshire: A Report on Excavation and Recording in the 1970s' in *Britannia 30*

Esmonde Cleary, A.S. (1989) *The Ending of Roman Britain,* Routledge

Faulkner, N. (2000) *The Decline & Fall of Roman Britain,* Tempus

Fincham, G. (2002) *Landscapes of Imperialism: Roman and native interaction in the East Anglian Fenland,* British Archaeological Reports, British Series 338

Foard, G., *An Archaeological Resource Assessment of Anglo-Saxon Northamptonshire (400-1066),* Northamptonshire Heritage

Frere, S. (1967) *Britannia – A History of Roman Britain,* Routledge

Fulford, M. (2000) 'Human Remains from the North Gate, Silchester' in *Britannia 31,* 356-8

Gerrard, J. (2004) 'How late is late? Pottery and the fifth century in southwest Britain' in *Debating Late Antiquity in Britain AD300-700,* Eds. Collins & Gerrard, British Archaeological Reports, British Series 365, 65-75

Gil, E., Filloy, I., Iriarte A. (2000) 'Late Roman Military Equipment from the City of Iruña/Veleia (Alava/Spain)' in *Journal of Roman Military Equipment Studies 11,* 25-35

Gould, J. (1999) 'The Watling Street Burgi' in *Britannia 30,* 185-198

Griffiths, N. (2001) 'The Roman Army in Wiltshire' in *Roman Wiltshire and After, Papers in Honour of Ken Annable,* Ed. Ellis, P., Wiltshire Archaeological and Natural History Society, 39-72

Hadley, D.M. (2006) *The Vikings in England – Settlement, Society and Culture,* Manchester University Press

Hartley, B. & Fitts, L. (1988) The Brigantes, *Sutton*

Hawkes, S.C. & Dunning, G.C. (1961) 'Soldiers and settlers in Britain, fourth to fifth century' in *Medieval Archaeology 5,* 1-70

Hawkes, S.C. (1974) 'Some recent finds of Late Roman Buckles' in *Britannia 5,* 386-93

Hendy, M.F. (1985) *Studies in the Byzantine Monetary Economy c.300-1450,* Cambridge University Press

Henig, M. (2002) *The Heirs of King Verica,* Tempus

Henig, M. (2004) 'Remaining Roman in Britain AD300-700' in *Debating Late Antiquity in Britain AD300-700,* Eds. Collins & Gerrard, British Archaeological Reports, British Series 365, 13-23

Henson, D. (2006) The *Origins of the Anglo-Saxons,* Anglo-Saxon Books

Higham, N. (1992) *Rome, Britain and the Anglo-Saxons,* Routledge

Hind J.G.F. (1977) 'The 'Genounian' Part of Britain' in *Britannia 8,* 229-234

Hingley, R. & Unwin, C. (2005) *Boudica, Iron Age Warrior Queen,* Hambledon Continuum

Hostetter, E., Howe, T.N., Allison, E.P. (1997) *The Romano-British Villa at Castle Copse, Great Bedwyn,* Indiana University Press

Johnson, S. (1989) *Hadrian's Wall,* English Heritage

Jones, B. & Mattingly, D. (1990) *An Atlas of Roman Britain,* Blackwell

Kemble, J. (2001) *Prehistoric & Roman Essex,* Tempus

Kilbride-Jones, H.E. (1980) *Celtic Craftsmanship in Bronze*, St Martin's Press

Laycock, S. (2006) 'The Threat Within', in *British Archaeology, March/April*, 11-15

Laycock, S. (forthcoming) 'Tribal Tension in late and post-Roman Britain'

Leahy, K.A. (1985) 'Late Roman and Early Germanic Metalwork from Lincolnshire', in *A Prospect of Lincolnshire*, Eds. Field, N. & White, A., Lincoln

Leahy, K.A. (1996) in *Dragonby*, Ed. May, J., Oxbow Monographs 61, 267-8

Leahy, K.A. (2007) 'Soldiers and settlers in Britain, fourth to fifth century – revised' in *Collectanea Antiqua: Essay in Memory of Sonia Chadwick Hawkes*, Eds. Henig, M. & Smith. T.J, 133-141

Leeds, E.T. (1945) 'Distribution of the Angles and Saxons Archaeologically Considered' in *Archaeologia 91*, 1-106

Liddle, P. (2000) *An Archaeological Resource Assessment of Anglo-Saxon Leicestershire and Rutland*, Leicestershire Museums

Limbrick, G. (1998) 'Frontier Territory Along the Thames' in *British Archaeology 33, April*

Lynn, M.A.B. & Jefferies, R.S. (1979) *The Alice Holt/Farnham Roman pottery industry*, Council for British Archaeology Research Report 30

MacDowall, S. (1995) *Late Roman Cavalryman*, Osprey

MacGregor, A. & Bolick, E. (1993) *A Summary Catalogue of the Anglo-Saxon Collections: Non-ferrous Metals*, British Archaeological Reports, British Series 230

Manley, J. (2002) *AD43, The Roman Invasion of Britain – a Reassessment*, Tempus

Malim, T. with Penn, K., Robinson, B., Wait, G. & Walsh, K. (1996) 'New Evidence on the Cambridgeshire Dykes and Worsted Street Roman Road' in *Proceedings of the Cambridge Antiquarian Society 85*, 27-122

Marzinzik, S. (2003) *Early Anglo-Saxon Belt Buckles*, British Archaeological Reports, British Series 357

Mattingly, D. (2006) *An Imperial Possession, Britain in the Roman Empire*, Penguin

Millett, M. (1987) 'Boudicca: the First Colchester Pottery Shop and the Dating of Neronian Samian' in *Britannia 18*, 93-124

Millett, M. (1990) *The Romanisation of Britain*, Cambridge University Press

Moore, T. & Reece, R. (2001) 'The Dobunni' in *Glevensis 37*, 17-26

Moorhead, T. S. N. (2001) 'Roman Coin Finds from Wiltshire' in *Roman Wiltshire and After, Papers in Honour of Ken Annable*, Ed. Peter Ellis, Wiltshire Archaeological and Natural History Society, 85–106

Myres, J.N.L (1986) *The English Settlements*, Oxford University Press

Niblett, R. (2001) *Verulamium, the Roman City of St Albans*, Tempus

Niblett, R., Manning, W. & Saunders, D. (2006) 'Verulamium: excavations within the Roman town 1986-88' in *Britannia 37*, 53-188

O'Brien, E. (1999) *Post-Roman Britain to Anglo-Saxon England: Burial Practices Reviewed*, British Archaeological Reports, British Series 289

Oppenheimer, S. (2006) *The Origins of the British, a Genetic Detective Story*, Constable

Ordnance Survey (1966) *Map of Britain in the Dark Ages*

Pearson, A. (2002) *The Roman Shore Forts*, Tempus

Potter, T.W. (2002) 'The Transformation of Britain from 55BC to AD60' in *The Roman Era, Short Oxford History of the British Isles*, Ed. Salway, P., Oxford University Press

Puttnam, B. (2000) *Discover Dorset: The Romans*, Dovecote Press

Robertson, A.S. (2000) *An Inventory of British Coin Hoards*, Royal Numismatic Society Special Publication 20

Robinson, P. (1994) 'The Late Roman Hoard from Blagan Hill, Wiltshire' in *Minerva 5, 4*, July/August, 14-15

Rodwell, W.J. (1975) 'Trinovantian towns and their setting', in *'Small towns' of Roman Britain*, Eds. Rodwell, W.J. & Rowley, R.T, British Archaeological Reports 15, 85-102

Rodwell, W.J. (1976) 'Coinage, oppida and the rise of Belgic power in south-eastern Britain' in *Oppida: the beginnings of urbanisation in barbarian Europe*, Eds. Cunliffe, B. W. & Rowley, R.T., British Archaeological Reports S11, 184-367.

Salway, P. (1993) *The Oxford Illustrated History of Roman Britain*, Oxford University Press

Salway, P. (2002) *The Roman Era, Short Oxford History of the British Isles*, Oxford University Press

Sealey, P. (1997) *The Boudican Revolt Against Rome*, Shire

Shotter, D. (1996) *The Roman Frontier in Britain*, Carnegie

Sims-Williams, P. (1983) 'The settlement of England in Bede and the Chronicle' in *Anglo-Saxon England 12*, 1-41

Sommer, M. (1984) *Die Gürtel und Gürtelbeschläge des 4. und 5. Jahrhunderts im Römischen Reich*, Bonner Hefte zur Vorgeschichte 22, Bonn

Stead, I.M. (1979) *The Arras Culture*, York

Stenton, F. M. (1971) *Anglo-Saxon England*, Oxford, Clarendon Press

Stevens, C.E. (1937) 'Gildas and the Civitates of Britain' in *English Historical Review 52*, 193-203

Suzuki, S. (2000) *The Quoit Brooch Style and Anglo-Saxon Settlement*, The Boydell Press

Swanton, M.J. (1973) *The Spearheads of the Anglo-Saxon Settlements*, The Royal Archaeological Institute

Swift, E. (2000) *The End of the Western Roman Empire, An Archaeological Investigation*, Tempus

Sykes, B. (2006) *Blood of the Isles*, Bantam Press

Taylor, A. (1998) *Archaeology of Cambridgeshire, South-East Cambridgeshire and the Fen Edge*, Cambridgeshire County Council

Todd, M. (1991) *The Coritani*, Sutton

Tyers, P., *Potsherd Atlas of Roman Pottery*, www.potsherd.uklinux.net/index.php

Tyers, P. (2003) *Roman Pottery in Britain*, Routledge

Van Arsdell, R.D. (1989) *Celtic Coinage of Britain*, London

Van Arsdell, R.D. (1994) *The Coinage of the Dobunni: Money Supply and Coin Circulation in Dobunnic Territory*, Oxford University School of Archaeology

Vermaat, R., *Dark Age British Earthworks – An Interview with Dr. Ken Dark*, www.wansdyke21.org.uk/wansdyke/wanart/dark.htm

Wacher, J. (1995) *The Towns of Roman Britain*, Batsford

Wade-Martins, P. (1974) 'The Linear Earthworks of West Norfolk' in *Norfolk Archaeology 36*, 23-38

Warner, P. (1996) *The Origins of Suffolk*, Manchester University Press

Watts, D. (1998) *Religion in late Roman Britain*, Routledge

Welch, M. (1989) 'The Kingdom of the South Saxons: The origins' in *The Origins of Anglo-Saxon Kingdoms*, Ed. Bassett, S., Leicester University Press

West, S. (1998) *A Corpus of Anglo-Saxon Material from Suffolk*, East Anglian Archaeology 84, Suffolk County Council

White, Sally (1986) 'A late Roman fixed plate buckle from Highdown, Ferring, W Sussex', in *Medieval Archaeology 30*, 91-2

Williams, D. & Vince, A. (1997) 'The characterization and interpretation of early to middle Saxon granitic tempered pottery in England' in *Medieval Archaeology 41*, 214-20

Wilmott, T. (2002) 'Roman Commanders, Dark Age Kings' in *British Archaeology 63, February*

Woodfield, C. (1995) 'New thoughts on town defences in the western territory of Catuvellauni' in *Roman Small Towns in Eastern England and Beyond*, Ed. Brown, A.E., Oxbow

Yorke, B. (1983) 'Joint kingship in Kent, c.560-785' in *Archaeologia Cantiana 99*, 1-20

Yorke, B. (1989) 'The Jutes of Hampshire and Wight and the origins of Wessex' in *The Origins of Anglo-Saxon Kingdoms*, Ed. Bassett, S., Leicester University Press

Yorke, B. (1990) *Kings and Kingdoms of Early Anglo-Saxon England*, Routledge

Yorke, B. (1993) 'Fact or Fiction? The written evidence for the fifth and sixth centuries AD' in *Anglo-Saxon Studies in Archaeology and History 6*, Oxford University Committee for Archaeology

Index